TRADING TACTICS

An Introduction to Finding, Exploiting and
Managing Profitable Share Trading Opportunities

DARYL GUPPY

Wrightbooks

DARYL GUPPY is also the author of:
Share Trading*, Trading Asian Shares, Bear Trading*, Chart Trading*, Better Trading*,
Snapshot Trading*, Trend Trading*, 36 Strategies of the Chinese for Financial Traders*

and the Australian editor/contributor to:
The Basics of Speculating* by Gerald Krevetz, The Day Trader's Advantage* by Howard Abell,
Options — Trading Strategies That Work* by William F. Eng

* Published by and available from Wrightbooks.

First published 1997 by Wrightbooks
an imprint of John Wiley & Sons Australia, Ltd
42 McDougall Street, Milton Qld 4064

Offices also in Sydney and Melbourne

Reprinted 1998, 1999, 2000, 2001, 2004, 2005 and 2007.

© Daryl Guppy 1997
Email: support@guppytraders.com   Internet: www.guppytraders.com

All charts created by Metastock© using data supplied by Electronic Information Solutions and Almax.

National Library of Australia Cataloguing-in-Publication data:

Guppy, Daryl, 1954-.

Trading Tactics: an introduction to finding, exploiting and managing profitable share trading
opportunities.

Includes index.

ISBN: 1 875857 51 6

1. Stocks - Australia. 2. Stock Exchanges - Australia. I. Title.

332.63220994

Cover design by Rob Cowpe
Printed in Australia by McPherson's Printing Group
10 9 8

Disclaimer

The material in this publication is of the nature of general comment only, and does not represent professional
advice. It is not intended to provide specific guidance for particular circumstances and it should not be
relied on as the basis for any decision to take action or not take action on any matter which it covers.
Readers should obtain professional advice where appropriate, before making any such decision. To the
maximum extent permitted by law, the author and publisher disclaim all responsibility and liability to
any person, arising directly or indirectly from any person taking or not taking action based upon the
information in this publication.

Contents

Preface

TRACKING THE GHOST OF EL DORADO

As a child I was enthralled by the abandoned rusting hulk of the El Dorado gold dredge stranded on Reedy Creek near Yackandandah and captivated by small clear vials filled with gold dust laboriously panned by an old prospector from mountain creeks in North East Victoria. Despite broken nails, aching muscles, erratic returns, the dirt, dust and heat, I have always found the lure of prospecting for metals and minerals irresistible. Now my prospecting tools are the computer, the stockmarket database, and charting software — and the lure is still irresistible. The dust is banished by air conditioning and only fingers ache from keyboarding. Yet the exploration principles remain the same.

The El Dorado sought by the Spanish conquistadores and described by Diaz in *The Conquest of New Spain* did not exist. Ours does. Every day the market surrenders a rich line of lode to the best traders. I wrote in *Share Trading* that we have a choice between a pot of gold and a working gold mine. In this book I explore some ways of finding the lode and bringing it on-stream to build a working gold mine. I am not a market wizard so the techniques in this book require no specialist skills. Like many traders who have moved from working for a wage to trading for a living, just duplicating my wages is enough to keep me happy. There are fortunes to be made — and lost — in the market. Better prospectors make, and keep, these fortunes.

This book is written for those who want to survive, and for those who, while not aspiring to market wizard status, would like to more aggressively manage market risk by finding, exploiting and managing trading opportunities. If you are prepared to pit your prospecting skill against those who have traditionally held the keys to the market, then this book will help equip you for the expedition.

Bull market conditions encourage novice traders. In a bull market the market pays for your mistakes as the general rise in stock prices allows for quick recovery of losses. In a bear market, you pay for them. Some of what is written in the following chapters may appear to be unnecessarily complex or detailed, but when the bear bites, these are the basic disciplines that separate the survivors from market victims.

The processes described in this book are easy in principle but some are very time-demanding if applied indiscriminately. We start with broad selection procedures and as the list of trading candidates narrows, apply more specialised trading tactics. These processes build on the routines and approaches covered in *Share Trading: An Approach to Buying and Selling* so this book does not cover old ground nor repeat old material, giving instead appropriate references to *Share Trading*.

Serious Trading

Trading is frustrating because, despite all the groundwork required before picking up the phone to enter or exit a trade, the market may still slip between your fingers.

Understanding the analysis, being in tune with the market, initiating and completing scanning processes and fine-tuning the financial aspects does not mean a trading opportunity will be revealed. The market does not owe us a living. Despite the hours of research, there is no guarantee that the stock will be available at the price we think is appropriate. There is no guarantee of any real trading opportunities being identified by our painstaking analysis. There may be none that match all our criteria.

This is annoying, but it is only fatal if we settle for second-best. As a private trader we do not have to trade. We can afford to wait until the best opportunities arise. This protects us from a market indifferent to our existence and survival.

There are always some market situations where the tools of technical analysis appear useless. This does not diminish the effectiveness of the tools. In the same way that a carpenter does not use a spanner to build a house, so a trader does not attempt to use technical tools in trading situations where they offer little help.

As traders we look for those opportunities compatible with the tools we are most skilled in using. To pretend that our particular tool kit will expose the secrets of all markets, or of any market segments, is foolish. As traders we want to identify our strengths, and weaknesses. By trading on our strengths, matching our trading style, and using the appropriate array of tools, we become better traders.

Success does count. Virtuosity is a theoretical skill if it does not wring financial rewards from trading. Trading approaches which mimic the apparent complexity of the markets are not always the best at understanding the markets. More difficult does not mean more accurate. Simple trading strategies score direct profits in complex systems so we aim in this book to dismember complexity into its simplest components. These lay the foundation for trading tactics.

A Road Map for Dismembering Complexity

Systems and systematic behaviour are at the core of complexity. Complexity is a dynamical system positioned on the edge of chaos where a single event — the butterfly effect — could tip it into dangerous instability and collapse. Survival depends upon the way the systems adapt to behavioural changes, moving forward along the cliff rather than to one side and over it.

Trading is on the very edge of chaos, riding alongside the market. Our survival depends on our ability to define our task and its components, to select the right tools and deliver appropriate solutions.

The core of every complex system has a dominant characteristic. The cyclone is defined by wind, the turbulence of a waterfall by water, the clash of market activity by numerical data. We measure the cyclone with an anemometer, the flow of water with a Dethridge wheel and the market with a price chart. No matter how you make your trading selection — fundamental, technical, accounting, financial or news analysis — your trading improves when you know how to read a price chart with its message of probability.

Joining the Rush

TRADING WITH THE BALANCE OF PROBABILITY, Chapter 1, goes to the core of every trading approach, matching the message of the chart with its implied information about probability. When some price combinations occur more frequently than others they signal a change in probability. The market throws up voluminous data, concealing this vital information. The cypher of understanding is the bar chart. The price bar, or candlestick display, is built on clear market emotions pointing to areas of increased probability. These MESSAGES FROM THE JUNGLE DRUMS track progress at the market battlefront and save financial lives.

Chapter 3, LASSETER'S REEF, brings the balance of probability to life in a sample trade, showing how basic understanding is matched with market reality. This is a model of the trading nuggets we hope to find and our search begins when we select the best time frame. TIME BITES CHARACTER, Chapter 4, shows how we focus short, immediate and long-term pictures into a single snapshot. The detail blurs as the structure emerges. Different time bites are used to confirm analysis across multiple time frames and so further stack the balance in our favour.

Prospecting for Trades

Armed with an idea of how our trading opportunity might look and how we might recognise it, we are ready to start SEARCHING FOR LOVE AT FIRST PROFIT. Some traders choose to follow an accounting path. We give them guide information in NO ACCOUNTING FOR ALL TASTES and explain how their path joins with ours when it comes to assessing and managing the trade.

We plunge into the jungle of technical indicators. This style of trading is a complex activity built on foundations of layered simplicity. We deconstruct some of these complex processes so we can rebuild them in a way that uniquely suits our trading style and financial requirements.

This is database mining at its finest. We consider the value of EYEBALL SEARCHES which provide an essential reference point for every trading decision. We place this near the beginning of our search and also return to it towards the end. Some choose to use this bar chart analysis only at the end of their search but the techniques do not change. Other chartists look for TECHNICAL TRUE LOVE — SEARCHING FOR RELATIONSHIPS between price patterns and daily price bars. Other technical traders prefer PERFORMANCE SEARCHES as the best way of quickly finding trading opportunities. All these techniques use common concepts to bind complex groups together. Working with simplicity provides the keys to complexity.

This understanding lets us build effective criteria for speedy searches that quickly find the best trading candidates. Some search criteria are spelled out for you to copy into your charting or market software package. Those who want to fiddle and fine-tune further will find specialist publications listed in the text.

The nuggets uncovered are still untested in the crucible of the market. We consider a new indicator used as AN ASSAY TEST — LOOKING FOR LIFE in Chapter 10. This combines our understanding of market behaviour with data analysis to identify points of explosive price action. Price data is objective, but our analysis of it is not. There are always TWO SIDES OF THE SAME COIN and we examine ways to identify and ultimately overcome our personal predisposition for gloom or glee. With this ghost acknowledged we finish the assay test interpretation and application with INDEX HUNTING to match nuggets of trading opportunity with markets.

Supplementary Numbers

Discovery is nothing without exploitation. Our selected trading opportunities, mined from our database, come in different shapes and sizes. Not all trades are created equal and in THIS LITTLE NUGGET GOES TO MARKET we examine the calculations required to rank the candidates from good to better and then best. The best satisfy our financial objectives. We breathe life into risk whenever we open a trade so PINNING A NUMBER ON RISK gives us an important advantage in validating financial objectives.

The key to successful exploitation of our hard-won trading opportunities comes in the shape of USING DEPTH OF MARKET. This unfamiliar collection of figures is too often ignored by traders, yet it opens a wealth of tactical information. We show some ways to understand and use it to our advantage. This puts profit in our grasp and most times we stop here. Sometimes we are able to step beyond this analysis crossing into the world of derivative trading. This gives us A LEVER TO LIFT THE WORLD so we explore the power of leverage delivered by specific warrant trading tactics.

Failure is a Handmaiden to Success

We cannot just go through the motions of trading. It is not a mechanical process. Trading is hard, demanding work. It requires a thorough working knowledge of the market, of trading techniques and of money management. Above all, it requires a psychological mastery of ourselves. At some stage every prospecting expedition comes to resemble a pilgrimage. Trading imposes stresses quite different from those experienced in any other job, and many would-be traders find that it is these psychological factors which defeat them.

The way we think about ourselves has a significant impact on the way we trade. Trading slides into OVER-TRADING when we abandon planning for movement, mistaking activity for purpose. Successful traders recognise this escape mechanism, and put it in the background so it does not distort their trading activities.

Behind every decision the trader makes there lurks a plethora of past sins and prejudices. Failure waits on every trade and there are factors other than the analysis of the trade that have a significant impact of our trading success. Stop loss is good in theory but difficult in practice. Success depends on knowing the difference between NERVES OF STEEL — OR CHICKEN WIRE. We look at matching stop-loss points with our nerves to improve stop-loss execution. Puffed with success from other financial activities some traders mutate into a market bully, sabotaging their own success. The market ignores COMMAND AND CONTROL strategies so if you find yourself nodding in agreement, then heed the warning.

These are hidden hands driving, or sabotaging, our decision making. Get to know them well because they are our trading companions always hitch-hiking a ride with success. Such hidden attitudes cast a pall of darkness over our trading activities, shadowing the way to failure. We can neither eliminate nor ignore them, so we must learn to live with them.

The most dangerous shadow of all is the unconscious belief that trading is a game of chance where anyone can walk off the street and take money from the market. GAMBLER OR TRADER? takes a professional look at trading behaviours suggestive of pathological gambling. Written specially for this book by a US private trader and psychologist, Paul I. Munves, this chapter cuts authoritatively to the core of the gambling trader's self-deception. It is not pretty reading, but nor are the consequences of gambling in the markets.

We are not alone in this expedition. Others search alongside us for nuggets. Some of them are real competitors but most are temporary participants. We want to emulate the survivors but few are initially aware of the INSIGHT AND IRONY this involves. This book is only an introduction to some of the tools used in trading tactics. It does not complete the question "I am a trader because ..." That is your task and the prospecting expedition turns out to be as much about this as it is about finding trading opportunities.

Finally, for those contemplating exploration in FOREIGN JUNGLES we provide a brief guide to the important differences between the operation of Australian and US markets.

An Introduction, Not a Guide

The procedures detailed in the following chapters are only one selection from many ways to approach the task of analysing the market for opportunities. Our purpose is to provide you with an introduction to a variety of approaches to encourage you to think more clearly about your current methods, or to help you make sense of the bewildering volume of market data. We want to provide you with the tools to finance, equip, explore, develop and exploit your own trading opportunities.

I have endeavoured to answer many of the questions raised in readers' email sent through www.ozemail.com.au/~guppy and in comments from those who attended Trading Workshop seminars. Thanks must go to Will Evans from

PJW Brokers, David Barnes, Bill McMaster and my parents, Ted and Patricia, who laboured through the original manuscripts. My wife, Marion, continued to demand an impossibly high standard of plain English, particularly in relation to apostrophes.

If you are reading this book I assume you are a serious trader or that you are serious about trading. This book assumes you have a working knowledge of the language of charting. Computerised charting tools sit, or soon will sit, on your desktop. This book will show you how to use them more effectively and give you search formulas to program direct into your computer.

We approach trading as a business so we must be systematic in the way we go about the many tasks associated with trading. This introduction will help you organise these tasks into a daily routine to take you quickly to the best of the current trading opportunities whether they be found in Lasseter's Reef, King Solomon's gold mines, El Dorado or your own private mother lode of market data.

Every journey begins with a small step. We set out to explore for nuggets of trading opportunity but, like every prospector, we also discover a great deal more about ourselves. Trading involves many perils and this book aims to prevent the first step becoming a stumble.

Run with the bulls. Hunt with the bears. Trade well.

Daryl Guppy
Katherine, NT
November 1997

Part I

JOINING THE RUSH

1

TRADING WITH THE BALANCE OF PROBABILITY

To trade or not to trade is the basic question. But is profit the only answer? Many novice traders think so.

Experienced traders learn that trading is the aggressive management of risk made possible by understanding the process of finding, exploiting and managing trading opportunities, financially and mentally. Regularly traders journey into the market jungle to mine nuggets of opportunity, returning with them to trade for profit. Successful traders understand the landscape and risk, and are properly equipped. The novice, equipped with little other than enthusiasm and a dream, walks into the jungle with an eye fixed on profit. Lacking tactical survival skills, few of the latter return.

The client casualty lists from brokerages fill pages with the names of those who thought profit was the only answer, and failed. This book is for survivors. If you want to keep your name permanently off the casualty list you must equip yourself with the best prospecting equipment. Simply aiming for a profit is not enough.

To protect profits and minimise losses you make better use of your tools, use your time efficiently and listen carefully to the roar and whimper of the market crowd. Like Ulysses, who wanted to hear the call of the sirens but avoid being lured onto the rocks, we consider ways to listen to the siren call of greed without coming to grief. We look at how to identify trading opportunities, some methods to analyse only the most promising and how the supplementary numbers from the market are used to confirm the promise of profit.

Later we examine some ways to detect the sound of distant thunder as the crowd stampedes through the marketplace. The market is a master pick-pocket and, while profit beckons, failure has its hands in our wallets. How much it takes depends on our trading tactics.

This is a prospecting expedition into the market jungle and before taking the first steps we require some understanding of the landscape. What strange shapes await us, what unusual growths, what behaviours? How will we measure and judge them against our own experience? Do we equip for snow, or sand, or dense foliage? The answers decide the tools, the protective equipment, and the way our expedition travels. Consider this first section as an expedition briefing for a land seen but improperly understood.

Our chosen landscape is peppered with probability and shape is delivered in bar charts. In this landscape lie the nuggets, so it pays to spend some time exploring these conditions before stepping into the market jungle. You could skip ahead and start the expedition immediately. When you decide you cannot make sense of the jungle shapes feel free to return to this expedition briefing.

Successful trading means having the balance of probability on your side. Good trading is about achieving financial objectives. Later we look at some specific ways to identify this balance, set financial objectives and control risk by tilting the balance in our favour. Before doing this we need to renew our acquaintance with probability, and later with the way this appears on a chart.

You cannot control the market, but you can control your entry into the market and your exit from it. Successful trading places these control points near levels of greater probability.

Probable Odds

Tell people you trade the market, but don't believe in gambling, and you have the perfect stand-up comedy routine. The laughter says a lot about general ignorance of odds and probability and perhaps why so many wannabe traders become investors. Trading against the odds, or the balance of probability, is a one-way ticket to financial ruin so understanding the concepts builds better trades.

Probability has an unfortunate historical relationship with gambling. Gambling and trading do not mix and when we talk about the balance of probability below and throughout the book, we use the term in a very specific non-gambling sense. The concepts of probability did start with games of chance but they now play an important role in understanding risk. The concepts are applied to the construction of bridges, the planning of space flights and understanding the impact of pollutants on the environment.

Forget for a moment the gambling connection because a pair of dice is still the best way to reveal the basic concepts. Between them they have twelve faces and each number from 1 to 6 occurs once on each, or twice between the pair of them.

There are a total of 36 different outcomes. The Renaissance gambler and mathematician, Girolamo Cardano, worked out the combinations and they are shown in column C, Figure A.1 in the annex to this chapter. Experienced traders note the dominant feature of column C immediately — the bulge in the middle. Most of us need more time to study the table before we see there are more ways to get to some results than to others. Looking at column A we see that throwing a 7 can be reached by six combinations, or favourable outcomes, but throwing a 12 can only be reached with a single combination.

This information provides the basic calculations necessary for determining the odds and probability of any outcome. The *odds* of an event happening is the ratio of favourable outcomes to unfavourable outcomes. These are detailed in column D. Using 7 and 12 again, we see the *odds* of throwing a 7 are six throws to thirty while the *odds* of throwing a 12 are one throw to thirty five.

In contrast, the *probability* of an event occurring is the ratio of favourable outcomes to the total number of possible combinations, shown in column E. Staying with 7 and 12, the *probability* of a 7 is six throws out of thirty six. The *probability* of a 12 is one throw out of thirty six.

Odds or probability – the distinction is subtle. Those who are unsure of the distinction can find more detailed discussion in the annex at the end of the chapter. This naturally raises the question of trading or gambling. The distinction is important. Get it wrong and the jungle claims another victim. If you suspect you might be gambling then the tests in Chapter 20 will help.

From the trader's perspective, what is important in the dice example is the way results tend to clump in a particular level. Whether we choose to measure the odds, or the probabilities, we still reach the same conclusion: some outcomes are more likely than others. In market terms, reaching some profit targets is easier than others. We choose to run with probability because, as explained below, trading thrives where the total number of possible combinations is large.

This observation is at the very core of successful trading. When traders look at price action they notice immediately that prices tend to clump in particular areas. This suggests some outcomes, some price levels, are more likely than others, or at the very least, more persistent over time than others. When we refer to the balance of probability for the remainder of the book, this is essentially what we mean.

The market is more complicated than a pair of dice. In every trade we deal with two aspects of this complexity. The first is the absolute limit in the number of possibilities for the direction of price.

In the market, in one sense, there are only four possible outcomes or events. The price will increase, or decrease, remain the same, or the company will be delisted. They are always 1 out of 4. Or to put it another way, the odds of losing money are 3 to 4 because only one result – a rise or favourable price move – will leave us with more than our starting capital. We cannot change these outcomes, so we cannot change the odds. No trading approach puts the odds in our favour so we must look to including probability in the best solutions.

The second aspect of market complexity is the theoretically infinite combinations of possible results above zero. Prices could range from a fraction of a cent, like Australian penny stocks, to thousands of dollars for a single share in Warren Buffett's US-based Hathaway Fund. A theoretically infinite universe of combinations is daunting, but it provides the trader with a solution because some combinations occur more frequently than others.

Whether you feel more comfortable moving with the odds, or considering the probabilities, is not as important as recognising that building trading decisions around the tendency of some outcomes to occur more frequently than others is a winning strategy. Your primary concern is to find the best way to identify any bulge — the balance of probability — in the market similar to the bulge in Figure 1.1.

Fig. 1.1
The probability bulge picture.
A pair of dice

Possible results	Number of possible combinations to reach each result	
2	W	1
3	WW	2
4	WWW	3
5	WWWW	4
6	WWWWW	5
7	WWWWWW	6
8	WWWWW	5
9	WWWW	4
10	WWW	3
11	WW	2
12	W	1

The graphic presents the same information as the figures in column C, Figure A.1, but is easier to understand. Here the balance of probability is heaviest at 7 because this result can be reached by more combinations than those required to throw a 12. Both the odds and the probabilities are weighted towards 7. Traders look for similar weightings in the market, and price clumps and trends provide the clues. Charting provides the same graphic representation of otherwise abstract figures.

The first clue is the ability of prices to move steadily in one direction for weeks or months.

Now the total number of possible combinations is not open-ended. Some combinations have extended persistence over time, either as consolidation areas where the same price re-ocurrs frequently, or as trends. These reference points reduce the ratio of possible combinations and favourable outcomes.

This tendency for prices to trend attracts us to the profit opportunities and tells us where the balance of probability is weighted. If we eliminate gross market manipulation, then what creates this probability?

The probability of one direction of price action over another is not equal and is related to the way prices have behaved in the past. Price has no memory, but the buyers and sellers who decide the price do have memories, some pleasant and many bitter. Just as it takes a long time to forget the theft of money, investors cluster around price levels where they have lost money in the past. A gift of cash is more readily forgotten and levels where profit was taken in the past have less impact than levels where losses were realised.

The strength of these memories and the number of people who have similar memories help to establish the probability of price behaviour. Our purpose here is to understand how to recognise this strength and use the probability to our advantage.

The way price behaves in the past, and in the future, is a function of fear and greed. Fear paralyses while greed galvanises. Fear makes us hold on while prices fall, and greed encourages us to chase rising prices. Fear and greed 'load' the dice and when the trader develops tools for understanding where and when the loading takes place he can make sure the balance of probability is very much in his favour.

Price action is recorded as a database of numbers and the newspaper stock report pages list the results. In primary school, students sometimes cut up these pages and use them to make cityscapes of skyscrapers, or more recently, used in ANZ advertising, for cutouts of backhoes and factory buildings. This is as close as many people get to making a picture from printed market information — unless, like accountants and other number crunchers, they are at home with figures.

The mathematician uses numbers to calculate the odds, and the probability. Fund managers use post-modern portfolio theory to hedge against market risk. The private trader finds it difficult to calculate these intensely mathematical solutions. A page full of numbers is difficult to understand.

Mere mortals, traders included, find it easier to see the probability — the bulge — in graphic form. The price chart draws the picture and outlines the cluster of prices in the same way as Figure 1.1 shows the bulge. Deciding when the balance of probabilities is in your favour is made easier on a chart, but only if you can put aside some preconceptions and learn to read the language of the chart.

Picture Perfect

The Antarctic has weird snow shapes sculpted by the wind, the desert sun-blasted rocks. Our landscape resembles that of a little-known Disney educational cartoon on maths. It did little to improve American arithmetic skills, but its enduring image is of a man in a landscape of distorted numbers, towering 7s and 5s, rather like a Sesame Street nightmare. The market jungle replaces vegetation with elegant price bars, thickets of candlesticks and clumps of moving averages against bluffs of charting.

Charts affront many traditional market players, from company directors, to brokerages and brokers, to mums and dads. They appear to devalue their hard-won research and knowledge by suggesting prices can be understood independently from the fundamentals of the underlying company or economy.

Some chartists confirm this divide by relying almost exclusively on obscure number relationships, often expressed as cycles and recurrent angles. Some fundamental traders add their bit to the division by emphasising that only detailed financial understanding of the company's books, with a dash of informed knowledge about company secrets, can allow the trader to take profitable positions in the market.

The truth lies somewhere in between. I rely primarily on charting and technical analysis as the basis of my trading decisions. This horrifies one of my brokers, but he has learnt to live with it. I use these methods to identify my trading opportunities. You may use other methods, but when it comes to assessing the trade we need information that only the chart can provide. It is beyond question that an ability to read a price chart will improve your trading.

A judicious mix of both disciplines makes for better trading. A price chart conveys very specific information in the same way a balance sheet reveals very specific financial information. Both displays — graphic and numerical — sometimes reveal more than their authors intended. Both displays are easily misunderstood.

No matter how you research, and finally reach, a trading decision you must eventually analyse and assess the trade financially. When the trade is entered, the open position must be managed to achieve financial objectives. The price chart, not the newspaper, gives you the basic information needed to undertake this planning process. Later we will look in detail at these procedures.

For now it is sufficient to understand that neither the entry nor the exit from a trade is determined by changing PE ratios, by management structures, by product litigation, profit forecasts or food poisoning scares. These certainly are events which trigger a decision to buy or sell, but they do not set the price the trader receives. Better traders make an exit based on the most recent price activity. Except in apocalyptic events, such as October 1987, few market professionals unload stock at any price. Instead they use current price activity to make an informed decision about the best possible exit price. Private traders emulate this and the chart, as a record of prices, is an indispensable trading tool.

Please remember, when a chart is used as some type of computerised ouija board it is just as accurate, and useful, as ouija board forecasts.

Let us very briefly consider the types of information conveyed in a price chart and what it does, and does not, tell us about the security we are considering. We need to decide if the bulge is fat profit, or dangerous flab.

Here's Health

When we check our financial health we reach for our wallet. Many market participants check the price chart in the same basic way.

"What causes a stock price to go up or down?" asks a self-confessed rookie trader in the Compuserve Investors' Forum. Another passenger in the same boat "SS StockRookie" suggests price might be linked to demand for products the company makes. Either they are purchased or they sit on the shelf and this affects the price of the company in the market, he suggests. This thinking implies a link between the line on a price chart and the financial health of the company. In this understanding the price chart morphs into a balance sheet in graphic form. The daily cash value of our wallet is put into a graph.

This unsophisticated explanation is usually dressed up more attractively. This reasoning is used to explain why the Queensland Metal Corporation price should increase after Ford Motor consummated the deal one magazine described as a marriage made in heaven. If share price was the bridesmaid it slipped heavily on the steps to the altar, immediately falling 32% from $1.51 to $1.02 before recovering.

Attractive in its simplicity as this line of reasoning may be, when stripped to the basics the picture is less pleasing. Ashton Mining shows the unattractive side of this simple explanation. It is a diamond producer and explorer with its main hole in the ground in the rugged Kimberley in the north west of Australia. Figure 1.2 shows a price chart of Ashton Mining in a standard bar chart format. In this five-month chart period the price of Ashton Mining varies dramatically. In twelve days from point A to point B, Ashton Mining adds 23% to its market value. The price increases from $1.74 to $2.15.

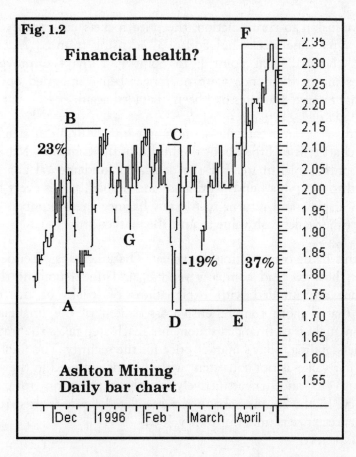

Fig. 1.2

Financial health?

Ashton Mining
Daily bar chart

What does this tell us about the health of the company, about the strength of its management, the size of its inferred diamond resources or the state of the cartel market for its products? We can speculate a great deal on this, but it is very difficult to establish a precise relationship between changes in any of these fundamental factors and the share price.

Perhaps they did add significantly to their inferred resource estimates. Perhaps, in this instance, we can accept an increase of 23% in the underlying value of the company over 12 days, no matter how improbable it seems.

However, five weeks later, this prosperous company loses 19% of its value in six days, plunging from point C to point D – $2.11 to $1.71. We are justified in asking if the diamonds added to inventory in December were found to be paste in February? What does this price action tells us about the health of the company, its management and its markets?

To add confusion to contradiction, the price rockets back to beyond its old level and after nine weeks has added 37%, rising from $1.71 to $2.34 as shown by the rise from point E to point F. Perhaps improved security procedures meant diamonds were no longer being smuggled out the front gate, or that reserve estimates had been upgraded again.

These wild swings in a basically sound company confirm our suspicions that the price chart tells us little about the health of the company. Market price is a bean counter's nightmare. For the dedicated fundamental analyst, at this point he throws up his hands in disgust and despair, wipes every chart from his screen display, and returns to the raw balance sheet numbers pitting his estimate of the wallet cash value against the market price.

He does this by de-constructing the wallet. The process is described in many articles on how to read company reports, and understanding the balance sheet. They are studded with explanations of 'tricks of the trade' and warnings that a more comprehensive assessment of the financial position requires an analysis of financial statements. Each step takes the trader further from understanding today's market price for the security. The final calculated figure of 'fair value' is not consistent with the price printed in the stock pages so we turn to another attractively simple explanation to explain the discrepancy. In the simple version the calculated figure is used to decide if today's market price is under or over valued.

The further we go down this path, the more subjective the result becomes because vital financial information is hidden, or unavailable, to everyone who wants to attempt these calculations. The Australian Stock Exchange (ASX) asks for full disclosure, but this does not apply to commercially confidential material so the analysts must guess at what is concealed. The better analysts often get it right and are paid accordingly.

Getting it right does not mean picking the current market price. This style of analysis is used by brokerages to 'price' a new float. They have full access to financial details that under other circumstances they can only guess at, or imply from other public documents. They almost decide what goes in the wallet. Yet, the first trades on listing show some spectacular differences between the brokerage valuation and the markets valuation. Of 61 recent floats listed in *Shares* magazine 34% are trading at less than their float price and 62% are trading above, while 4% are going nowhere.

This style of analysis has an important place, but we need firmer footings when we trade the market with trading on our mind. I am suggesting that it is less useful from a trading perspective in the same way that the official valuation on your house bears little relationship to the price it brings on the open market. If you use price charts as a measure of the contents of your wallet, then you miss the essence of the advantages charts bring to trading.

Going back to our wallet explains why. If we lose our wallet the insurance value is more than just the cash inside. It includes the credit cards, the sentimental picture, the ticket stub and the PIN number ineffectively disguised as a fax contact. It includes some measure of the potential future value of the wallet to the thief, particularly if he uses our credit cards. We readily accept different measures of value and apply them in different circumstances.

The price chart records the insurance value rather than a daily count of the cash in the wallet. The chart display is a barometer of the market's feeling about the company and the potential future resale value of shares purchased today.

The Chart Says So

The chart is a graphic representation of the market's valuation of the security at a particular point in time. Each point on the chart, such as point D, Figure 1.2, captures in the traded exchange the exact market valuation of Ashton Mining.

This is not a valuation of fundamental worth reached after a simple addition of its assets and the subtraction of its liabilities. This is not a simple count of the cash in the wallet or diamonds on the shelves. It is an estimate of how much shares in this company are going to be worth sometime in the future.

When the transaction takes place at D the seller believes Ashton Mining is doomed. He is bailing out because he believes prices will go much lower. He is taking his loss now before it gets any larger in the future.

The buyer has exactly the opposite conviction. He believes, for whatever reason, be it fundamental or technical, that the price is going to increase in the future. He is happy to get a bargain entry into an improving price. The seller is pleased because the exit saves him from further loss. Time will tell who will be happy and who will be regretful, but for this very instant each person on either side of the transaction believes he has done the best that is possible in his circumstances.

This understanding of market activity — of this trade — tells us nothing about the current status of the company, about its inferred resources, its management, or its audit report. Point D on the chart is never designed to give us this information. This point tells one thing only — this is how the market of buyers and sellers felt about the value of this security at this precise point in time in relation to its future potential. This valuation is a measure of market sentiment.

When we understand that the bar chart measures market sentiment by using market price, then we have a solution that allows the fundamental trader and the technical trader to make the best use of a chart with a price plot.

Price is primarily a measure of sentiment, not a measure of worth. If we do use it to measure company worth, such as when it is incorporated into a number of financial ratios such as price to earnings, price to net tangible assets, or debt to equity, we still end up with a result reflecting current market sentiment rather than a balance sheet.

Defining the Balance

Gold fever brings together a rich assortment of prospectors from all walks of life. The portals of the Stock Exchange building draw crowds in the same way, all impatient to start their expedition. Those determined to survive know at some point they will be called to make, or take, a price in the market. The decision puts the balance of probability with them, or against them. In a landscape shaped by probability success goes to those who use equipment to make or take this price from within a bulge, rather than those who select a price from more slender territory. Getting behind the price bars offers an advantage.

Annex to Chapter 1

ODD LOTS

Calculating the odds is the first step in calculating the probabilities. The mathematical groundwork distinguishing odds from probability was done in the Renaissance by Girolamo Cardano. Writing in *Against the Gods*, Peter Bernstein maintains that Leonardo da Vinci was fascinated by the concepts, even though he would fail a year three arithmetic test today. Leonardo spent many hours with Cardano until he finally understood the problem. If he understood the concepts then the following primer discussion should not present too much of a challenge to today's calculator and spreadsheet-enabled trader.

Toss two dice, put money on the outcome and we enter the world of odds and probability. And it is not as far from this common wager to trading the financial markets as many people think. The probabilities of any outcome become different from the odds of any outcome in subtle ways.

Before we calculate the odds, we need first to determine the list of possible results. Each of the pair of dice has six faces giving a total of eleven possible results. Throwing a 0 or a 1 are not possible results. The lowest possible result is a 2 (one dot plus one dot). The highest possible result is a 12 (six dots plus six dots). This gives eleven possible results. All the possible results are shown in Figure A.1, column A (page 16) — if only life, and trading, were so amenable to a similar process of neat tabulation.

Calculating the odds of any number between 2 and 12 appearing after a throw depends on the total number of possible outcomes, or the opportunity set. As our Renaissance scholar Cardano told Leonardo da Vinci, the odds are the ratio of favourable outcomes to unfavourable outcomes. If we want the number 7, a favourable result, then there are thirty other possible combinations in the opportunity set representing unfavourable results. In modern terms the odds of any turning up the number 7 are six (favourable results) to thirty (unfavourable results), or more commonly expressed as 1 to 5 (30 divided by 6).

Why not 6 to 36 (1 to 6)? We are saying that out of a total of six throws one of them will produce a 7 because there are six combinations out of a possible thirty-six combinations that give this result. The total of throws needed is six — one favourable outcome plus five unfavourable outcomes.

The full list of favourable outcomes is tabulated in column C, Figure A.1. The ratio of favourable to unfavourable outcomes, the odds, are in column D.

CREATING PROBABILITY

The probability of an event is the ratio of favourable outcomes to the total opportunity set. The difference is important. Calculating the odds compares favourable outcomes to unfavourable outcomes. Calculating probability compares favourable outcomes to all possible outcomes. Leonardo, like many high school students and 'wannabe' traders, had difficulty in understanding the difference. I imagine Cardano dragged the dice out yet again to illustrate the difference.

The divergence between odds and probabilities appears in the ways the outcomes can be reached. There are thirty-six possible combinations, or ways, of reaching those eleven results. Column C, favourable outcomes, shows the number of combinations required for each result. Some results, such as number 12, only occur from one group of combinations — six dots and six dots. At the other extreme, number 7 is a result reached by six different combinations. They are: 6+1, 5+2, 4+3, 3+4, 2+5 and 1+6. For those who do their mathematics simply, the total number of favourable outcomes is equal to the total opportunity set.

From these calculations we create a table of probability. It tells us there are six possible combinations that give a result of number 7. This is six out of the thirty-six combinations available. This ratio of favourable outcomes to the total opportunity set is written as a probability of 6/36. The probability of a 12 occurring is found in just one combination out of the thirty-six available and written as 1/36.

We make these calculations because we know the limits of the total opportunity set — lower limit 2 and upper limit 12 — required to produce the total opportunity set.

At a more complex level we can perform similar calculations for a pack of cards, or for the market. The professional card player knows these probabilities, recognises them instantly and uses them to his advantage. The trader does the same by recognising market conditions that tip the balance of probability in his favour.

In transferring the discussion of odds and probabilities from the dice to the market, we shift from 'favourable outcomes' to 'events'. The father of Modern Portfolio Theory, Harry Markowitz, showed the mathematics required for this is much more powerful than a simple calculation of odds and probabilities. Although we know the effects of these events it is more difficult to attach a value to them. The extent of a rise is theoretically infinite, and a fall is limited only by zero. The total opportunity set is ill-defined so the calculation of probability which looks at the ratio of favourable outcomes to the total opportunity set is difficult, if not impossible, to complete.

This level of financial mathematics is beyond the scope of our discussion and readers who wish to follow this in more detail should refer to *Against the Gods*, or *Hedge Funds* by Richard Hills. Those equipped with the appropriate guidance equipment can make their way through *A Treatise on Probability* by John Maynard Keynes.

Extended discussions of risk and probability in wider contexts are found in *Taking Risks: The Science of Uncertainty* by Peter Sprent and *Lady Luck: The Theory of Probability* by Warren Weaver. The relationship between odds and probability form the basis of some linked trading and money management approaches. David Caplan in *Trade Like a Bookie* deals with these types of approaches in detail.

Difficult or not, the trader needs a rule of thumb to estimate the ratio of favourable outcomes to the total opportunity set — the probability. The way prices clump at particular levels suggests outcomes with a higher than normal probability. We shift the balance of success when our trading strategy is based on moves from clump to clump. This rule of thumb serves the private trader well.

Fig. A.1 The probability bulge by the numbers.
A pair of dice

A Possible results	B Total opportunity set	C Favourable outcomes	D Ratio of favourable outcomes to unfavourable outcomes (must add up to 36)	E Ratio of favourable outcomes to total opportunity set
2	36	1	1 to 35	1/36
3	36	2	2 to 34 1 to 17	2/36
4	36	3	3 to 33 1 to 11	3/36
5	36	4	4 to 32 1 to 8	4/36
6	36	5	5 to 31	5/36
7	36	6	6 to 30 1 to 5	6/36 (1/6)
8	36	5	5 to 31	5/36
9	36	4	4 to 32 1 to 8	4/36
10	36	3	3 to 33 1 to 11	3/36
11	36	2	2 to 34 1 to 17	2/36
12	36	1	1 to 35	1/36
		▶	**ODDS**	**PROBABILITY**

Total opportunity set is the
total of favourable outcomes 36

16

2

MESSAGES FROM THE
JUNGLE DRUMS

J ungles give cover for the daily battle 'red in tooth and claw.' In the very best adventure books the battle progress is reported by jungle drums. Our search for trading nuggets in our chosen jungle takes place against a background battle for the bulge.

Unlike the Bastogne battle of the same name there are no dramatic explosions, no flickering of artillery on the horizon nor screeching tank treads through the fog. During those frantic days in December 1944 the airwaves carried desperate, confused, static-ridden messages reporting the progress of the battle. The modern financial market battle for the bulge is fought by silent proxy with numbers dancing across the screen in dealing rooms, brokerages and on home computers. In this battle, progress is reported accurately by the price bar.

People make prices and we would like to know what they are thinking today. If many people make many prices at the same level the bulge gives us clues about probability. If we understand how they thought in the past then we have a guide to their future thoughts. We want to buy at today's prices and sell at a profitable price in the future. Any information that helps to establish the most probable profitable future price is particularly useful so we scan the price bars for messages written by other traders.

Although most people are more familiar with a line chart as a basic screen, or a newspaper price plot display, it is the bar chart that provides the best starting point for understanding price action. It shows all the important elements of price action for the selected period. Experienced traders are so accustomed to the bar chart they run the risk of forgetting what it means and so miss important clues by stepping straight into complexity and ignoring the simply profitable.

Too often we rush into the fray, using analysis to jump from the bar to our favourite indicators. We rush to manipulate price data by smoothing it with averages, by looking at the way today's close relates to the close of several periods ago, we track the momentum in relation to volume, or to its previous rate of change. All of these are valid ways to understand the information provided by the market, but the bar chart — or candlestick chart — is the only price plot combining all the most recent price data in a single screen display along with the probability bulges. The picture is not quite as clear as Figure 1.1 but it is our starting point and time spent here brings rewards.

Constructing a Bar Chart

Graphically the bar on a bar chart — and its Japanese equivalent, the candlestick — is a scratch on the screen. These two styles of price plot provide the same information, and despite their cultural differences, are read the same way. Unless noted, the remainder of this chapter assumes bars are interchangeable with candlesticks.

Both plots link the four basic price details — the open, the close, the high and the low — for the selected period. Although the period can be as short as a few minutes, or as long as 13 weeks or more, for this discussion we treat it as a single trading day.

Markets are a moveable feast so traders range up and down the table from the opening price. Buyers entice sellers to lower their prices. Sellers encourage buyers to bid up.

The price bar shows the major points in the course of sales during the day. A small horizontal slash, or bar, is made to indicate the opening price. A vertical line is drawn to the right. It extends down to touch the lowest price where trades actually take place during the day. The line is extended upwards to mark the highest point during the day where trades actually took place.

The close of the day is marked by a horizontal slash on the right hand side of the vertical line connecting the high and the low. These horizontal bars give the chart plot its name and Figure 2.1 illustrates the process. An up day or a down day is shown by the position of the left hand open bar in relation to the right hand closing bar. Some screen displays show up days in blue and down days in red.

These construction techniques are slightly modified for traders involved in bond and futures markets, or intraday traders, where there is no open price. We look at these later in this chapter.

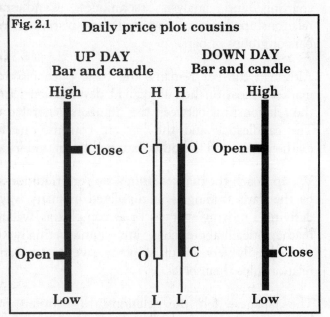

Fig. 2.1   Daily price plot cousins

UP DAY Bar and candle

DOWN DAY Bar and candle

There are always sellers holding out for higher prices and buyers too mean to pay the current price. Their orders are in the ASX Share Automated Trading System (SEATS), and recorded in the depth of market information. These prices, above and below the actual high and low for the day, represent possible prices that were never achieved.

We will explore the messages contained in this information in Chapter 15.

Reading a Bar by Candlelight

A candlestick price plot is constructed in much the same way as a bar chart plot. Instead of showing the open and close as a horizontal bar to the left and right of the vertical line they are shown as parallel horizontal lines at the top and bottom of a rectangle. These are joined to form a box, or body, of the candlestick as shown in Figure 2.1. Up days are shown as an outline, or white, box. The box is filled in on down days, usually with red ink. Any price movement beyond the open or the close, is shown as a single vertical line rather like the wick on a candle. Hence the European name 'candlesticks'.

The candlestick approach diverges from the European development of charting and analysis techniques. Candlestick charting emphasises relationships between bars and their placement relative to other individual bars or groups of bars.

Although the bar remains the basic price plotting tool used in European markets, most of the subsequent developments in technical analysis explore the relationships between the numbers generated by price and volume data. The candlestick and the bar are cousins, one fed on a rigorous diet of mathematics, and the other fattened by an understanding of relationships.

We approach the market from a western tradition so the data series produced by the day's trading is manipulated in many ways. It may be as simple as deriving a moving average, or as complex as Williams' %R. These essentially mathematical approaches are quintessentially European, and although undoubtedly very useful, skip some very important insights offered by price relationships themselves.

The Japanese felt the relationships between prices — the relationships between consecutive candle bars — provided information about the way the market was likely to develop. Their understanding of the market battle places less emphasis on raw figures.

The names given to candlestick relationship patterns sound exotic but they are shorthand for common patterns. If the description suits the mood — dark cloud cover for reversal patterns — then so much the better. Where the pattern name — such as harami cross — is less familiar to European ears, then the ability to easily use candlestick charting as a pattern recognition tool may be diminished for the casual user.

Modern software overcomes this problem to some extent. Specialised software such as CandlePower 5 from North Systems or Candlestick Forecaster scans for many patterns identified by candlestick chartists. Common software packages, such as Metastock, scan for a limited number of patterns.

Modern practitioners of candlestick charting, Steve Nison, *Japanese Candlestick Charting Techniques* and Greg Morris, *Candlepower*, have taken these patterns and explained them in terms of modern European psychological, or demand and supply, analysis. This aids our understanding of candlestick charting, but it should not diminish the importance of the original pattern recognition strengths. The strength of the candle comes from the light it throws on market relationships, not from number crunching.

No matter how you decide to make your trading decision, the bar, or candlestick, chart most fully displays the price action of the day. In theory, it simply answers the question "How much is this security worth today?" If the day's price action is encapsulated in a single line — where the open, high, low, and close are all equal — then the bar chart does give a simple answer to the question.

Understanding the pricing of a security is not as simple as walking into a shop to buy a box of biscuits off the shelf. We might go shopping *for* Coles Myer, but we are not shopping *at* Coles Myer. This is not a set price exchange. Although we know the price charged yesterday, there is no fixed price today, and even more disturbingly, there is no fixed price for tomorrow. Price changes during the day, and the slice we select impacts on our future profits. This makes trading both possible and exciting. Trading takes advantage of price differences by using negotiated trade prices to enter and exit a position.

We all have opinions about the market and about particular securities. They are so much hot air until the strength of our conviction forces us to take, or not take, action. The moment we decide to enter or exit the market — the moment we place an order, whether it is filled or not — we condense the hot air into a more concrete activity. The volume of orders sitting in the market provides important information about the commitment of traders. Everyone talks, but only a few commit.

The moment our trade is executed a new slice of information is added to the course of trades. Our buy or sell order perhaps sets the high, or low, for the day. Our opinion becomes an irreversible part of the day's trading activity.

We expect to make money and we back our opinion with cash. Now our opinion counts, no matter how well informed or ill-informed it may be. Other traders act independently and the combined price activity reflects the way a committed crowd of people feels about this particular security at this point in time. It is not a price decided by a third party. This is not a box of biscuits. This price is alive and it changes, grows, and morphs in direct response to the urgings of the crowd that buys and sells during the day. The jungle is alive with noise and we use the bar chart to filter our chosen noise from the background static.

Understanding a Bar

Each bar or slash on a bar chart measures a different slice of crowd sentiment. To understand how it does this we ask questions about each of the price elements. Who sets the open, the high, the low, and the close?

Before we answer the question we must deal with one issue. If there are no trades today, then how do we show price? Some data suppliers leave the space blank. As discussed more fully below, some bar charts do not show an open. They start the plot with the first traded price for the day, building a high-low-close bar only.

The more common approach is to show the untraded price as the same as yesterday's close and we use this in all of our chart examples. The starting bar on the left hand side is set at the same level as yesterdays close unless the stock is traded immediately on the open. For the moment these distinctions need not distract us other than to note that the first traded price for the day is the open and the comments below apply to it.

Who Sets the Open?

This is perhaps the least important of all price elements. It is most commonly set by the novice traders or part-time traders. It is set by those people who download the prices overnight, or read them in the paper, and decide to buy or sell because the stock looks good. They ring their broker on their way to work, placing their first orders before the market opens. They act on conclusions based on yesterday's information without waiting for verification from today's initial price action.

Market earthquakes are the exception. When institutions panic they act like novice traders. Anyone who tried to ring their broker on Tuesday April 1 after the Dow tumbled over Easter 1997 will recognise the phenomenon. The hour before and after the opening of trade was swamped with orders, choking phones lines and rewarding brokers who had three ears.

The open is also set by traders who have long-term orders sitting in the market. This includes those trading on support or resistance levels as discussed later. The orders are designed to take advantage of the trader's long-term analysis of the probability of prices reaching a specified level.

Some orders are simply forgotten. Lazy or inattentive traders may have placed orders weeks or months ago based on price activity at the time. Through inattention they neglect to remove the orders from the SEATS system and when the price returns to this level they unexpectedly find themselves the proud owners of a security they no longer really want.

Generally the orders filled on the open do not come from full-time traders. This makes the open the least reliable guide to the direction of the market and the feeling of the crowd.

By the end of the first hour the professional traders move fully into the market and set the direction for the day. They confirm overnight trading decisions against the current price action as it develops. These orders are placed by those with access to current market information. The character of the trading day changes as the professionals enter. They help to set the other price elements; the high, the low and the close.

Who Sets the Low?

This is set by the most pessimistic seller — by the bears. They believe the market will only go down, so they want to abandon their position as quickly as possible. The buyers are either long-term bulls waiting for a bargain, or institutional traders taking an intraday position at the best price available in relation to the open.

For all intents and purposes, it is not possible to short fully-paid ordinary shares on the ASX, so this downward pressure is not a result of short selling as it is in the United States. This is an important difference because most US trading books assume downward pressure is a result of short selling. In Australia it is more likely to be the result of institutions reweighting portfolios, fund managers taking a loss quickly, or other traders or investors either taking a loss, or more likely, trying a save a profit.

In other markets where short selling is permitted, then this downward pressure is driven by the desire to make money rather than to minimise losses. Bears are motivated by optimism rather than pessimism because they want to make money from falling prices. The desire to make money drives the price action differently and the presence of market makers complicates the picture further. In some ways this slice of price action holds a weaker message than the same slice in markets where falling prices translate into losses.

These markets do have equal liquidity in either direction because profit is possible from any price move. In the Australian market where a loss is the more probable outcome of a price decline, sellers find it more difficult to match with buyers because the buyers cannot immediately benefit from the price decline. Not only are they buying the future, but they are buying a future where prices must increase before they show a profit on the trade.

The growth of derivative-style trading with warrants may scar the Australian market landscape. These financial products do allow traders to short the market. If the ASX permits selected ordinary shares to be shorted then the jungle landscape will change again. The comments and conclusions drawn from the US market about bear characteristics will gain increasing relevance.

Who Sets the High?

This is set by the most optimistic buyer. He believes prices are going to keep on rising, so he wants in at almost any price. In a rising market, these are institutional buyers who are moving size — share parcels worth $100,000 or more. It is also enthusiastic private traders including those who have caught the lunchtime news, or who have been watching the price movement on their screens. When the big money agrees with them, this will set an up day.

Most Importantly, Who Sets the Close?

This is the most significant of the price elements and is used as a benchmark to assess both the direction of prices for the day, and the strength of the price move. The last 20 minutes of trade is the most hectic period of the day. It is dominated by traders who watch the market because it is their job to do so, or because their primary income depends on it. By definition these are the professionals. The amateur trader is still hard at work on his day job and is unlikely to be able to duck out for a quick cigarette and a peek at a SEATS screen.

The close is also set by intraday traders who usually take their profits towards the end of the day. True day traders do not carry open positions overnight. Short-term traders with a one to four-day time frame, will also close out positions if they feel the market might reverse direction overnight. No matter which way you slice it, the close is set by the smart money, by savvy traders taking profits, or cutting losses, or by those positioning themselves to take profits in the near future.

The close is generally considered to be the most accurate representation of the market's feelings about the stock on the day. So why not use a line chart based on the close?

The range between the price elements gives trading clues vital for the best possible entry or exit. This is the daily reality of the market and it destroys many fancy theoretical calculations. This also applies to groups of bars. The long and the short of it tells traders more than any single line can ever do.

Special Bars Open 24 Hours

We hinted above that not all bars look the same. These equity bar chart construction techniques are slightly modified for traders involved in bond and futures markets, or intraday traders, where there is no open price until a trade takes place. Price bars in these markets look like Figure 2.2, showing the high, low and close for the selected period.

Day traders face a different challenge from position traders and these specialised price bars do a specific job. The day trader is the direct offspring of

Jessie Livermore and the other great tape readers. They watch the market action during the day, reading the tick information to find the market's intentions. Gary Smith, a US trader, gives a fascinating blow-by-blow description of this style of trading in *Live the Dream by Profitably Day Trading Stock Futures* and also in the May 1997 issue of *Technical Analysis of Stocks and Commodities.*

The day trader's intention is to enter and exit a trade between the market open and close. He carries no overnight positions. Traders who do carry overnight positions are more properly short-term traders.

A daily bar chart using a single bar to show the action over the six hours of trading is of little use to the day trader. Instead, they arbitrarily divide the day into segments and plot the price action in each segment. These segments may be as short as one or three minutes, or more commonly five minutes, and stretch to 10, 20, 30 and 50-minute periods. The choice depends upon the market being traded.

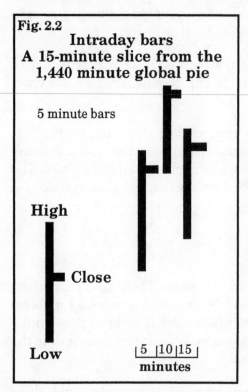

Fig. 2.2
Intraday bars
A 15-minute slice from the
1,440 minute global pie

5 minute bars

High

Close

Low

|5 |10|15|
minutes

The first bar in Figure 2.2 is part of an ongoing five-minute price plot. The top of the bar is the high achieved in this five-minute time period. The low is the low traded in this five-minute time period. The close, the right hand slash on the bar, is the price at the end of this five-minute period.

The next bar in the series does not have an open because the price plot starts only with the first traded price in the next five-minute period which is not necessarily at the same level as the previous close. The beginning of this period is instantaneous. When the clock ticks to the next five-minute period the chart point moves one bar to the right and makes no entry until a trade is made. What is important in this plot is the lowest and highest points and the final closing price, in the selected period.

This style of bar charting offers clear advantages for these intraday traders. For position traders active in bond and other markets where the standard price bars show high, low and close, the picture is distorted when some data feed and charting software packages calculate an artificial 'open' for each day. The method used to calculate the 'open' varies and inevitably impacts on the accuracy of the data when shown either as a standard bar or as a candlestick display.

This has several consequences for the way the jungle drums report the battles and the way we search for the balance of probability.

Although not an issue now, the first of these consequences comes with the eventual move to 24-hour continuous markets. This will tend to make many accepted bar charts – O, H, L, C – look more like the bars used in intraday trading – H, L, C. In practice these bar charts can still be usefully constructed to show an open with using an artificial calculation.

Markets may be traded 24 hours a day, but brokerages are not that active. Futures contracts are traded in the US on the New York Stock Exchange (NYSE). Australian traders can participate directly in what for us, is overnight trading. The New York Exchange opens day trading at 8.10 am and closes at 2.30 pm. The overnight session runs from 4.00 pm through to 8.00 am. The Sydney Futures Exchange (SFE) provides a continuous open market by trading 6.00 am to 10.00 pm Australian time. US traders wishing to trade in this period must participate in what is for them, an overnight market.

In following this sequence of Exchange hours around the world we find a surge of early orders as trade begins in each local region. This effectively establishes an 'open' and about six hours later at the end of the trading day, in regional local time, there is another surge of orders, effectively creating a 'close'.

In effect each regional open and close of trading floors creates a distinctive open and close blip on the price action. For all practical purposes these blips can be used in building a bar defining a single 'day' of trading. In any twenty hour period, there may be three to four such 'days'.

Trading other 24-hour markets is made more difficult by Exchanges having different procedures for determining the open and the close for the day. This has a significant impact on price data but is of limited interest to ASX traders. Australian traders involved with US markets can follow a full discussion in the annex to this chapter.

The nuances of bar chart construction in 24-hour markets impact on the chart display and on some trading tactics. These changes do not significantly alter our understanding and interpretation of information provided by the bar chart — support, resistance, trendlines — and the subsequently derived and calculated indicator information — moving averages, stochastics, oscillators. Day traders using 3 and 30-minute charts base their trading on the same understandings as position traders who use 6-hour — 10.00 am to 4.00 pm — charts.

Using a Bar

Understanding the information in a single price bar, no matter how constructed, lets the trader make a better entry or exit from a trade. The bar chart tells us how the smart money, the significant money, is positioned in relation to the extremes of emotional feeling about the security. Smarter trading suggests we should be travelling in the same direction as the smart money because it shows us where the balances of probability lie in any single trading period.

These important clues about the attitude and orientation of the smart money are instantaneous and are displayed immediately at the end of every trading day. You get the close at the same time as the institutional traders and every other private trader. You get to act on it at the same time as everybody else — when the market opens the next day. The jungle drums are heard by everybody and the message is in the beat.

The bar chart captures the beat of the market jungle and gives us information to confirm or deny our initial identification of a trading opportunity. For the fundamental trader, the bar chart is perhaps the last stopping point before the market is entered. For the technical trader, the bar chart is the starting point for all other analysis. The next chapter quickly looks at the way a bar chart builds a trade.

A Bar in Every Market

Equity, commodity, currency and the growing derivative markets are different in their rules, procedures, risk profiles and tactics. Many say the great divide between the equity market and other financial markets is the concept of a zero-sum game. Many commentators and traders believe trading any financial market is a zero-sum game with a winner and loser every time — what I win, you *must* lose. This difference is claimed to be so great that any discussion about equities cannot be relevant to other markets. On the surface this makes the bar chart analysis techniques discussed above appear less relevant to these markets.

Every market provides the data needed to build a bar chart. In the same way the various codes of football are all united by a single common feature — teams chasing a ball — markets are united by price activity. The bar chart as a means of recording price activity is common to all markets so the artificial divide between equity and other financial markets is unimportant because the bar chart always provides us with the same type of information about the player's emotional reaction to current price. It does not tell us who takes money from whom nor describe the distribution of spoils.

Nor does it tell us how traders feel about the type of game they are playing — rugby or soccer, equities or commodities — so we don't use a bar chart in this way. In some important ways the philosophical argument about zero-sum games, while entertaining, is largely irrelevant to understanding the message. The bar provides concepts, such as support and resistance, equally valid for equity trading and for commodities or currencies in financial markets. A developing triangle pattern speaks the same language on a five-minute currency bar chart as it does on a weekly equity bar chart.

Our belief about the trading arena we choose, be it zero-sum or not zero-sum, changes the way we approach the market and the trading strategies we prefer. The battlefields are different, but the emotional messages contained in the price dispatches from the front are the same. The balances of probability — the bulges — are exposed in any bar chart. Building a trade from this information is the basic entry point for every trader no matter which market he trades.

Every prospector builds a grub-stake to finance the next prospecting expedition. In the gold mining towns they flash some sample nuggets. Or, like the enigmatic Australian prospector Harold Lasseter, they build these into tales of a reef with "the yellow stuff in it as thick as plums in a pudding". No briefing on the dangers of the jungle would be complete without a sample nugget to re-ignite those with faltering courage. The next chapter gives shape to the nuggets we expect to find. You risk your own capital so it pays to put a more definite shape on the imagined pile of dollars hiding in the market jungle.

Annex to Chapter 2

WHEN A CLOSE IS NOT A CLOSE

Foreign markets use common terms, but the meaning is not always the same. Sometimes we decide the distinction is not important, but unless we are aware a distinction exists we cannot make an informed decision. The closing price is vital to most charting and technical analysis indicators.

The CNN feed used by Australian television stations invariably shows the New York Exchange finish the trading day with the bell. Actual close of trade is not this simple and data showing the close for the NYSE, and other markets, is not always as accurate as we intuitively believe.

Systematic trading usually requires an entry and exit as close as possible to the target price. Variations in end of day data prices affect the results of technical indicators. Delays in real-time data updates on the screen, based on reports of trading activity in the pit, affect profit margins. The differences particularly affect those trading US futures contracts and markets.

A few seconds before the official closing time all Market On Close[1] orders are executed at the market price. Trading ends only when all such orders have been executed so trading may go some time beyond the official closing time. Trades are settled within a closing range. The simple average of the price range is the settlement price and this may be different from the official close used by data vendors.

To add confusion in futures markets, the closing session for different contracts begins at different times, extends for different periods, and varies from exchange to exchange. New York Coffee's closing session lasts for five minutes, while the Chicago Mercantile Exchange normally starts 30 seconds before the official closing time. Currencies on the same exchange have about 60 seconds. Traders using Market On Close orders must know the individual closing times for their contract.

Settlement vs close — does it matter? If your search takes you to this part of the jungle the difference is an additional hazard. A bar chart based on the

---

[1]A more detailed discussion of US market orders and of the differences in trading environments of the ASX, NASDAQ and the NYSE are covered separately in the Appendix, Foreign Jungles.

close can be significantly different from a bar chart based on the settlement price after the bell. The impact of these differences will depend on your style of trading and the way you place orders. You should know which price your vendor supplies as it affects the way your data matches with reality.

NOT THE OPEN TOO

If the distinction between the close and the settlement price has not set your head spinning, then rotational openings should do the trick. Futures traders active in US markets using the open to set decisions on an intraday basis face significant challenges.

Like the close, all market orders placed before opening time are executed at the market. Prices are quoted as an opening range rather than a price. The closing time of the opening session is when all pending market orders have been filled. The simple average of this opening range is quoted as the official open price.

Many data vendors use the official open price as the open in their daily updating service. Many traders prefer to use the first actual trade as the open. Not knowing which price your data vendor uses is not always fatal, but it is dangerous.

This confusion is compounded with rotational opens on New York markets. The official open starts with trading in the front month contract. Trading opens for a short period, then stops. The next month out is opened for a short time, and then closed. This continues until all contract months have established an opening range. Once the rotation is completed trading in all contracts are opened simultaneously and the actual full day's uninterrupted trading commences. The time between the official open and the actual simultaneous open, ranges from a few minutes to nearly half an hour. Off floor screen traders locked out for 30 minutes are at a disadvantage on days of high volatility.

Phillip York of QBL Funds Management gives an extreme example taken from June 27, 1994. He tells how the Coffee markets opened at 9:15 a.m. after a weekend freeze in Brazil:

> *"The July contract opened at 175.00 and in the next 60 seconds established an unprecedented opening range of 7.00¢, from 173.00 to 180.00."*

Trading stopped as the opening rotated to the next month out:

> "*A full 35 minutes later, trading resumed at an 'unofficial' opening price of 161.00. The difference was a full $7,125 per contract from the high of the Opening Range.*"

Burned by this confusion between official and actual opening prices, some traders only use the second actual open when all contracts are reopened simultaneously. On a tick by tick basis the day trader can pick this. The position trader relying on end of day data gets unreliable signals unless he knows how his data vendor plots the open. And it is no wonder that it is sometimes easier to draw the bar without a slash on the left-hand side.

3

LASSETER'S REEF

Armed with two concepts — the balance of probability and the structure of a bar chart plot — we are better equipped to find and assay trading nuggets than many of our competitors. Life in the market jungle does get much more complex, but with this information alone we can find and build a better trade.

We know a single bar tells us where the smart money, the big money, is positioned, moving with or against the trend. We enhance the probability of success if we move in the same direction. In the same way, the behaviour of a group of bars creates a similar probability bulge. In the first chapter Figure 1.1 bulged enticingly at the number 7. The same attractive bulges pop out in Figure 3.1. We have deleted the price scale to make it easier to focus on the way prices move. On the jungle battlefield of uncertainty these are the touchstones of trading success.

Every prospector shows samples. Some, such as the reef samples produced by Harry Lassetter, are misleading. Others, perhaps from Great Central Mines' Bronzewing find, are truly exciting. We show you an example below, along with ways to judge real gold from fool's gold. This nugget comes from the region we intend to explore.

This sample uses the bar chart alone. We establish profit targets, entry points and stop loss levels based on a framework of probability. A plain vanilla analysis of the General Property Trust (GPT) chart uses this trading framework to give us an advantage over those who do not understand the bar chart. No matter how complex our analysis may later become, the probability bulge is the trading touchstone at the beginning and end of every trading decision.

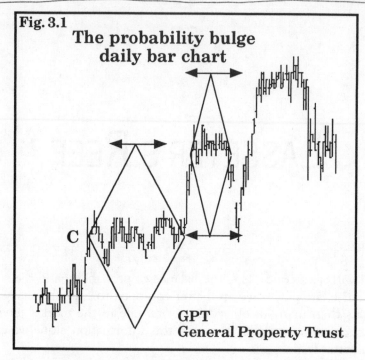

Fig. 3.1

The probability bulge daily bar chart

C

GPT General Property Trust

What stands out from the GPT daily bar chart? Even a cursory look shows information not easily obtained from any other source. Prices seem to clump at particular levels, moving sideways, before moving up, or down. Newspaper price quotations, even when collected together over a few days, do not reveal this information so clearly.

This is the major bar chart advantage. Immediately we see prices tend to spend some time moving in a tight trading band before taking off, usually dramatically, to establish new levels that later also develop into tight trading bands. These observations give the trader enough information to take advantage of trading opportunities.

With GPT, support and resistance — the probability bulges — provide a simple trading strategy. Support and resistance are important concepts and we will return to them in Part II. For the moment we merely want to take advantage of this behaviour so only a brief definition is needed.

When prices fall, support defines the level where they pause. This level forms when buyers enter the market because they think the stock is attractively priced. With GPT, the lower limits of each band are support levels. They are well defined and easily marked as shown on Figure 3.2.

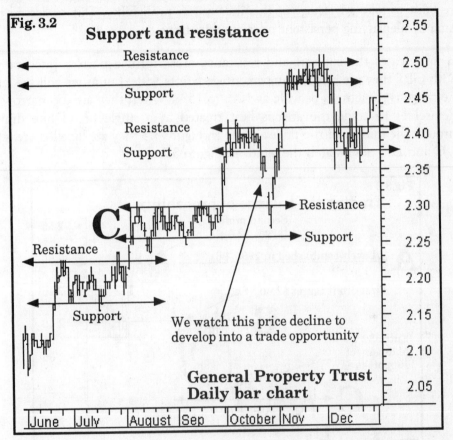

Fig. 3.2 **Support and resistance**

Resistance
Support
Resistance
Support
C
Resistance
Support
Resistance
Support
We watch this price decline to develop into a trade opportunity

General Property Trust Daily bar chart

2.55 2.50 2.45 2.40 2.35 2.30 2.25 2.20 2.15 2.10 2.05

June | July | August | Sep | October | Nov | Dec

Resistance is similar to support. It defines areas where prices reach a consistent peak before pulling back. The level forms in the opposite way to support. Resistance levels happen when sellers unload stock because they have made their desired profit, or because they feel the stock will not go any higher. Again, with this chart, the areas are unusually well defined. The middle trading band, or consolidation area, between these upper and lower levels is labelled C. Traders thinking ahead by looking back will note how these correspond to the double-headed arrows in Figure 3.1.

Persistent Probability

Using the language of probability we observe there are areas where specific price combinations have persistence — short-term trends — or extended persistence — long-term trends — over time. Gold travels along river beds, but gathers in the hollows. The simple vibrating riffle tables in every gold room are built to take advantage of this increase in probability. Our trades do the same by identifying persistent price combinations.

In most cases the support and resistance areas form a narrow price range. With GPT they are only a few percentage points wide, but as we will see later the range is sometimes as wide as 10% to 15%. When they are too narrow in themselves to trade the area is best treated as a single broad line drawn through the middle of the price action. In Figure 3.3 they are labelled areas A, B, C and D. These match the bands in Figure 3.2.

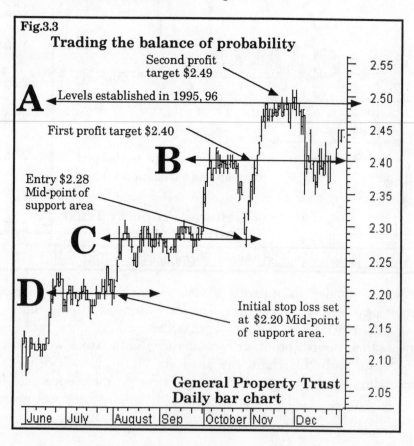

Fig.3.3
Trading the balance of probability

Second profit target $2.49

A — Levels established in 1995, 96

First profit target $2.40

B

Entry $2.28
Mid-point of support area

C

D

Initial stop loss set at $2.20 Mid-point of support area.

General Property Trust
Daily bar chart

June | July | August | Sep | October | Nov | Dec

2.55
2.50
2.45
2.40
2.35
2.30
2.25
2.20
2.15
2.10
2.05

A resistance level, such as the upper line in area C on Figure 3.2, or the centre line C in Figure 3.3 often becomes a support level and vice versa as the trend changes direction. Once the level is crossed there are a substantial number of new stockholders who have made decisions based on this level. They calculate their profits, losses, or break-even points from it.

Our entry strategy for GPT is simple. As the price drops from $2.40 in October we sense a trading opportunity developing as it moves towards level C. We all want to buy today's high performing stocks at bargain prices so we lie in wait where the balance of probability bulges. The nearest bulge is support level C and by setting an entry order at the midpoint — $2.28 — we have a good probability of being filled because prices have paused here in the past.

It is important to understand we are not buying the sudden price dip. This does not, in itself, signal a sound trading opportunity. We are buying the balance of probability that the price collapse will pause at one level rather than another.

We are not saying prices will necessarily rally from this pause, although we think they will on balance. We are saying prices will move, and when they do, they will probably move as far as an established support or resistance level and pause for a while. The total number of possible combinations is not open-ended. There are areas where combinations have extended persistence over time. Using these clumps or bulges as reference points, puts the balance of probability on our side because it reduces the ratio of possible combinations and favourable outcomes.

After striking these levels, the subsequent move will follow a similar pattern, up or down. This is not a rare jungle 'nugget', although it is often well camouflaged. Prices do not move in a random pattern. They do gather at points for extended periods, and thereby provide a smaller range of possible combinations. 'Nuggets' with these patterns are very valuable.

The well-defined support and resistance levels, A, B, C and D, also provide a simple risk control strategy. You should not trade unless you have a fully-developed strategy for managing risk in each and every trade. Later we will show how this is developed, but for the moment we want to briefly sketch how this GPT bar chart provides the necessary calculation points.

To manage this trade successfully we must fully plan the risk and the reward so there are no unpleasant surprises. The methods of planning and managing a trade are common to all trades. Trade with $2,000, or $2,000,000 — the principles remain the same.

These analysis steps may appear too basic for real trading. In fact they are more than adequate and form the basis of every trade. There is no set relationship between the time consumed by analysis and the trading outcome. Some wannabe traders fail to understand that hours spent does not necessarily translate into a correct answer and they pursue complex answers when simpler ones are also profitable.

In any trade we first set the conditions to tell us if our analysis is wrong. The second task is to set reasonable profit targets based on the bulges of probability. All of this information comes from the General Property Trust bar chart so we consider each step using Figure 3.3.

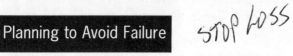

Planning to Avoid Failure   *STOP LOSS*

The trader must know when he is wrong. This trade entry is planned at $2.28 just above support and we must decide how much additional price retracement shows we have misjudged. These calculations are the first step and should be completed before the trade is opened so the scope for emotion in later decisions is reduced.

Our trading proposition accepts the basic odds — favourable outcomes to unfavourable outcomes — and measures them. From this pause area, prices will either fall towards the next support level or rally to the next resistance level. There is no shame attached to misjudging the direction of the price move. The real problems arise when we cannot admit the misjudgement because this prevents us from taking appropriate action. Sitting on a loss is not a sign of strength. It is a sign of weakness showing you do not have the discipline to take a loss.

This marks the difference between successful traders and unsuccessful traders. It is not the size of the profits, but the size of the losses. Successful traders control risk by taking small losses early according to a predefined plan. Unsuccessful traders are forced to take big losses usually under unfavourable circumstances because they need the money, because the paper loss is too great, or they need to be able to sleep without worry. It is the loser's law of the market. In Part III we look more closely at planning to avoid failure.

With this simple trade example, to avoid taking large losses we must quickly know when we are wrong. In this case, if the price pulls back below our intended entry around support at $2.26 — if there is a close below $2.26 — then we are wrong. The current support level would be broken and GPT past price history tells us when this happens the price will fall to at least the next support band at D. The midpoint of this band is $2.20 and an exit here shows a loss of 3.5%.

This is within acceptable limits so it sets the initial stop-loss point. It is a realistic stop loss because it uses the dynamics of the chart support levels to shift the balance of probability in our favour. If prices do fall, they are more likely to pause in this area than in other areas.

Caught on the Rebound

When to take profits !

The second step in any trade is setting reasonable profit targets. What is reasonable? Too often this concept is bounded only by our own greed, or limited by our fear. A price chart unemotionally defines 'reasonable' for each trade. Here we skip the depth of calculations involved because this nugget is just a sample of bigger trading treasures.

This sample GPT trade is based only on information supplied by the bar chart so the price action sets profit levels related to the bulges of better probability as shown in Figure 3.1. These are also significant support and resistance levels and profit targets set near them increase the probability of a successful exit at our preferred price.

The first bulge in probabilities is around $2.40, shown as area B in Figure 3.3. The return is 5.2%. As an initial target this is acceptable. The second bulge, area A, is around $2.48 to $2.50. A midpoint exit at $2.49 for 9.2% seems a reasonable target.

This is all very clear in retrospect in Figure 3.3, but not so clear in late October when these decisions about future price action are being made. The higher profit target — the second bulge at level A — was established by previous price action not shown in Figure 3.3. This level formed in April 1995, and again in June and July of the same year. More recently it was tested in March 1997 when prices approached this level several times but were unable to breakthrough to new levels. The people who make prices by buying at these levels have long memories so these combinations have extended persistence over time.

Armed with this information from the chart the trader already has a better risk control and profit strategy than those who do not use a chart. The trader was able to exit at a safely-calculated $2.49, taking a 9.2% return, because he knew in advance two vital pieces of information provided by the chart alone.

He knew what conditions would signal he was wrong. And he knew the conditions signalling success. He knew in advance how much he expected to gain, or lose. Instead of hanging onto the trade in hope, he exited cleanly with financial targets satisfied. Trading success was based on understanding how the balance of probability is used to enhance profits and limit losses. This separates the consistent trading winners and survivors from the losers.

The trader used the chart to locate the balance of probability of crowd action, and hence price action. By setting targets based on the way prices pause and consolidate at persistent levels he shifts the balance in his favour.

This simple analysis is just the beginning of assessing any trade. Successful trading requires more thorough research, sound analysis matched to preferred trading techniques, and specific methods of establishing the financial objectives and viability of the trade. All trades start with, and return to, this touchstone of the balance of probability.

The search for market gold is similar to prospecting for the real metal itself. Before venturing into the jungle, sensible new chum prospectors survey the terrain and talk to old experienced miners who have worked the ground. They gather clues about what to expect so they can get to the gold quicker than their competitors. This and previous chapters are the market equivalent of this pre-expedition research.

Next, novice prospectors determine the character of the deposits, be they alluvial, placer, or mother lodes. Finally new chum prospectors equip themselves with good tools for exploring the ground, with the best methods for assaying the quality of the find, and with a strategy for protecting the growing bullion. These are issues we will explore in the following sections after we have a method to define the character of our deposits. There are no shortcuts in this journey — unless you choose to follow Lasseter's footsteps to his mythical reef.

4

TIME BITES CHARACTER

The gold museum attached to Sovereign Hill in Ballarat houses a collection of samples gathered from the surrounding areas. From nuggety bits of pure hard cash, to fine flecks of dust and sandy grains, the sheer variety is surprising. This gold has character, be it forged in basalt furnaces, scoured by wind and rain or tumbled in polished glory along stream beds. Clearly more than a pick and shovel is needed to extract a fortune on this field.

Before we start the search for trading gold we need a good idea of the character of our reef. Does our gold come in nuggets, in rich veins visible in the quartz, or is it scattered like gold dust in a river bed stream? Although the metaphor is not strictly correct because our 'nuggets' are living events with character and behaviour, it serves as a useful way of thinking about the nature of our search expedition in the market jungle. Character determines the tools we use to detect and mine our potential fortune. Later we use specific tools to discover and unearth trade opportunities but our search is initially assisted by considering different time frames.

Gold nuggets nestle deep in the wrinkles of local geology and our trading 'nuggets' are hidden in layers of weekly, daily and day-by-day activity. This jungle includes a fractal landscape with small patterns repeated on a larger scale. Stocks have characters, or groups of behaviours, best seen on a weekly chart. They exhibit individual behaviours, best seen on a daily chart. They thrash with emotion on a daily basis. The time bite we choose as a screen display captures character, behaviour or emotional activity.

Each chart time bite captures a different glimpse of opportunity and from these we build a better picture of probability. Flip forward a few pages and check the weekly price plot for Woodside Petroleum (WPL), Figure 4.3.

The uptrend character is clear. Here is easy money. Most try to climb on board when the trend is well established. "Get me into something, anything, going up" they tell their broker in the middle and closing stages of a bull market as if the market is a one-way elevator to the roof.

When the same WPL chart is reduced to a few days, shown in Figure 4.6, profit opportunities look less certain. This is an emotional view and events are thrown out of proportion. Unlike other investments, or money-making opportunities, value fluctuates, sometimes wildly. Rationally traders know if they are on board this simple weekly trend evident in Figure 4.3, then price behaviour will trend upwards. Emotionally they are attacked by the rise and fall of prices shown on the daily chart and listed every morning in the newspaper. These contradictory feelings come from different time frames. A better understanding of the links between character, behaviour and emotion turns up many rough diamonds.

Securities, like those who trade them, do have character. They range from staid established giants to cheeky little start-ups. Prices develop characteristic groups of behaviours which impact on the probability of future behaviour.

Each bar on the price chart is related to, and depends on, the previous bar. Each daily graph of market emotion builds on the behavioural high or low of the previous day. The range of behavioural swings is constrained by the character of the security. Each time bite is a snapshot of market action — minutes, daily, weekly — and signals or confirms different trading opportunities. We need different trading tactics to suit each of them. This jungle includes thickets of time and open glades where only a few price bars thrive.

Elder thinks we should look @ charts in the following order: 1) weekly 2) Daily 3) A few days or ticks

Trading Time Bites

Dr Elder in *Trading for a Living*, codified these time relationships in the Triple Screen trading approach. It takes advantage of computer power and modern software to capture snapshots for further study.

The core essential of his approach is to trade in the direction of the prevailing trend while taking advantage of short-term favourable conditions to make the best entry, or exit, possible. Elder suggests we first look at weekly charts, then daily charts, then at just a few days or at tick data.

In practice we feel dwarfed in this jungle so we start with the middle view because this is the one most commonly displayed on our trading screens. Some software displays 150 trading days, or about seven months, of data as the standard default. Other software displays 260 trading days, or just over a year, of price history. The size of the screen view time bite is a matter of personal choice but I favour a year, or 260 days, of data. If I want to take a closer look at particular price activity I use the zoom function to expand the detail.

Use 260 days default

Why 260 trading days? Significant trends develop over extended periods and we want to trade in the direction of the trend. Shorter time bites sometimes give misleading clues. We want to see a wider range of sensible options. At times we might 'fade' the trend by taking an early position in anticipation of a trend change. As prices grope for the bottom, or snatch desperately at new tops, we take advantage of these early warning signs to buy or sell in anticipation of a new trend developing.

Although the turning point might be dramatic, it can also be a whimper. Some stocks break out of the trend and race sideways for weeks or months, trading in a narrow band, forcing our trading capital to take a rest. Stand too close and the action loses significance. Stand too far away and the detail eludes us. A year of daily activity on the screen strikes a balance.

Daily Time

The time bite contained in the initial screen view sets our focus in more ways than one. The first subconscious judgements made here heavily influence our analysis of other time frames. If our first look at the data is too narrow, we lose perspective. Significant price moves get lost in a welter of daily price activity. Insignificant price moves gain unwarranted stature because the context of their performance is too narrow.

Just how vital is this, or is it an exercise of academic importance? The impatient prospector is satisfied with the nuggets he sees at first glance. A fortune awaits those who take a longer view. In market terms the following charts of Woodside Petroleum show the advantages of each time bite. The bar labelled 'A' is the same bar in each view. We look for a buying decision based on the analysis of each chart.

I prefer a 260-day time bite but many traders use the smaller default screen display. For comparison, we start in Figure 4.1 with a 150-day view. The questions we ask are the same. How strong is the new downtrend[1] and how long will it last? The last bar, A, shows a small rally in the short-term downtrend in place since January. It looks too weak to jump on board. This 'nugget' is passed over.

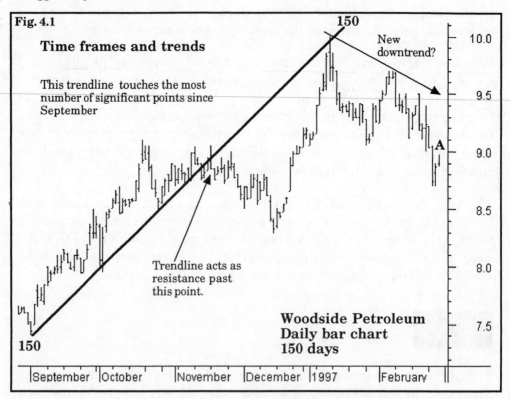

Fig. 4.1

Time frames and trends

This trendline touches the most number of significant points since September

New downtrend?

Trendline acts as resistance past this point.

Woodside Petroleum Daily bar chart 150 days

September | October | November | December | 1997 | February

---

[1] See Chapter 6 in *Share Trading* for more details on how trendlines are constructed.

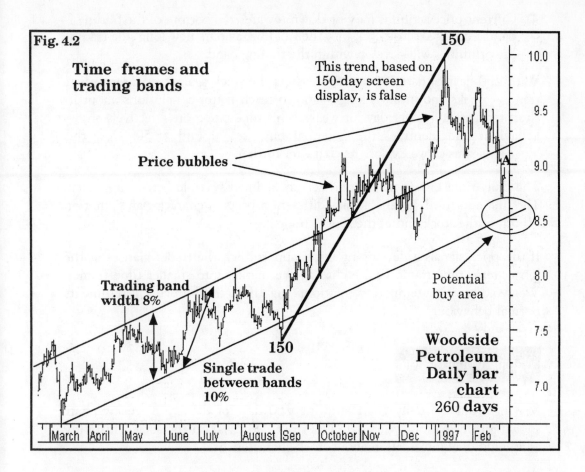

Fig. 4.2

Time frames and trading bands

150

This trend, based on 150-day screen display, is false

Price bubbles

Trading band width 8%

150

Single trade between bands 10%

Potential buy area

A

Woodside Petroleum Daily bar chart 260 days

March April May June July August Sep October Nov Dec 1997 Feb

10.0
9.5
9.0
8.5
8.0
7.5
7.0

Turn to my preferred screen displaying 260 days of data for the same stock, in Figure 4.2, and the analysis changes. The trendline dominating the 150-day chart, shown here as a thicker line, is a purely short-term trend. The real trend constraints for WPL are established by the trading bands. Additional information available from this time bite includes:

➲ Prices move in a trading band about 8% wide. A single trade is reasonably expected to return about 10% as prices move diagonally between the trading bands.

➲ In the last four months prices bubbled above the upper trading band. Bullish buying pushed prices to extremes. This is a change in behaviour and the upper trendline of the trading band acted as a support line. Bubbles retreat to this line, then rally again.

○ Current price action is moving down towards the bottom of the trading band. As prices settle back into their old behaviours new long side trading opportunities will develop within the trading band.

With 260 days of data it is easier to assess the stock against its intermediate trend – weeks and months long – and to reach better conclusions about its short-term trend – over days or weeks. This time bite more effectively shows behaviour and identifies the potential buy area around $8.50. Now this 'nugget' gleams so we explore its character further.

The daily time bite is the second screen of Elder's Triple Screen approach. The first and third screens display different aspects of character and emotion – both of the stock and of those who trade it.

If the price signals a developing trade opportunity, the trader glances at the longer-term time frame before chasing the market into smaller time frames. We avoid buying a temporary emotional high if we think price will resume its normal behaviour.

Weekly Confirmation

Moving from the daily chart showing 260 days of data to a weekly chart showing three to four years data (750 to 1,000 days) on the screen instantly adds additional information about stock characteristics.

The weekly view, Figure 4.3, puts current behaviour into a wider character context. This time bite confirms current behaviour is consistent with the well-established trend. Now the combined trading information derived from Figures 4.2 and 4.3 includes:

○ The downside is limited by the long-term trendline. Also confirmed by Figure 4.3. The slope of the trendline is consistent across time frames.

○ Prices move in a broad band. Prices bubbled above this band in late 1996 but returned to the band in early 1997. Both time bites confirm this.

○ The height of the weekly band width is about 15%. Trading returns approach 19%.

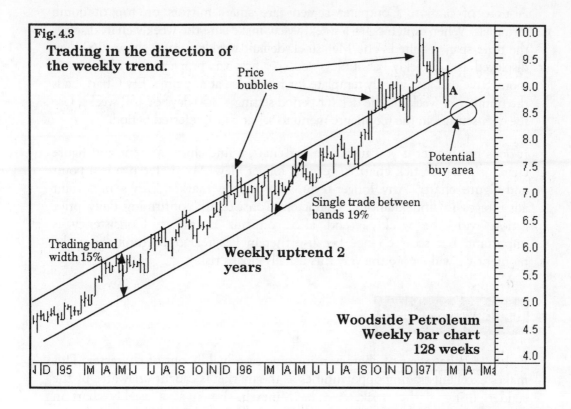

Fig. 4.3

**Trading in the direction of
the weekly trend.**

Price
bubbles

A

Potential
buy area

Single trade between
bands 19%

Trading band
width 15%

**Weekly uptrend 2
years**

**Woodside Petroleum
Weekly bar chart
128 weeks**

J D 95 M A M J J A S O N D 96 M A M J J A S O N D 97 M A M

The agreement between these two time bites points to the balance of probability. In deciding how to extract this 'nugget' we make additional notes:

⮑ Only a few sales take place on the bottom trendline before prices move upwards again. Buy orders are best placed early just above the trendline in anticipation of a rapid rebound. This characteristic behaviour appears in both long and short-term time frames.

A buy zone is indicated at $8.60. The buy zone slides up the trend line as price action is added, moving the bars to the right. A sell zone based on the upper trend line also slides to the right as new price bars are added.

⮑ Each trade returns around 10% in the short term, but better returns are available by waiting through several cycles of rebounds between the trading bands.

Woodside Petroleum is not an erratic character. With consistent behaviour across two time frames we can confidently trade in the direction of the trend and take advantage of a temporary price pullback during the day.

A note of caution. Computer screens are smart mirrors on top of dumb terminals. When switching to a weekly view make sure the weekly chart displays the time span required. The Metastock default weekly format shows 260 days displayed as 52 weekly bars unless you specify x-axis properties as 750 days or more. Save this as a weekly template for future use at any time. Ezy Chart loads the number of weeks as the default period setting – 150 days or 150 weeks. Use the data settings in the Configure menu to select your preferred period.

It does not matter if you turn to a bar chart, a line chart, a point and figure chart or a candlestick chart to get this longer view. My preference is a point and figure chart.[2] Any longer-term view of the market brings important advantages in understanding character. Consistently confirming daily price action with the weekly trend also confirms character. Consistency is important, but so is change because therein lies real opportunity. For the moment we will ignore the way this usually cloaks risk.

Bad Boys Make Good

Bad boys behave out of character, in some cases wildly out of character. This makes excellent trading opportunities as the market is caught unawares by the sudden firing of the stock. Arcadia Minerals shown as a weekly chart in Figure 4.4 is a sleepy stock in long-term hibernation moving between well-established support and resistance bands. A simple trading strategy, buying support at $0.07, selling resistance at $0.14, returns around 100% over 12 to 18 months.

In mid-January 1997 the market Prince Charming gave this sleeping beauty a kiss and the price sat bolt upright. This was a dramatic change from the previous characteristics of the stock on a weekly basis, and of behaviour on a daily basis.

Several successful trading approaches became redundant overnight. New approaches were recruited and they are outlined in Figure 4.5. When the character of the stock changes, we must change our trading tactics. If we do not understand how to read character we cannot select the appropriate tools and will continue to trade the stock as it was rather than as it is.

---

[2] See Chapter 9 in *Share Trading* for discussion of how point and figure charts are constructed and used.

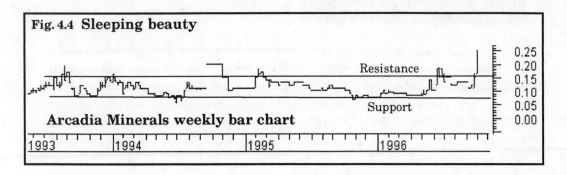

Fig. 4.4 Sleeping beauty

Resistance

Support

Arcadia Minerals weekly bar chart

0.25
0.20
0.15
0.10
0.05
0.00

1993   1994   1995   1996

Schizophrenic stocks destroy complacency. Arcadia switches character in the February to April period and support and resistance trading is king again. Most times we trade when the behaviour of the security is consistent with its character — but not always. Understanding the appropriate context of price activity gives you an important edge.

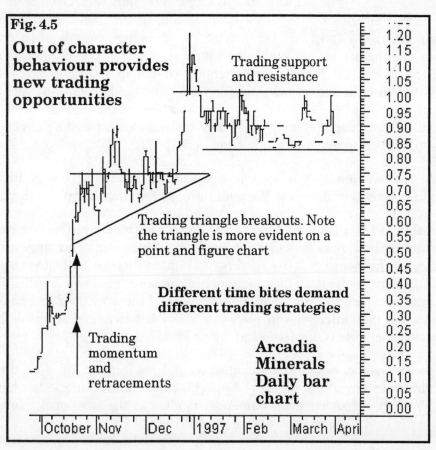

Fig. 4.5

Out of character behaviour provides new trading opportunities

Trading support and resistance

Trading triangle breakouts. Note the triangle is more evident on a point and figure chart

Different time bites demand different trading strategies

Trading momentum and retracements

Arcadia Minerals Daily bar chart

1.20
1.15
1.10
1.05
1.00
0.95
0.90
0.85
0.80
0.75
0.70
0.65
0.60
0.55
0.50
0.45
0.40
0.35
0.30
0.25
0.20
0.15
0.10
0.05
0.00

October Nov   Dec   1997   Feb   March April

Day by Day Emotional Extremes

The trade decision is based on character and behaviour, but the actual trade is based on the emotional activity of the security. This is Elder's third screen and the smallest time bite. Here we zoom in on the immediate emotional dimension. There are many tools used to assess the strength and stability of this emotion, and some of them are discussed in later chapters. Here we consider only how this last, and shortest, time bite helps establish a better trading perspective.

Exactly how tightly we micro-manage depends on our trading technique. Day traders use minute by minute data drawn from the course of trades. Some position traders use depth of market information in ways discussed in Chapter 15. Most position traders use the message in the price bars to get a better entry.

As position traders we want the best possible entry into WPL consistent with the current behaviour of the stock. The previous time frames suggested $8.50 as a potential buy area and because we know volume is small when prices touch the line, we set our buy price a little above, at $8.60. We finesse this decision further by paying close attention to the most recent days' price activity. Using the screen zoom function we bring the last few days into full screen focus as with Figure 4.6 to give a clear view of the emotional balance of the forces of demand and supply over the most recent trading days. This close to the action we smell fear and taste greed.

Every tool we use at this level is designed to understand the immediate emotional activity of the stock. We want the most favourable entry or exit point.

Our objective is a favourable entry just above the trendline. The immediate pressure pushes prices low after the open on February 28. This suggests the decline has further to go so we need not bid up, or chase prices higher to get a position. On the basis of the emotional information conveyed by this price bar, and using our knowledge of the behaviour of the stock over several time frames, the buy order stays in place just above the trendline at $8.60. Two days later the order is filled as prices dip to $8.55 .

Proposed trading tactics are modified to take advantage of the current emotional activity of the stock. The information contained in the last bar of the Woodside chart confirms our understanding of the emotional character of the stock giving us the confidence to leave the buy order in place.

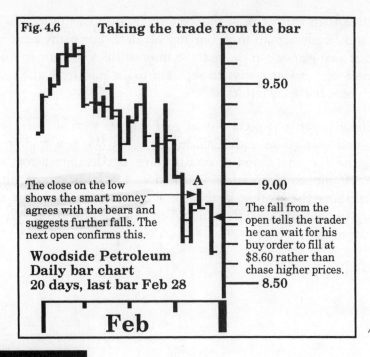

Fig. 4.6 **Taking the trade from the bar**

— 9.50

The close on the low
shows the smart money
agrees with the bears and
suggests further falls. The
next open confirms this.

A

— 9.00

The fall from the
open tells the trader
he can wait for his
buy order to fill at
$8.60 rather than
chase higher prices.

**Woodside Petroleum
Daily bar chart
20 days, last bar Feb 28**

— 8.50

Feb

*DAily 260
DAyS
14s*

Choose Your Time

Most traders start with a daily chart and this sets the focus for our search for
trading opportunities. We want behaviour consistent with character. The
identification techniques discussed in the next section are all based on 260
days of daily chart information.

If your trading approach is based on the character of the stock then weekly
charts form the primary basis of your search for trading opportunities.
Intraday traders use the daily chart and a real time data feed to understand
the emotional activity of the market crowd mapped by current price activity.
Your choice — character, behaviour or emotional activity — decides the type of
trading strategies you use, and the range of applicable trading tactics.

The choice of time frame is a personal one, but please choose one
consistently. When particular trading approaches are suggested by the
behaviour of the stock a quick check against the characteristic of the stock
over different time frames will confirm if the proposed trading approach is
appropriate and realistic, or unachievable. We aim to trade in the direction of
the prevailing trend by taking advantage of favourable price behaviour to
make the best entry, or exit, possible given the balance of probabilities.

Our objective is to extract only the best trading opportunities, theoretical, potential, and finally actual, from our market data. For many reasons, what looks good at first glance can prove to be impractical after further study. The next section looks at some ways to separate fool's gold from the real metal and ways to read the assay results.

In the Ballarat region prospectors won gold nuggets with shovels, gold dust with pans, and gold grains with California cradles. We win trading gold by confirming the size and shape of each trading opportunity across multiple time bites. Equipped with this knowledge we know more than our competitors about the market landscape, the lay of the land, the way our 'nuggets' are formed and how they hide. We join the gold rush with a better chance of survival.

Part II

PROSPECTING
FOR
TRADES

5

SEARCHING FOR LOVE
AT FIRST PROFIT

When the gold rush starts thousands flock to the fields hoping to strike it rich. From the goldfields of Ballarat last century and Tennant Creek in the Northern Territory in the 1930s, to modern-day rushes in the Gawler Craton or the Mt Isa Mineral Province, the scene is the same. Armed with everything from spades and metal detectors, steel panning dishes and makeshift cradles to reverse circulating and rotary air blast drill rigs, the hordes rip apart the landscape. Every patch of country within pegging distance of any find is considered prospective. Digging just anywhere does not bring results and the best prospectors spot the high probability areas.

Over geological time nuggets of gold are broken from the surrounding quartz matrix and tumbled along stream beds creating alluvial fields. Armed with a single bit of information — gold is one of the heaviest metals — experienced prospectors select a pile of river sediment, from just the right spot.

Inexperienced scroungers, like those in the background of an S. T. Gill painting of the 1850 Victorian Goldfields, indiscriminately mine the same ground for profit and find nothing. The difference is not due to luck but to systematic searching for preferred characteristics. The shape of the stream indicates areas of better probability — the shape of market data does the same.

Traders mine market data, searching systematically for chosen characteristics. Although bulges figured prominently in the previous chapters, the weight of the balance of probability is shown on charts in several different patterns. The most significant of these is the trendline, closely followed by its cousins, the family of triangles. Other indicators, calculated from price data, are designed to show when price action moves away from the range of more probable outcomes and towards another set. Oscillator-style indicators rely on oversold or overbought conditions to signal this shift in balance.

The security we want looks good on the chart. This is the first step in selecting the most promising ground. The sorting process can be simple, or it can be complex, but in each case our objective is to identify those opportunities where the balance of probability favours an entry. This can range from spotting a breakout from a downtrend to finding the best entry point in an established trend. The search focus is primarily on the entry. Once suspected nuggets are selected we clean them up and test them for quality. These processes, particularly with the eyeball search approach, are often intertwined, but for this section we will try to separate them as we look at some search methods and develop some lists.

Start Digging

Some people claim the search is so exciting because they don't know what they are looking for. These people are not successful traders. You must know what you are looking for, and in digging through market data there are five necessary steps, ranging from identifying the trade, analysing it and subjecting it to financial analysis, to assessing the potential trade against market conditions and managing the open position until the trade exit. Each step produces a list, each one progressively smaller than before. We will build, use and refine these lists throughout the remainder of this book. Briefly, the first screening grids in this digging expedition include:

1 The size of your trading capital. You cannot trade every opportunity, so you are financially limited.

2 The decision you make about the amount of data you include in your initial search. It could be the entire market, or just a market segment.

3 Trading style. This rules out some trading approaches in favour of others.

Even if you specialise in a single market segment — resources, industrials, banks, the top 100 — the amount of information available over even just a few years is formidable. This is more so if you have the entire market available to you. And more data is added every day. Miss a few days of data collection and the charts change dramatically. Instead of mining the data heap, it overwhelms you.

Splitting this heap into a smaller pile is an obvious first step and in taking it you are assisted by lack of trading capital. You do not have the capital to trade every trading opportunity although this does not prevent some from attempting this feat. Just arbitrarily creating a smaller pile is a waste of time unless you have a system to separate the nuggets from the heap.

Scanning the database to extract trading opportunities aims to build a pile small enough to reasonably handle in a day, and still leave time for trading. The size of the pile, or list, will depend on your analysis skills and the charting software. Programs such as Metastock and Ezy Chart supply tools to quickly analyse data. We look at how these are used later because these tools are of little use unless you know what you are looking for.

With a clear idea of what we want to find — a gold nugget — our search is more efficient. What we are looking for — a heavy metal — will determine exactly how we look. We want to find a trading opportunity so we look for signs showing the balance of probability.

The first database scan aims to weed out stocks not meeting our criteria. The technical trader uses different criteria from the more fundamentally or financially-based trader. Most traders combine the two styles, but with a greater preference for one. The efficiency of your search tools should match the size of your database and your style of trading. A bigger shovel will not help if you have no other objective beyond making a profit. Like the inexperienced scrounger in the river bed, you will find less.

The first search develops a list, or perhaps several lists. These are the stocks which command your closer attention. Later we will look at how the trader puts these under the microscope using a range of indicators and techniques, but for the moment we want to take the first steps in reducing our growing heap of market data to a manageable size.

Getting Comfortable With Style

Every trader feels more comfortable with some trades than with others. Some prefer secure trades based on support and resistance bands. Other feel more comfortable trading with long-term trends, while another group takes early positions in anticipation of a breakout.

Which trading style is comfortable for you depends very much on your trading personality. If the trading style is inconsistent with your personality, with your overall financial situation, or with lifestyle constraints, then you set yourself up for failure. Good traders are not only in tune with the market, they are in tune with trading opportunities matching their personality and lifestyle. I would find it very difficult to day trade and to write books about trading. As a position trader I have this time.

A person who is more at home with making and taking decisions based on considerable analysis is unlikely to be a successful day trader where rapid decisions are made based on hunches, experience and a feeling for the precise mood of the market at that instant. This sounds so obvious we expect only a few people to fall into this trap. In fact many people reach for the money before considering if it is consistent with their style. The goldfields are dotted with inexperienced scroungers wielding expensive metal detectors.

In a broad sense you have three initial choices for your approach to the market. Matching personal style with choice will determine how you approach the scanning process. The choices are:

- ➲ Chase the pot of gold
- ➲ Use one trading technique applied to multiple market sectors
- ➲ Master one market sector and look for multiple opportunities using many trading techniques.

The Pot of Gold

Chasing the pot of gold is exciting, fast-moving, and most often unsuccessful. Just as a few lotto winners encourage the losers to try again, the few pot of gold trading successes sometimes receive enough publicity to make it appear that this is the rule, rather than the exception.

This approach aims to identify fast-moving stocks with rapidly increasing prices. Jumping on board requires good judgement, perfect timing and nerves of steel. Experienced traders make this approach work very well. By trading with leverage supplied by options, warrants or some other derivative instrument, small movements in the underlying stock are multiplied into significant gains.

Inexperienced traders have less success. Their buying helps to drive prices higher. Often they buy from experienced sellers who are selling into strength. The 'blowoff' chart pattern, Figure 5.1, shows this activity. The experienced trader takes it as a warning, while the inexperienced trader sees it as an opportunity.

Chasing the pot of gold is a legitimate trading approach, and later we look at some specific techniques used in this trading approach.

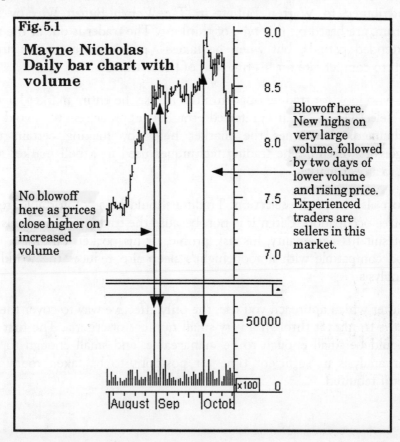

Fig. 5.1

Mayne Nicholas Daily bar chart with volume

No blowoff here as prices close higher on increased volume

Blowoff here. New highs on very large volume, followed by two days of lower volume and rising price. Experienced traders are sellers in this market.

One Technique Many Markets

The second option uses just one, or perhaps two, trading approaches. The entire market is searched for stocks fitting the criteria. The initial search might uncover 40 opportunities, and the next, based on the second technique, might uncover 40 more. The mass of market data is quickly sorted into a smaller pile with a preliminary list of 80 stocks.

The limits of this approach for private traders are reached quickly. Use three or four preferred trading approaches, and you could end up with a hundred stocks or more on the preliminary list.

Some traders overcome this disadvantage and look for comparatively rare combinations of market circumstances. When these occur they commit large sums confident these uncommon circumstances yield predictable results. Some of the techniques described by Peter Lynch in *One Up on Wall Street* and attributed to Warren Buffett in *The Warren Buffett Way* by Robert Hagstrom, are based on this type of thinking. The trader is out of the market for extended periods, but when he takes a position the returns are large enough to compensate for his time out of the market.

Those who look for trading opportunities across the entire market have to be more selective in their preferred trading approaches to avoid being overwhelmed. Sometimes the market helps by making certain trading strategies less useful. The trading techniques used in a bull market are not suited to a bear market.

Comfort also helps the selection. Trading should be a comfortable, relaxing, stress-free occupation. Often it is not, because the trader uses methods which do not suit his personality, his risk profile, or his pocket. Finding a trading method compatible with a good night's sleep also reduces the workload of data analysis.

No matter which approach you use, the only effective way to cover the entire market is to filter it through a very small number of criteria. The first search list should be small enough to be manageable, and small enough to permit further analysis in sufficient time for positions to be taken today in the market if required.

Identifying a profitable trading opportunity based on yesterday's data is good. Finding it too late to be able to buy the stock at the preferred price is annoying. Watching the stock price move exactly as you thought it would — but without you on board — is vastly unsatisfying.

More Trades in One Market

The third option concentrates on one market sector and searches for a variety of trading opportunities. In *Share Trading* we suggested a private index built from around 200 stocks. Using a utility for Ezy Chart this index is automatically updated and charted like any other stock.

How you define the sector is not important. It might be on the basis of size — the top 100 — on the basis of industry — resources, banking — on the basis of volatility — stocks with a standard deviation or beta value greater than one — or just your collection of personal favourites and brokerage recommendations. Here the trader makes a prior choice to physically limit the amount of data analysed and ignore other trading opportunities.

In return he expects to have more time to consider many more trading approaches and to act on his analysis.

Using this approach we scan for stocks meeting a variety of conditions consistent with a variety of trading approaches. This might include stocks approaching breakout conditions, those hovering near support areas, and those showing unusual price and volume relationships. It does not matter if we end up with four or five lists. Each list is short because it is drawn from a limited market selection. Invariably there will be duplicates, so the final combined list is small enough to examine in detail and to apply the results during the current trading day.

More importantly, by limiting our activities to a smaller database we are able to start with the most powerful search method of all — the eyeball. A chart has one overwhelming advantage — the price relationships are easily comprehended. Instead of a jumble of figures we see a chart which is readily understood at an intuitive level. The trader uses this advantage when he eyeballs a chart.

The eyeball has limits, usually imposed by its owner — fatigue and speed. This powerful search technique cannot be applied to hundreds of charts on a regular basis. It is best suited to a small number of stocks, selected and scanned regularly.

Lists of Shopping Lists

We make shopping lists, or sort and reduce market data into smaller piles, so we can focus on the main task without being distracted. Supermarkets have specialists designing shelf layouts to distract us from our shopping list. They are often successful, but nowhere near as successful as the market with its daily specials.

The market distracts easily because scanning the database has one major disadvantage — the shopping list must be prepared freshly each day. Each scan, or search, or Metastock exploration usually compares the current day's data with previous data. Some software packages, such as Ezy Analyser, allow you to set the parameter dates for the search.

If you do not scan for two days then past trading opportunities will not always be identified in today's search. Trade situations develop and mature over a period and to miss the development of critical points does have an impact on trading. Playing catchup is no substitute for timeliness so finding the perfect daily special is no good four days after the event.

In developing your scanning routine, factor in the frequency of your searches and the impact this has on identifying developing and newly-emerging trading situations. If you use a weekly shopping list then accept that you miss the daily specials. This does not matter if you did not intend to shop for them. It does matter if your trading techniques rely on daily specials.

Traders must chop market data down to size in a consistent way. By reducing the analysis load to a manageable level we quickly concentrate on only the most exciting and most promising trades showing a better probability of success.

Trading success is reached by many different routes but it helps to follow a consistent path when it comes to identifying trading opportunities. Before we focus on trades with the best probability we narrow the field using any of the four search options covered in the following chapters along with examples.

The options include eyeball, relationship, performance and accounting searches. This list is not an exhaustive, nor an in-depth survey of the search patterns available. It is an introduction to each of the major groups of techniques available so you can more quickly move in the direction that suits your trading style.

Charting software tempts with built-in search and exploration parameters. Metastock users have six search criteria on their default list. Ezy Chart users have 11 buy and sell default criteria installed for them. Users can adjust, modify and add to these starting lists but searches are more effective if you are aware of what you are measuring with each indicator. The following chapters discuss these directions. Remember, our objective is to find the best opportunities quickly so we have time to assess them and to take action before trading closes for the day.

Finding the nuggets is the first step and before we move off into an unfamiliar financial landscape we consider two paths leading to the mother lode.

6

No Accounting
for All Tastes

opies of the Berkshire Hathaway annual report are snapped up by brokers, private investors and financial commentators as soon as they are released. Warren Buffett, arguably currently amongst the worlds most successful fund managers, uses a fundamental approach and he makes no secret of his methods. Like the renowned Benjamin Graham, on whose style he bases his own, Buffett's approach is succinct: Find good companies which are undervalued and buy them. Janet Lowe looks more closely at Benjamin Graham's investment strategies in *Value Investing Made Easy* and Robert Hagstrom brings the approach up-to-date with *The Warren Buffett Way*.

It is this approach, and variants, which dominate the Australian broking industry. Most brokers specialise in providing advice based on a close analysis of fundamental market factors in industry sectors, or the balance sheet of individual companies. Many private traders pit their accounting skills against those of the brokers and the company accountants looking for the discrepancies in valuation. If we use this approach we aim to select a few trading — not investment — candidates from the broad mass of market data.

We suggested in the previous section that no matter how you make your initial stock selection, when it comes to actually buying the stock, and later selling it, the bar chart provides you with invaluable information not obtainable elsewhere. In the following chapters we look more closely at ways to use this information to delve into the mass of market data and locate the best nuggets of trading opportunity.

In this chapter we stand, ready to begin our jungle prospecting expedition, on the edge of an escarpment looking out over the financial landscape below. Like every prospector we hope to see gold-bearing country where we can strike it rich, so we look for well-worn tracks through the jungle trees. There are two paths leading down into the valley and we will take my preferred path in later chapters.

First, let us consider the choice in paths. Like many others, I place comparatively little weight on the fundamental bookkeeping style of analysis in my trading decisions. It is not my intention to set up a straw man called fundamental accounting analysis, only to then knock him down. This path does have problems and I choose to highlight these because they confirm my choice of trading approach. As a serious trader your are entitled to understand why I choose to take one trading path rather than another, particularly as this book concentrates on that path alone. In later chapters we explore the dangers and shortcomings of the path I prefer.

Many fundamental traders use charts to back up their analysis, and for market timing. Many technical analysts combine vital fundamental information with chart signals. Jack Schwager, the US futures trader considers this in two books, *Schwager on Futures: Fundamental Analysis* and *Schwager on Futures: Technical Analysis*. Although in this book we treat this as two distinct paths many traders successfully combine these approaches. Your approach will be an individual blend drawn from each.

Poised on the edge of the escarpment, this chapter provides a signposted summary introduction to the other path. There are many writers more qualified than myself to guide you fully down this path should you decide to follow it. Finding the nuggets using this style of search employs different techniques but, like the technical search methods covered in detail in the following chapters, the paths converge where the nuggets are found. Both have the same objective — to find the best trading opportunities in the shortest possible time, and quickly enough, to be able to buy them before they go up too far or too fast.

Financial Camouflage

For those taking the fundamental accounting path the primary search tool is balance sheet analysis powered by an understanding of market fundamentals and company fundamentals. The search light is provided by insider, or timely, knowledge and aims to capture "Sound companies that are undervalued".

Fundamentally sound is a concept torn in three directions.

First, a company requires results to impress the market and existing shareholders. This reflects the core business of the company and a sound bottom line has advantages. Various accounting conventions make this concept more fluid than is comfortable, sometimes delivering unbelievable results. QBE Insurance was so annoyed with the official reporting standard — AASB1023 — that for a time they filed two separate financial reports to the Stock Exchange. Using the official accounting standard QBE profits rose in one financial year by 78.5%. Using the Directors' preferred accounting standard, profits for the same period rose by only 15.1%.

A brokerage cottage industry is built around correctly interpreting the results delivered by accounting conventions. This is set to expand with ASC approval of a revised standard on equity accounting which will change some annual multi-national and international company results by millions of dollars. When big business and regulators cannot agree on the correct standard then the small trader faces a huge task in cutting through a company financial report to find the 'real' fundamentals.

Second, the concept is further torn as the company would prefer that public results did not give away any competitive advantage. Commercially sensitive information is legitimately concealed in balance sheets, company reports and newspaper briefings. One of the great brokerage games of hide-and-seek is built around the search for this information before the rest of the market hears of it. Rumours, rumours of rumours and early news breaks are the lifeblood of this game.

Taxing Times

Third, and most significantly, the fundamental concept is distorted by taxation requirements. The best financial results are achieved when the costs of production are reduced. Publicly this focuses on labour costs, but privately taxation is just as significant. Balance sheet items are shifted where possible to minimise taxation impacts.

Personally, most of us have an ambiguous relationship with the tax department. You think they want more than their fair share and the tax department thinks you understate taxable income. This personal battle has more tricks and turns than a barrel full of monkeys.

On a corporate level the battle is fought in silks and backed by the best of the big six accounting firms because company accounts correctly presented reduce tax liabilities. Incorrectly presented, the same financial information can create a massive tax bill. The battle on the tax front contributes to bottom line profits no less significantly than the battle for customer loyalty, increases in labour productivity and commodity price or currency fluctuations.

It is too easy to dismiss the significance of this factor, but those raising capital in the US, for instance, must prepare financial information under US rules and the impact is significant. When Daimler-Benz agreed to recalculate its 1993 profit according to US rules the DM615 million profit under German rules became a loss of DM1,839 million. Naturally, national statutory company accounts tend to exploit the most advantageous tax strategy so the same company may be an attractive proposition in some environments and a dog in others. Tax is a production cost and like all costs, corporations legitimately seek to reduce them wherever possible.

From our position on the escarpment, when we survey the landscape this creates a significant problem because corporations do not keep two sets of books. If we could see the set showing true profit as distinct from the set prepared with taxation in mind, we would make better decisions about the fundamentals of the company. Instead, as outsiders we try to unravel the reasoning behind the structuring of specific company transactions into taxable, or non-taxable, categories. We try to second-guess the auditors, the accountants, and the taxman. Some of us, and some brokerage analysts, do this very well and these conclusions can provide a shortcut in our market search. Most of us do not have, and cannot reasonably expect to acquire, these skills.

Without a guide the financial landscape is covered in an accounting jungle hiding the mountains and valleys. Somewhere the jungle hides a massively wealthy Porgera gold deposit, or equally, a frightening Bre-X financial hole in the ground. *The Accounting Jungle* by Bill Jamieson is the first field guide new explorers should carry along with their metal detector.

Do It Yourself Ratios

With these caveats in mind we turn to an overview of fundamental search material. This metal detector uses financial ratio information from columns in the *Stock Exchange Journal* or from the last six columns in the *Australian Financial Review* market reports. Some of the nuggets are found in the following six ratios.

1 Price/NTA

By comparing price and asset backing per share the ratio gives an indication of whether the shares are trading at a premium or at a discount. The theoretical calculated value of the company's tangible assets are divided by the number of shares on issue. The Net Tangible Assets (NTA) per share figure is divided by the current share price and expressed as a price to NTA value. A figure of one means the company is valued in line with its net tangible assets. If price/NTA is greater than one the share trades at a premium, and at a discount if the figure is less than one.

The search engine, or metal detector, starts to screech when shares trading at a price/NTA discount are uncovered.

2 Debt/Equity

This compares the level of company debt with ordinary shareholders' equity, net of any intangibles. A company with $4 million in debt and $2 million of shareholders' funds has a debt/equity ratio of 200%.

Lower debt/equity ratios are not always better as companies making good use of borrowed funds for expansion can offer attractive trading opportunities. Generally lower debt/equity readings are noted by our metal detector.

3 EPS

Earnings Per Share (EPS) is measured in cents per share and represents the amount of profit made, equivalent to each share on issue. This ratio is also called a Return on Shareholders Funds or Return on Equity.

As a way of measuring current performance this is often listed as Current EPS and Latest Year EPS. The current period includes the latest financial reports while the latest year is the final figure for the last financial year.

Stocks showing an increase in Current EPS register on our metal detector.

4 Dividend, Dividend Yield and Franking

This is a simple rate of return calculation from dividend payments. It is calculated by dividing the rolling yearly dividend per share by the share price and expressing the result as a percentage.

Dividends per share is the historical rate of dividends paid per ordinary share. Results are shown as Current Final and taken from interim reports. Previous Year results are taken from the last full financial year.

Bigger is usually considered better and these bumps are noted in our search.

Franking is usually shown as %F. Fully-franked dividends are shown as 100F and partially-franked dividends by 65F if they are 65% franked. If fully-franked dividends are an important part of your investment strategy then tune your detector to pick these up.

5 EBIT

This is Earnings Before Interest and Tax and when divided by the figure for sales we have an EBIT Margin. This shows the proportion of sales contributing to company profit. Appropriate margins vary across industry groups so we must fine-tune our metal detector for each sector.

EBIT is also used to calculate the company's ability to generate profits from its assets. As with the EBIT margin, generally higher is better, but our metal detector should be tuned to the general level applicable to each industry group.

6 Current and Quick Ratio

The current ratio measures the theoretical ability of the company to repay short-term debt. A ratio of less than one suggests the company may have difficulty so again bigger is generally better. The same outcomes apply to the quick ratio, but this is calculated by dividing current assets less inventories, by current liabilities.

These ratios, and a number of others, are derived from the relationship between market price and the internal financial activity of the business as reported to the Exchange or as inferred through other accounting announcements. Many of these broadly form the basics of a Capital Asset Pricing Model (CAPM) approach. The critical discussion in *Blueprint For Investment* by Richard FitzHerbert is a handy introduction to the intricacies of the CAPM approach. Readers looking for greater detail about this style of analysis for individual stocks can turn to *Sensible Share Investing* by Austin Donnelly or *How The Stock Market Really Works* by Martin Roth.

You might decide the CAPM approach does clear the jungle. If so, use the analysis methods discussed in detail in the books mentioned above, but remember when the time comes to make your buying decision, and later the selling decision, that the bar chart provides you with invaluable information unobtainable anywhere else.

Balancing Acts

Reading a balance sheet has more twists and turns than a modern thriller and we do not intend to re-invent this particular plot. The financial sleuth uses Martin Roth's *Analysing Company Accounts* and *Understanding Finance: Balance Sheets* by William Lee Johnson as detectives' bibles.

The balance sheet is a snapshot of the company's finances at a single point in time, typically June 30. The profit and loss statement covers a selected period, a quarter, a half year, or a financial year, and shows how profitably it has operated in the period. In a broad sense, the profit and loss report tells us if the company has made money in the last six months, while the balance sheet lets us know if it still has a lot of debt left to service so high profitability will have to continue. The cashflow statement is a summary of cash received and paid out by the company.

Some thriller-style balance sheets use many twists and turns developed in the 1980s, including:

➲ The capitalisation of interest on projects of uncertain value when completed.

➲ The valuation of shareholdings in associated companies at market value when the share prices of those companies is influenced by the market activities of other associates.

- Unrealistic valuation of assets, particularly property, so book value is poorly related to market value.

- Using 'equity' accounting to inflate profit figures when little of the 'equity accounted profit' is actually available to the company.

The balance sheet search for concealed golden opportunities is painstaking, time consuming, and for those like Warren Buffett and Peter Lynch, ultimately very profitable. In addition to the books mentioned above, *Accounting For Non-Accountants* by Philip Stanley and *Finance For Non-Finance Managers* by Eric Smith are useful introductory references for those who put the latest thriller to one side in favour of a night with the company reports. The topic is a hardy perennial in *Shares* and *Personal Investment* magazines and in the financial pages, so we do not intend to duplicate the excellent work done by others.

Compared to the demands of trading, these balance sheet and ratio searches are leisurely pursuits and ideally suited to an investing approach that does not place as much emphasis on timing market entries for short and intermediate-term trades. Despite this investment emphasis, many traders are looking to link CAPM-style analysis with trading tactics. They want to trade the best stocks rather than the best trades so our purpose is to find the most efficient means to search through masses of market data to identify the best stocks. Some affordable software packages work with the CAPM and balance sheet approach.

Software Bloodhounds

This idea of finding undervalued stocks and staying with them until they sell at their true value, or perhaps even beyond, is a constant theme of established investment advice. The financial relationships are old. What is new is the development of extensive databases and the software to access them. This not only makes the search easier and cheaper; it puts the tools into the hands of clients, rather than advisers, and gives an advantage to traders, rather than brokers.

Indeed some software packages, notably the Royals Sharefinder software and the most recent version of Windows on Wall Street, use these factors in scanning stocks. The Ezy Analyser module can also do a search assessing stocks against this criteria.

Sharefinder is close to a 'grey box'. Buy and sell signals are generated automatically, but unlike a black box trading system, the relationships between each of the factors is clearly explained. Additionally, the user is given limited opportunity to manipulate the parameters. The user is presented with results determined by the software but must decide if he will buy the recommended stock or do further toolbox technical analysis.

We believe the recommendations made by such software trading programs need to be further analysed against the specific financial and trading objectives of the user. Ways to do this are discussed more fully in Part III.

Windows on Wall Street, and the Ezy Analyser module, are toolboxes. The user manipulates the parameters to suit his favourite ideas, and the software scans, sorts and ranks the data according to these user-defined criteria. They are a more powerful analysis package for those who wish to combine chart, technical and fundamental analysis.

However, there is a major shortcoming. Both these software packages, and others operating in the same way, require more than just a data stream providing open, high, low, close, volume and perhaps open interest information. The data provider must also supply the basic information necessary for the calculation of PE ratios, NTA, EBIT, etc. Windows on Wall Street uses a US data stream and has no Australian equivalent. Emerging Australian software packages are finding difficulty in obtaining this information in electronic format and private traders will have trouble accessing this relevant information for the entire market. Ezy Portfolio Manager is moving to solve this problem.

Taking a Different Path

For many people involved with the market, this fundamental and accounting approach is the primary source of trading information. Our purpose here is to understand that if you use these factors as part of a trading decision, then they need to be ranked and sorted in much the same way as other important price and volume data. This ranking will help to identify the better trading opportunities.

The significance and weighting you attach to each of these accounting factors will depend on your trading objectives. When you prioritise these to your satisfaction then the search to create the initial list of trading opportunities is rapid and effective. In Chapter 13 we show how to bring the trade to fruition using charting information and in Chapter 14 how to assess trades against our financial objectives.

From where we stand on the escarpment at the beginning of our journey, there are two paths leading down into the valley. Although not mutually exclusive most traders choose to follow one path more closely than the other. If you decide to follow the path outlined above then I cannot guide you, so please read the recommended guidebooks. The other path, my preferred one, follows R-plot, performance, and eyeball signposts. This path we explore more completely in the following chapters.

Both paths meet wherever gold is found. Readers taking the CAPM and associated paths should rejoin us in Chapter 11.

7

EYEBALL SEARCHES

T he bulge of probability concept, shown in the grouping of number combinations based on a dice throw, was transferred to the support and resistance levels shown in the General Property Trust chart, Figure 3.1. This plot used a visual chart pattern to highlight probable entry and exit points. Identifying and understanding such patterns relies on eyeball recognition.

The eyeball search rests on simplicity and when completed, presents a short list of the best trading candidates. A sample typical eyeball list with notes, drawn from 200 resource stocks, is shown in Figure 7.1. Everybody has eyeball software and it is very powerful when used in conjunction with a computer screen.

The eyeball search is the simplest of all the search techniques and it must be used at some stage in the trading process. Those taking the entire market defer this eyeball search until the last steps in assessing trading opportunities.

For them this is when the number of candidates is reduced enough to make an eyeball search time-effective. Traders who rely on fundamental analysis eyeball the charts to select timing clues.

Fig. 7.1	**Extract from an eyeball search list with notes**
	A	B
1	Stock name	comments
2	ASH	SUP-1.90 RESIST-2.15
3	CAR	SUP-.24 RESIST-.29
4	EBR	UPSLOPE TRIANGLE RESIST-.28
5	FTU	DOWNSLOPE TRIANGLE SUP-.044
6	GSE	RESIST -.19
7	LHG	TREND BREAKOUT 2.29
8	MIM	TREND BREAKOUT 1.55 TARGET 1.80
9	NBH	RESIST BREAKOUT 3.90
10	PEM	SUP - .78 RESIST - .84 THEN .90
11	PTZ	RESIST/SUP .93
12	SCN	DOWNTREND BREAKOUT .15 TARGET .175

I track a small segment of the market — 200 to 300 securities — so the eyeball search is always my starting point. It takes 10 minutes to look through these bar charts. With such a small number I grow to know each of them so I quickly skip those that have been out of contention for weeks.

Despite claims from the computer industry, the eyeball has not been replaced by a software replica. Pattern recognition software is improving and some traders use it to search their database and identify a multitude of patterns. Here the danger lies in the large jump between recognising the pattern and building a causal link between past and future price activity.

SuperCharts software lets you 'paint' a series of bars to show other occurrences of the same pattern. It is a very powerful feature, but fails to establish any causal link between the pattern and future price action. Metastock contains a similar feature. We use other tests to prove the validity of the links. The computer helps but it cannot do these tests automatically. We use this type of pattern recognition software to supplement the eyeball scan by expanding the number of securities that are scanned quickly. The resulting list should be subjected to a further eyeball evaluation before moving onto other techniques.

The Eyes Have It

What do you look for? The most powerful technical patterns are trendlines, support and resistance levels and the triangles they produce. These are the four basic pillars of technical analysis, and although they sound complex, they are usually easier to see than they are to describe. The chart examples used below are typical examples drawn from a variety of market sectors.

Recognising any of these patterns is a judgement call. Recognition of the patterns is difficult to program in a mathematical sense. A trendline is a basic concept so software developers have grappled with mathematical descriptions. Many software packages feature automatic trendlines, but rarely do they look 'right' so every package also allows you to also draw them by hand. The eyeball is still supreme and a search for these simple patterns filters out many unattractive trading prospects. The search is rapid, it is judgemental, and by its nature, it is approximate — limitations willingly accepted in return for a small bundle of stocks that warrant much closer attention.

Finding these patterns does not require an advanced degree in mathematics. Good software speeds up the eyeball scan. Metastock users flip through charts by clicking the Next Security button. Ezy Chart users select Auto Display linked to live charts. Starting with the first security in their database, experienced eyeballers spend three seconds or less on each chart searching for visual evidence to support intuitive conclusions about the nature of price activity. They look for a definite trend, a support or resistance level, and for obvious triangle formations. They navigate towards the balance of probability using weekly patterns to point the way. When behaviour is consistent with character the probability of selected outcomes is enhanced.

Building on Support

Support and resistance offers significant information about the balance of probability as shown in Chapter 3. Remember, support is formed when buying pressure consistently overcomes selling pressure at a particular price level. Resistance is created when selling pressure overwhelms buying. When prices reach the resistance level so much stock is on offer that buyers need not bid any higher.

To find these levels start with a weekly bar chart. Note where prices hit a level several times and rebound, and you find support or resistance. The chart of the television company, Beyond International (BYI), in Figure 7.2 shows a clearly-defined support level at $3.00. This is a clear-cut line, but more often it is a narrow area a few cents wide. We suggested in *Share Trading* that point and figure charting is a very useful way of confirming support levels, but many weekly bar charts also show this fairly clearly.

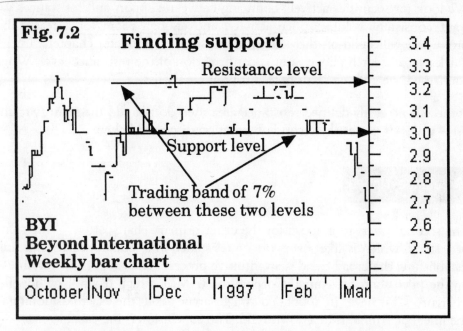

Fig. 7.2 **Finding support**

BYI
Beyond International
Weekly bar chart

In establishing these lines the key factor is the limit of the price bars. The lines are pencilled in where price bars consistently finish, or start, their price moves. The line in Figure 7.2 is drawn just under the extremities of the down price moves from November 1996 to March 1997. On all charts in this chapter, for clarity, the line is drawn slightly below or above the actual level.

The building contractor, Watkins Pacific (WTP), in Figure 7.6 also shows a support level. This ranges between $0.205 and $0.22, shown as dotted lines. A thicker line plotted at the midpoint of this range, around $0.21, provides a working guide.

As BYI comes up in our eyeball scan we note the support area of $3.00 on a scratch pad. With WTP we note $0.21. Two additional observations are needed before adding these stocks to our preliminary list.

First, look for a nearby resistance line or level and write down its value. Beyond International shows resistance at $3.20.

A stock on support and moving sideways in a consolidation pattern offers few trading opportunities. When the trading band — the distance between support and resistance — is only a few ticks high, the trade is unprofitable. The trading band in Figure 7.2 shows almost a 7% gross return.

We look for securities actively bouncing between support and resistance. We want consistent volume, price activity, and enough room for a reasonable profit. We will build on these analysis steps in detail in later chapters. In this quick eyeball search all we want is confirmation of the resistance level. When confirmed, we add the security to our preliminary list.

If there is no easily-defined resistance area then do not add the security to the list — unless it passes the second observation discussed below.

A Balance Tipped

The second observation looks for the other primary chart pattern — the trend of a stock, which is like a support or resistance line, but tipped to one side. Establishing the broad trend is an intuitive process. The trend shown in line A on the price chart for Amrad Corporation (AML), a high technology hopeful, in Figure 7.3 is never in doubt. You might argue about the exact positioning of the line, but Amrad is in a downtrend. The conclusion is inescapable.

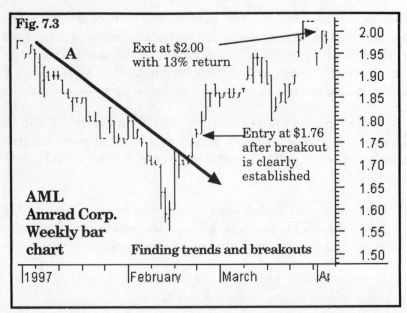

Fig. 7.3

A

Exit at $2.00
with 13% return

Entry at $1.76
after breakout
is clearly
established

AML
Amrad Corp.
Weekly bar
chart   **Finding trends and breakouts**

2.00
1.95
1.90
1.85
1.80
1.75
1.70
1.65
1.60
1.55
1.50

1997   February   March   A₁

We look for a close outside the trendline because this tells us a breakout may be taking place. Which side of the trendline we use depends on if we want to trade long or go short. In a downtrend, a long position is taken on a breakout to the right hand side of the trend. A short trader looks for breaks on the right-hand side of an uptrend.

List only securities with definite trends and, at first glance, unequivocal breakouts. This simple and effective process selects only the best and the most obvious trading opportunities. This does not mean they are unprofitable. The obvious is often surprisingly profitable.

In February 1997 Amrad Corporation clearly changed direction. Spotting the breakout from the downtrend is easy and we do not need to confuse the issue with high-tech charting techniques and advanced technical analysis. The obvious is often profitable, with an entry at $1.76 and an exit at $2.00 returning 13% over six weeks.

Later in the analysis process you might decide the stock has moved too far to make a good trade, or perhaps there is too little upside. These decisions are made at others steps in evaluating the trading opportunities. In this first search we build a broad list reliant on our judgement. If the trend is not immediately visible, then it is probably not there, or if it is, the trading opportunity is weaker.

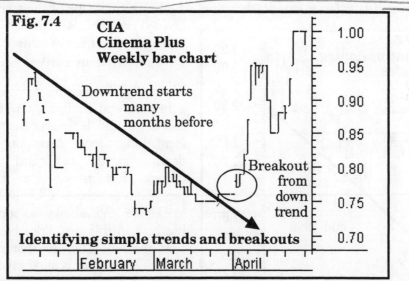

Fig. 7.4 — CIA Cinema Plus Weekly bar chart — Downtrend starts many months before — Breakout from down trend — Identifying simple trends and breakouts

Trendline breakouts sometimes last for several months, or years as the leisure company, Cinema Plus (CIA) indicates in Figure 7.4. Breakouts are often sudden and decisive. To catch them we must eyeball the charts regularly, two or three times a week. This is not a time-consuming chore when applied to a small list of stocks. We develop the small list either by initially selecting a small market segment to follow, or by using the last list culled from a search of the entire market using the methods covered in the following chapters.

Trading is more of an art than a science. Trendlines can be defined mathematically, but if they don't look right then we have little confidence in the signals they generate. This is not a magic picture where we squint and half focus our eyes to see the hidden image. If it is not there at first glance, then it is not there. Do not lose sight of the objective of this first search. We want a short report listing all major trading opportunities.

Hot Tips

When sloping trendlines intersect horizontal support or resistance lines they form triangles. These are the focus of our second qualifying observation in the eyeball search for support and resistance levels. If the support level is well defined, and it forms the base of a triangle defined by the trendline, then add the security to your list.

Triangles are attractive because they suggest increased probability of price action and to a lesser extent, direction. The horizontal edge of the triangle is divided into thirds. On each of the remaining figures in this chapter these divisions are marked '‡'.

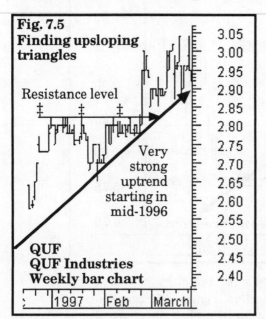

Fig. 7.5 Finding upsloping triangles

Resistance level

Very strong uptrend starting in mid-1996

QUF
QUF Industries
Weekly bar chart

1997 Feb March

3.05
3.00
2.95
2.90
2.85
2.80
2.75
2.70
2.65
2.60
2.55
2.50
2.45
2.40

The probability of strong price action is highest, and strongest, towards the end of the middle third of the triangle formation. Good breakouts often develop in the last third of the triangle but they have reduced probability of success. QUF Industries in Figure 7.5 shows a successful breakout in this area. Price breakouts from the very tip of the triangle tend to be weaker. This is a judgement call and if your initial list overflows with trading possibilities, then securities moving towards the very tip of a triangle pattern should be ignored.

Two of the triangle patterns, upsloping and downsloping, feature a horizontal edge created by either support or resistance levels. The food group, QUF Industries, shows the way the top of an upsloping triangle is formed by the resistance line at $2.83. The sloping side of the triangle is formed by the trendline.

This is a simple visual pattern, and as it develops the full triangle is projected into space. Watch future price activity to confirm the projected triangle. The breakout from the QUF triangle in February is substantial, and takes place in the last third of the formation.

Returning to the building contractor Watkins Pacific in Figure 7.6, the chart shows both an upsloping triangle and a downsloping triangle. We noted above that $0.21 formed a support line. This is a useful observation, but when we combine it with the downsloping trendline drawn from the high at $0.27 a clear triangle develops on a weekly basis. As this triangle develops it is a signal to keep an eye on this stock. Aggressive traders took early positions in January 1997 at $0.21 in anticipation of a breakout. Conservative traders took positions at $0.22 once the breakout was established.

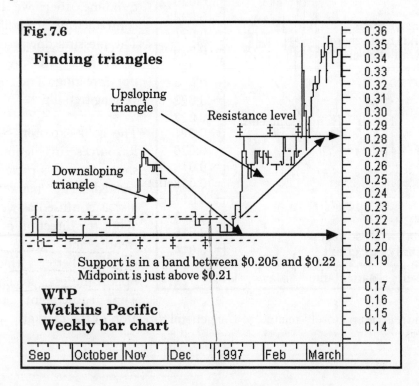

Fig. 7.6

Finding triangles

Upsloping triangle

Resistance level

Downsloping triangle

Support is in a band between $0.205 and $0.22
Midpoint is just above $0.21

WTP
Watkins Pacific
Weekly bar chart

Sep | October | Nov | Dec | 1997 | Feb | March

In this instance, the triangle developed fully and was followed by a strong breakout. This is unusual and underlines the need for traders to track stocks regularly. The chart also shows a resistance line at $0.28. This defines another triangle top and the short-term upsloping trendline defines its upward slope.

Eyeballing these patterns built from the interaction of support and resistance lines, and trend lines, is not a complex process. As the patterns develop, the securities are noted on a scratch pad list for further analysis.

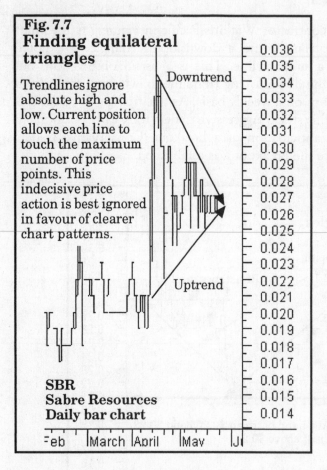

Fig. 7.7
Finding equilateral triangles

Trendlines ignore absolute high and low. Current position allows each line to touch the maximum number of price points. This indecisive price action is best ignored in favour of clearer chart patterns.

SBR
Sabre Resources
Daily bar chart

The third pattern, an equilateral or symmetrical triangle, forms when two contradictory trendlines meet. When it is almost as easy to draw an upward sloping trendline as it is to draw a downward sloping trendline, then we have contradictory trendlines. The pressure down seems to balance the pressure up, creating two converging trendlines.

The gold explorer, Sabre Resources, in Figure 7.7 shows how this pattern is created. The market is just as confused as we are about the direction of the trend and there are usually better trading opportunities available. The subsequent price direction is often closely related to the general direction of the market.

Triangles are hot tips because they flag an increase in price activity. A matrix of probability and price direction in prevailing market conditions is shown in Figure 7.8. This is covered in more detail in Chapter 12. The trader fits this into the charting context, matching probability of action with probability of reaching price targets.

Eyestrain

Useful as it is, the eyeball search has some serious limitations, usually imposed by its owner. Fatigue, wishful thinking, or seeing, and the upper limits of speed mean this powerful

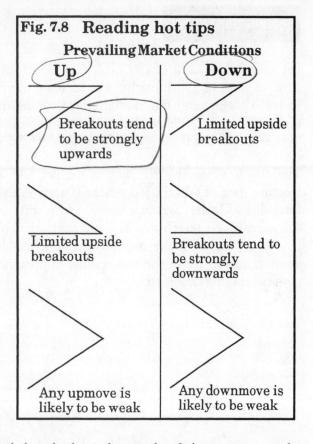

Fig. 7.8 Reading hot tips

Prevailing Market Conditions

Up	Down
Breakouts tend to be strongly upwards	Limited upside breakouts
Limited upside breakouts	Breakouts tend to be strongly downwards
Any upmove is likely to be weak	Any downmove is likely to be weak

technique cannot be used with hundreds or thousands of charts on a regular basis. Use it to regularly search a small number of stocks.

Beginners have more success searching for one feature each time — support, or trendlines, rather than both. With practice it is easy to check for both features in a single glance.

The eyeball search effectively develops an initial list of trading candidates but searching a database with more than a few hundred stocks is impractical. In later chapters we will show how this list is reduced further by better analysis. Searching larger databases calls for software able to evaluate each stock against selected specified criteria. Then these selections are eyeballed before moving to a deeper level of analysis.

The eyeball scan is so useful it is included in every trading decision. We all look at charts, but really seeing them is a different skill.

Beyond the Eyeball

Let us not lose sight of our objective. Confronted with massive amounts of data we must establish methods to separate the nuggets from the overburden. Fail to do this, and our working days, or hours, are consumed by fruitless activity, forever tantalised by missed trading opportunities. There are nuggets in this jungle, but finding them is generally hard work.

Traders downloading the entire market use software to uncover stocks meeting specific criteria. Judgement is apparently elbowed to one side by rigid formulas. Unless we are very clear on our trading objectives the software-driven search lets us build fantastical myths. Remember, no matter how complex we make this process this search expedition simply aims to develop a short list of the best trading opportunities rather than a long list of possible trading candidates.

8

TECHNICAL TRUE LOVE -
SEARCHING FOR RELATIONSHIPS

A s with every prospecting expedition, many traders are consumed by
the belief that some tools will help them see beyond the surface to the
reality beneath. The geologist Mark Creasy has a reputation for
spotting surface blows indicative of deeper geology and mineralisation. The
Central Victorian goldfields vibrate with the screech of metal detectors
searching for the reality below the surface clays. Eyeballing the charts is only
one of many ways to mine our database. The remainder of this section deals
with mining much larger fields, usually the entire market. The techniques are
also applied effectively to smaller market segments.

The nuggets we seek are securities where the balance of probability suggests a
change in direction. We cannot use the power of the computer to mine our

database for price and volume history unless we know what we are looking for. There is no signpost reading: "Profit Here."

The software manuals provided with Metastock, SuperCharts and other charting programs have extensive sections devoted to search formulas. A multitude more are available from Internet sites including www.guppytraders.com. They are all valuable tools but not particularly useful in unskilled hands. This and the following chapter are not toolboxes. We show some sample tools, but only to explain how they work effectively with one type of market geology rather than another.

Effective database mining relies on two significant types of market geology — relationship plots (R-plots) and performance-based plots. Both use raw price and volume data. Most tools belong in either one of these categories. Selecting the best tool from the correct category box is an important step towards trading success.

R-plot approaches rest on simple relationships between the open and close, and volume. They rely on the price plot and price patterns visible on the charts rather than on indicator results. Every result is a market price that could have been traded. These are Mark Creasy's surface blows indicating a deeper reality.

Performance-based approaches manipulate, smooth, average, or extrapolate the data. Like an aero-magnetic survey the search is for numerical results indicating a probability balance. The search looks for a distinctive signature hoping the owner is nearby.

When we look at the value of a moving average, typically used in performance-based approaches, we come up with a figure that is not necessarily a price traded in the market today. The moving average may give a value of $5.90 with the stock trading between $6.00 and $6.10. Traders could buy or sell at these prices, but not at the moving average price of $5.90.

These performance, or indicator, results are one step removed from the market and give the trader a different category of information about market activity.

In contrast, R-plot searches give the trader information drawn from the range of price activity actually experienced on the day. These results are much closer to the actual market activity, and are more useful in some circumstances. Although the line is often blurred, it is a useful distinction to remember.

Charting the Basic R-plot

The basic R-plot tells us which stocks have performed best over a selected period. This is simply a powerful application of the computer's capacity to search, compare, and rank information in a database. This basic scan trawls through our stock list, ranking them by comparing today's price with previous points. The search identifies nominated high, or low, achievers, but leaves the task of interpretation to the trader.

There are many basic ranking criteria. Among the most commonly used are:

1 Best performers today compared to yesterday.

2 Best performers over the past three or five days.

3 Best performers over the past week or two, or for three weeks.

4 Stocks making new high or new lows.

Remember, we use the power of the computer to identify potential trading opportunities so we can analyse them at depth at a later stage. The list should be small enough to make in-depth analysis possible. Figure 8.1 lists the top five stocks selected from the Resources sector on each of the first two search criteria.

Fig. 8.1   R-plots
Finding the top performers
Resources sector
Metastock Exploration results

1 day performance			3 day performance			5 day performance		
1	IRO	35	1	CFR	72	1	CFR	138
2	MGG	26	2	RRS	60	2	IRO	84
3	TMM	20	3	IRO	56	3	RRS	60
4	NTS	15	4	ABR	38	4	GSE	33
5	GTM	14	5	PRM	36	5	DEF	30

Metastock users can modify the default Performance, Daily exploration in the Explorer Module to scan the periods they prefer. The exploration formula is:

Column A
CLOSE

Column B
ROC(CLOSE,1,percent)
Column C
ROC(CLOSE,2,percent)
Column D
ROC(CLOSE,3,percent)
Column E
ROC(CLOSE,4,percent)
Column F
ROC(CLOSE,5,percent)

Results can be sorted by performance over a selected number of days.

Ezy Chart users search for new highs or lows in any defined period using Ezy Analyzer and the Select Criteria function. Figure 8.2 shows stocks making new yearly highs after a search of the entire market. Criteria Design details read:

The High Price of today is the highest it has been in 280 days

Fig. 8.2
R-plots
New yearly highs
ASX entire market
Ezy Chart Analyser
results (extract only)

Making new yearly highs

1	CRG	$12.50
2	CSL	$8.10
3	DAH	$0.35
4	DAT	$2.23
5	DEF	$0.28
6	DJW	$3.10
7	EEC	$1.60
8	EME	$2.92
9	FAF	$1.12
10	FLT	$3.15

Just knowing which stocks are moving quickly, or making new lows, is useful trading information not easily extracted from other sources. On the same day that Cluff Resources (CFR) added 109% to its value in a single trading session, the *Australian Financial Review* listed Goldfields as the top performing stock, up $0.10 or 5%. The information published in much of the daily press is taken from a reduced database built from the most popular and well-known stocks. This pre-selection is inadequate for trading purposes because it excludes too many stocks.

In most cases the trader will want to examine basic R-plot results a little more closely before committing his time to further in-depth and time-consuming analysis.

Advanced R-plots

All R-plot searches compare price activity against a predetermined pattern, or another data element, such as volume activity. They do not compare indicator results.

The most commonly-used advanced R-plots include:

1 Inside days

2 Gap days

3 Out of range days with a close near the high

4 Price and Volume breakouts

Advanced R-Plots usually compare one day's price activity to a previous day or group of days. An inside day, for instance (Figure 8.3), is created when the high and the low are within the high/low range of the previous day. The significant feature is the way the price bar relates to other price bars — smaller, larger, or built on changes in volume.

There are many other R-plots. The equivolume chart, for instance, uses changes in the width of the bar to plot changes in volume. How useful these other R-plots are depends on your trading style and technique. The key is to decide what you are looking for before you select the search criteria.

Most modern charting software comes equipped with default search criteria. Many people use these defaults indiscriminately and by using something different you may find a useful corner to give you an edge over the main crowd. Equally, by using the defaults as a starting point, the trader further refines the initial selections by assessing them against his own specialist criteria. The examples that follow are not a complete list of possibilities. The purpose is to show how such R-plot factors are incorporated into a data search so you can make better use of your favourite factors.

Inside Days

An inside day is when the day's price activity — the range from the low to the high — falls within the range of the previous day's price activity. Both the bar and candlestick chart displays in Figure 8.3, Faulding FH and Co (FHF), have inside days marked. This is an important reversal pattern when it occurs within an established trend. Further confirmation is required, but by searching for this we add the security to our watch list.

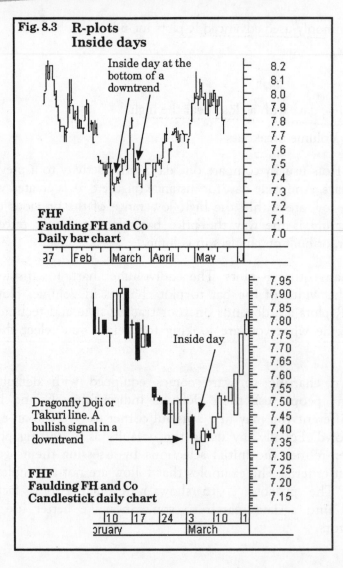

Fig. 8.3   R-plots
Inside days

Inside day at the bottom of a downtrend

FHF
Faulding FH and Co
Daily bar chart

97 Feb March April May J

Inside day

Dragonfly Doji or Takuri line. A bullish signal in a downtrend

FHF
Faulding FH and Co
Candlestick daily chart

10 17 24 3 10 1
bruary   March

This R-plot is also readily identified as part of a candlestick bullish and bearish Doji day pattern. On a Doji day the open and the close are equal. The bullish or bearish character are created by the length and direction of the 'wick' above or below the Doji.

Using a weekly candlestick approach and trading from the long side, we are interested firstly in a Dragonfly Doji shown in the bottom section of Figure 8.3. This is most significant in an established downtrend, particularly so when the end of the trend is signalled by a particularly disastrous day. Prices dip dramatically, appearing on the chart as a very long tail, but there are only a few frightened sellers left, so prices close equal to the open. This price action shakes out the last sellers, setting a new low. Find this, and we watch the stock the next trading day for confirmation.

The significant confirmation is when prices open and close within the range of the previous day. This creates an inside day and it suggests sellers are refusing to participate in the market unless they get a better price. This is a change from a market dominated by fear – I'd better sell now in case prices go lower – to a market discovering greed – I will hang on because things are going to get better.

The inside day often acts as a leading indicator, giving the trader advance warning of a price volume breakout. The warning is derived from the relationship between bars of price activity. FHF shows an inside day at the very turning point of the downtrend. This relationship is enough to add FHF to a watch list of potential trading opportunities. For comparison purposes, the same inside day following a Dragonfly Doji is shown as a candlestick chart plot.

As a long-side trader you want to select those opportunities developing into worthwhile entry positions for new trades. Scanning for an inside day uses the Metastock Explorer function. A search formula is as simple as selecting Inside() from the Analysis Tools.

The Ezy Analyser formula is a clear two-step command reading:

> The high price of today is less than the high price of yesterday
> AND
> The low price of today is greater than the low price of yesterday

Searching for Candlestick patterns is usually straightforward but in this case Metastock does not have a default Dragonfly Doji day tool. We have to build one using logic and several Candlestick categories in the Functions list. The following Exploration formula shows the construction process for this and other custom formulas:

```
Column A
Close
Column B
If(LongLeggedDoji(),1,0)
Column C
If(LongLowerShadow(),1,0)
Column D
If(Doji(),1,0)
```

This Metastock Exploration will return a boolean answer for each stock examined. Stocks meeting the search criteria appear as 1, while those failing the test return a 0 result. The formula element — ,1,0 — tells Metastock to do this, but in everyday English the 1 is read as Yes and the 0 as No.

The logic of three simultaneous searches defines the dragonfly day. In plain English, any stock that returns 1 in each of the columns must be a dragonfly day because:

➲ The day will have a very long tail above or below the Doji — a Long Legged Doji in Column B; and

➲ The tail is below the body of the day — Long Lower Shadow in Column C; and

➲ The open and the close are the same — a Doji day in Column D.

These logical conditions define a Dragonfly Doji and are included in the Explorer Filter Column as:

```
When (colB,=,1) AND When (colC,=,1) AND When(colD,=,1)
```

Complexity is built from levels of simplicity; an issue which becomes more important in the next chapter. Our purpose here is to show how Japanese candlestick charting is particularly adept at identifying R-plot patterns. If you feel price R-plots are important, or perhaps the most important factor, then learning how to construct search criteria is important. If you do not have this skill then specialist software such as North Systems CandlePower5 may save a lot of time.

Gap Days

A gap is when price closes at, say, $15.90 and then opens the next day at $16.09, as in area A on the BHP daily bar chart, Figure 8.4. This gap is 19 cents wide. In area B the previous bar closes at $16.82 and the next bar opens at $16.93 — a gap of 11¢. Prices can gap up, or gap down, and some analysts believe that each gap must be closed or covered. Closing the gaps means prices subsequently cover the gap in price activity, as shown with price bar C and D. This leads to specific trading strategies, but before they can be applied the trader must isolate those stocks showing gap activity.

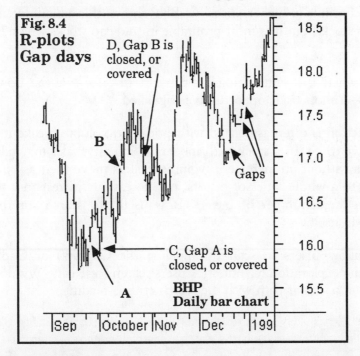

Fig. 8.4 R-plots Gap days

D, Gap B is closed, or covered

B

Gaps

C, Gap A is closed, or covered

A

BHP Daily bar chart

A gap is a chart set-up, or an R-plot, between one bar and another. A gap up is created when buyers are so eager to get stock they bid ahead of other buyers in the market. During the day prices leapfrog forward as selling dries up. When sellers see hordes of buyers at $15.90 they know they can probably ask for $0.20 more. In this boiling market someone amongst the buyers will break ranks, meeting the asking price.

When trade closes for the day, both buyers and sellers review the situation. Not all market participants watch the action during the day. Many are position traders, or investors, taking positions based on end of day data, on broker's advice, and on the information they glean from the television or financial press. Sellers who were in the market withdraw their orders when they see the acceleration of prices. They hope to get a better price. Buyers who know nothing about the stock decide to join the action. They jump the line with bids at a higher price for the open of trade. Other informed buyers who particularly want a position place opening bids higher than the previous day's close.

On the next open the first sale takes place when bid meets ask. Higher bids create a price gap up. The price gap is confirmed only if all subsequent trades for the day continue at higher prices. As BHP shows, this action does develop in blue chip stocks, but it is most profitable in mid-cap stocks where liquidity is more erratic.

Of course, when the same thing happens in reverse — a gap down in a downtrend — a short trade opportunity is signalled.

This price action is often associated with price and volume breakouts, but it does not have to be. In a stock with moderate liquidity, sales may take place at gap prices without an increase in volume. Sellers move their ask prices up in response to a whole series of factors, not necessarily in response to being chased by a large number of buyers. It is useful to search for this data relationship in itself.

Metastock allows users to scan by applying the GapUp() or GapDown() formula to the exploration. Candlestick users search for Rising Windows. Ezy Analyser takes a similar path with the search criteria reading:

> The low price of today is greater than the high price of yesterday

The criteria is reversed to find gap down days.

Edwards and Magee in *Technical Analysis of Stock Trends* presented the classic interpretation of the gap phenomenon. They include specific trading strategies for each. You may decide to concentrate on common gaps, or exhaustion gaps, or runaway gaps. Analysing and categorising the gap is a later trading decision. In this initial search we look for any gap because selecting them hones the list against our specific criteria.

This is not a useful method when dealing with stocks with a spotty price activity. Stocks with extremely low, and intermittent, volume activity often show gap-like behaviour. With so few sellers and so few buyers, sales are irregular, and often without any intervening price activity. Many of these stocks will show up on a search based on gap criteria. Weed them out by looking at the charts to determine if the gap-like activity is the usual price behaviour.

Out of Range Days

When the range of daily price movement is greater than normal it points to an imbalance between buyers and sellers. If the direction of the imbalance is upwards it suggests prices will be bid higher to satisfy the demand because the supply (sellers) is limited. If the supply was greater then all buyers would buy at lower prices.

Out of range days blur the distinction between an R-plot and an indicator. This concept considers the 'range' of price activity between the open and the close and compares it with the previous range. This is sometimes a straight-

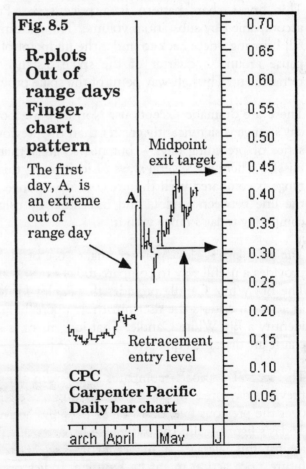

Fig. 8.5

R-plots Out of range days Finger chart pattern

The first day, A, is an extreme out of range day

A

Midpoint exit target

Retracement entry level

CPC Carpenter Pacific Daily bar chart

arch April May J

forward intuitive process. With Carpenter Pacific (CPC) shown in Figure 8.5

there is no doubt price bar A is much larger than the normal range of price activity.

This is an extreme example and although very easy to see, such price activity provides few useful signals to the trader. The price has moved too fast for the trader to jump on board. If we use end of day data we are disadvantaged because the spike may be a singular event, and not the beginning of a prolonged upmove. Only future price action tells us if it is worth jumping on board after the inevitable retracement. However, this type of development, as shown with CPC, is a frequent occurrence in mid-cap and speculative stocks. A single massive out of range day provides the clue and trading this type of move is hair-raising, but very profitable.

This finger chart pattern is a price spike. Prices show massive ranges, accompanied by substantial volume. The pattern is completed by a dramatic fall bringing prices back to under the midpoint of the initial spike. Often they pause around a quarter of the spike distance and traders enter on this retracement. The half-way point of the spike provides an exit target.

These are dramatic exceptions. Normally we look for the situation where a day's range is significantly greater than the previous day's — or an average of a series of preceding days — but not so great that the trading opportunity is missed. There are several ways of identifying this. In the first R-plot today's range is compared with the previous day's range. The second approach blurs the line between R-plots and indicators by using a calculated average and comparing today's range with it.

The standard R-plot approach makes use of Japanese candlestick because it provides a useful way to compare today's range with the previous day's range. The Big White Candle provides this R-plot for Metastock users. When used as a search criteria the user must rely upon the judgement of the software to identify a Big White Candle. That judgement is sometimes faulty, and those charts are discarded quickly.

The second approach compares today with the calculated average range of previous days, reached by taking the difference between the high and the low over the previous five, or 10 or 21 days and converting this to a single figure. Today's figure — also the difference between the high and the low — is plotted against this average. A higher figure suggests the day's range is larger and future price action might be building. Indicators that work like this include

BIG White CANDle

Average True Range and ADX style analysis which plot the difference between today's range and the average range over a defined previous period.

Notice how we are drifting from R-plots to indicators. This drift alters the way we search the data and affects the search results. The constant danger is when the search delivers a result different from the one we intended. There is nothing wrong with searching for gold nuggets and ignoring the odd valuable streak of silver exposed in the process. There is something wrong when the search ignores the gold and only selects the silver. If we use indicators to find what are essentially R-plot conditions then we sometimes miss the nuggets and find the silver instead. The silver ADX indicator reacts slowly because it is based on averages. The gold R-plot trading opportunity is signalled sooner with a Big White Candle search. The search must match objectives with methods.

The R-plot delivers a simple visual message flagging the potential for further price action and suggesting an appropriate entry price. The performance indicator moves away from this simple message, placing today's price in a wider context more suited to a different style of trading.

For our purposes it is enough to know you can make this criteria as simple — a Big White Candle — or as complex — an Average True Range indicator — as you wish. Adjust the parameters to suit your trading needs.

Price and Volume Breakouts

Financial writers make some rather artificial distinctions between market information — fundamental, charting, technical. Good traders use a combination of each to enhance their trading style by identifying those perfect, or near perfect, opportunities matching their ideal trading conditions.

Volume is the fuel driving the market. An uptrend, to survive, must be nourished by new buyers and fed by cautiously reluctant sellers. Consistent volume is important. To topple the existing trend there must be a surge of buyers, or sellers, capable of changing the price.

The change in price and volume provides the groundwork for this R-plot, but to explore it the trader needs indicator-like tools.

Volume is usually shown as a histogram, with solid bars. Volume charts yield clues when volume is out of character but this is hard to decide. The jagged pattern needs smoothing so in this case a mathematical solution is better than a visual one.

The key in using volume as a search criteria is to measure today's volume against consistent past volume calculated on a long-term average, for instance where the volume is 50% above the 50-day moving average. Price breakouts are selected on a percentage approach basis, perhaps where price has increased 5% or greater over yesterday's close.

The search is not meaningful unless we define criteria to match our trading intentions. A search of an entire market may need to be repeated several times using slightly different criteria. I look for short-term breakouts where the price increases 5% or more over yesterday's close. I match this with stocks where volume is 50% above the 50-day moving average.

The Metastock formula is:

```
ColA CLOSE, ColB REF(CLOSE,-1), ColC ROC(CLOSE,1,PERCENT)
ColD VOLUME, ColE MOV(VOLUME,50,EXPONENTIAL), ColF
((VOLUME-MOV(VOLUME,50,EXPONENTIAL))/MOV(VOLUME,50,EXPONENTIAL))*
100, Filter WHEN(COLC>=5) AND WHEN(COLD>=COLE*1.5)
```

Those using Ezy Analyser select the default Volume Trend with Highest Close. This shows all stocks where the volume has increased steadily over the past four periods and where today's close is the highest close for those four periods. By selecting Criteria Design users can manipulate the standard values to suit their search requirements.

With around 2,628 securities, including options and warrants, the Ezy Analyser takes less than five minutes to identify all securities meeting these default criteria. Figure 8.6 lists the top seven selected from an entire market search, along with a chart of Fimiston Mining (FIM).

My trading style determines the structure of the R-plot and the Metastock search parameters. These are not default search formula. They are modified to reflect my particular beliefs about market behaviour. Your beliefs about the market, and your trading style, will differ from mine so the final formula settings you use will be different as a result.

My objective in setting the cut-off figure, such as 5% or 50-day volume average, is to eliminate as many stocks as possible, and to include only those with a real possibility of becoming useful trading opportunities. Some bigger fish will slip through the net, but we ought to catch enough to give us a feed for the day.

The choices we make in setting the search criteria should all assist in excluding those stocks which are least likely to develop into trading opportunities in the immediate future.

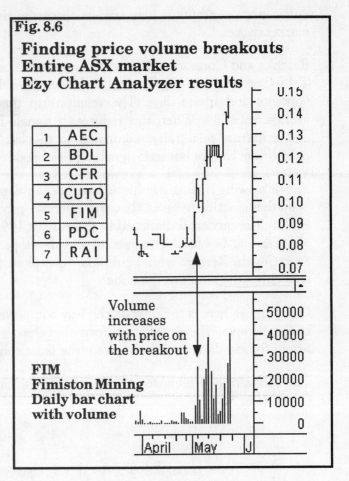

Fig. 8.6

Finding price volume breakouts Entire ASX market Ezy Chart Analyzer results

1	AEC
2	BDL
3	CFR
4	CUTO
5	FIM
6	PDC
7	RAI

Volume increases with price on the breakout

FIM Fimiston Mining Daily bar chart with volume

Buying Into Complexity

We look for nuggets, and the search can be as simple, or as complex, as we choose to make it. The search is productive as long as we do not lose sight of our objective. In the same way that a 180-tonne capacity Caterpillar 5230 Excavator is just a pumped-up spade, the search for NR4 conditions used by US futures traders Linda Raschke and Larry Conners is conceptually in the same R-plot class discussed above.

The NR4 conditions understand that a market tends to move swiftly from periods of price consolidation to new levels. The high volatility, narrow

4-day range conditions, help traders recognise this market setup before the market moves.

Raschke and Connors combined the narrow range 4-day pattern discussed by Toby Crabel in his *Day Trading With Short Term Price Patterns* with historical volatility and inside days. The relationship they use looks at the 50-day average volatility. When this reduces, it signals market agreement on value and a narrow price range compared to the last 4 days confirms this. The equilibrium cannot last so it signals a price break.

This is a swing trading technique based on an R-plot relationship. Defining it is mathematically complex, but the essential process is the same as for any R-plot. The process is discussed in the August 1996 issue of *Technical Analysis of Stocks and Commodities* magazine and developed more fully in their book, *Street Smarts*. Readers who would like to explore this concept further should read either the article or the book.

Our purpose here is to illustrate the way complexity is derived from common basic concepts. The exploration formula below is a long way from our first search for gap days, yet it builds from the same concepts.

The Metastock formula for NR4 with high volatility used by Raschke and Connors is:

```
Column A
Std(log(C/Ref(C,-1)),5)/Std(Log(C/Ref(C,-1)),99)
Column B
HIGH-LOW<Ref(LLV(H-L,3),-1)
Column C
HIGH<Ref(HIGH,-1)AND LOW>Ref(LOW,-1)
Column D
HIGH
Column E
LOW
Filter
colA<.5 AND (colB=1 OR colC=1)
```

Column A shows the ratio between 6-day and 100-day volatility. Column B shows a 1 (yes) if today is an NR4 day. Column C shows 1 (yes) if today is an inside day. The high and low, Columns D and E, help determine entry points.

Complexity does not guarantee success, but if complexity is built on a firm understanding of the concepts, it can be a very useful tool in identifying situations of high probability. By developing better search criteria we reduce our time in mining the ore body so we can spend more time polishing the nuggets.

The Preliminary List gets Bigger

Where to look and what to look for? The answers depend on the market you select, the tools you prefer and your trading style. The results can be selected after a search based on patterns most easily selected by the human eye, or on relationships between price, price ranges and volume. This *a priori* — before the fact — decision determines what is included in our preliminary list and how large it is.

Before returning a single cent of profit the trader must expend a fortune in search and analysis time. Performance-based searches, discussed in the next chapter, provide the last component of this constant search for trading nuggets.

A free list of ready-to-use Metastock exploration formulas is available from http://www.ozemail.com.au/~guppy and they are updated regularly.

9

PERFORMANCE SEARCHES

So far we have looked for nuggets of probability using direct evidence — the eyeball — and by spotting surface blows characteristic of gold-bearing country — R-plots. The boom in modern Australian mining is built on inferred results. Geological activity conducive to the formation of gold leaves a signature. The signature is an indicator, and often easier to find than the gold. When this approach is applied to our market search the danger lies in being so distracted by the signature indicator that we walk over nuggets in plain view.

In this chapter we look at the family of indicators and search approaches based on price performance. These performance indicators suggest a strong probability that price action is developing but, like modern gold exploration techniques, we need additional digging to confirm the resource. We cannot tell you which combination of performance indicators is best because your trading style is individual. Instead we show you how your choices determine the search results. If your choices are inconsistent with your beliefs about market activity then the nuggets will be elusive. Understanding the process builds a better search mechanism for identifying the balance of probability.

Unlike the R-plot, an indicator takes price data and manipulates it to reveal additional "hidden" information about the development of price action. For instance, by comparing the standard deviation range to previous trading days we build details about the speed and momentum of price that are not available through R-plot or eyeball searches.

The difference between the R-plot group and the performance indicator family is that an indicator reading is not a market price. It is a numerical value obtained from the result of a calculation. This is the key to working with technical analysis indicators.

Elder suggests in *Trading For a Living* that indicators fall into one of three categories — trend-following, oscillators and miscellaneous. This chapter concentrates on the way we use the first two without discussing a host of individual indicators at significant depth. Additional reading references are noted where appropriate. Later we provide a test for indicator success.

The way the indicator is constructed tells us what it is trying to measure. If it measures the same factors we want to measure, then it is safe to use it to set our scanning criteria. If it does not measure our preferred factors, then we should not use it because the results may become a dangerous threat to our trading. Powerful indicators give enticingly complex results and it is too easy to second-guess our otherwise sound analysis. Many traders succumb to the temptation to use a range of sometimes contradictory indicators because the names sound interesting, they are available on the software, or other people talk about using them.

Very broadly these two groups of performance indicators — trend-following and oscillators — are designed to answer two simple questions:

1 Where are we? — these are the trend-following indicators.

2 Are we breaking the speed limit? — these are the oscillators.

The first part of this chapter considers trend-following indicators. These are all based on moving average concepts and we show how this simple idea is layered into some of the most complex of indicators. All of them are designed to answer a single question: Where is price now in relation to price in a previous period?

From Zero to One and Beyond

Using the power of the computer to search an extensive database of securities is as simple as a few mouse clicks. Understanding the report results is more difficult.

Depending on the software used, some scanning results deliver a numerical value. Others use boolean logic returning either a 1 = YES or a 0 = NO. It would be a major step forward for Metastock and others if they could convert this 0 and 1 to plain English equivalents. By using the 'sort' function in Metastock the responses are ranked from highest to the lowest. This groups all the 1 — yes responses — together, making it easier to develop a useful list.

The Ezy Analyser returns a list of securities passing the search criteria. The user adjusts the sensitivity of the search by deciding the time frame. A search for stocks showing a moving average crossover might use a 5-day cut-off period. The database analysis only returns those securities where the event has occurred within the last five days. Users move from the list of selected securities to the chart of each one.

No matter how displayed, the "Yes" results suggest turning points where the balance of probability bulges at its thickest. These points are not always supported by the bar chart price action, but the idea is that the indicator either confirms or anticipates the shift. The initial task is to find the securities at turning points where an entry is signalled. Judging the next turning point for the exit is a different task discussed in Part III.

Where are We? An Average Answer

The old prospectors looked for specks of gold. By collecting enough specimens from several areas they determined an average concentration and the potential location of the mother-lode. More recently, some modern geologists watched Dyak tribesman panning specks of gold and extrapolated the Bre-X disaster. Other modern prospectors fly over a larger area, gathering extensive aerial data which is manipulated to give a better average indication of the size and location of the ore body. We have the same choice of market search techniques using performance indicators.

The trend-following group of performance indicators plot the current position of a stock against some previously calculated average position. The result tells us where we are.

Prices fluctuate, sometimes erratically. A plotted price line is constructed by snapshots of one price element — perhaps the close — and is a little like joining the dots. This line is made more useful when compared against past prices, on average. We want to know where we are in relation to a range of previous price activity. Simply looking back at past history is one solution.

Another plot compares today's price with the moving average of prices. Unfortunately price has four parts — open, high, low and close — so we must choose one to base the average calculations on. Most times we take the close, and create a pre-defined average range from this data. Many traders use 3, 4, 5, 7, or 20-day moving averages. Choosing a single element — the close, or high etc. — immediately reduces the amount of information available. As discussed in Chapter 2, a line chart is not as useful as a bar chart.

An alternative solution combines the four price parts into a single 'average' figure. Choosing the median price — the mid-point between the high and low for the day — captures additional information about price, more than any other single data point, such as the open. This price data relationship has a value plotted on a chart as single point. Calculate the value for each day in the past, join the dots, and the screen display plots a line in the same way as a closing price line.

We can further manipulate the median price by plotting the 10-day, or 15-day moving average of the value. Then we have a data point against which we compare today's median price. Conceptually this is not different to a closing line display plotted against a 20-day moving average. The difference is in the detail. We plot a median price against its 10-day average and learn something different about price behaviour.

This is essentially a simple calculation concept using an average of an average. The mathematics is more complex but this calculation task is ideally suited to the computer's form of high-speed idiocy. Often we make this calculation even more complex by the calculation method chosen for the moving average.

Data Manipulation

The choices include a Simple Moving Average (SMA), an Exponential Moving Average (EMA), and a Weighted Moving Average (WMA). Your choice may be based on simplicity and ease of use, or it may be more closely related to a specific belief about the market. With modern software all choices are equally easy so it pays to think carefully about the impact of each approach.

Does it really matter? Figure 9.1 lists the results of three Metastock Explorer searches using an SMA, EMA and WMA. The database of securities searched are the same, but the membership of each list is subtly different. New additions are shown in bold italics. One of these lists gives you a head start. Which one it is depends on how you match your choice with your beliefs. The search results should support and reinforce your trading strategy.

Fig. 9.1

Performance Indicators
Moving Average Crossover 3/10
All Resources
Metastock Explorer results (first ten only)

EMA results		SMA results		WMA results	
1	KGM	1	KGM	1	*HAR*
2	TRY	2	TRY	2	KGM
3	CNT	3	NDY	3	TRY
4	NDY	4	MIM	4	CNT
5	QRL	5	KCN	5	NDY
6	COG	6	AAA	6	QRL
7	MIM	7	MLG	7	COG
8	KCN	8	*AUG*	8	MIM
9	AAA	9	*EMP*	9	KCN
10	MLG	10	*GLD*	10	AAA

In *The Lion King* film the wise old monkey belts a young lion across the head with his staff. He tells the angry lion that the attack was in the past, so, according to the young lion's philosophy, it doesn't matter. Rubbing his head, the lion concedes that the past does have an impact on current and future events. In a similar way, I believe recent price data is more significant than less recent price data.

What happens today has a greater immediate impact on what happens tomorrow than do events of 10 or 20 days ago. As a result, I use an EMA calculation because it is consistent with my understanding of the market. My trading list comes from the first column in Figure 9.1.

Applying any of these styles of average calculations to a single data element — open, high, low or close — gives useful results, but they are not a simple traded market price.

The level of complexity increases when we use a relationship between price data. We might manipulate the data by selecting a median price. In this example if the low is $0.40 and the high is $0.80 then the median is $0.60.

Others prefer to use the mean price or what we commonly call the average. Continuing the example above, if the open is $0.42 and the close $0.64 then we have four observations — open 42, high 80, low 40 and close 64. The total is 226. To find the mean the total is divided by the number of data points giving a result of $0.565.

Plotting the mean against the median leaves a $0.035 gap. This is not insignificant if your trading method relies on signals generated by moving average crossovers.

The levels of complexity are almost infinite, and addictive. Other manipulations calculate the standard deviation and compare today's price activity with past activity. Some use the mean deviation to find the average absolute value of the difference between the population of data points and the mean.

Again, does it matter? The answer is yes. Figure 9.2 lists EMA crossover search results from the All Resources sector using the close, the median and the average, or typical, price. The results are ranked by the value above or below the crossover point, with zero values identifying the exact crossover. We have only shown the candidates' names. The difference in the make up of and order within the lists reflects the relationship between the price data selected as the basis of the EMA calculation. Opportunities noted in one list sometimes do not appear in either of the others.

When Walter Scott lamented "O, *what a tangled web we weave, When first we practise to deceive*", he wasn't talking about price data manipulation but the effects are the same. If you use an indicator based on complex calculations and price data manipulation make sure you understand and agree with the reasoning behind the structural choices.

Fig. 9.2
Performance Indicators
Moving Average Crossover 3/10 EMA
All Resources
Metastock Explorer results (first ten only)

Close price results		Median price results		Typical or average price results	
1	KGM	1	*GRM*	1	KGM
2	TRY	2	KGM	2	COG
3	CNT	3	COG	3	TRY
4	NDY	4	TRY	4	NDY
5	QRL	5	NDY	5	QRL
6	COG	6	*QRL*	6	MIM
7	MIM	7	MIM	7	AAA
8	KCN	8	AAA	8	KCN
9	AAA	9	KCN	9	MLG
10	MLG	10	*MLG*	10	*AUG*

Complexity is not always the best answer so do not select an indicator just because it is complex. Nor should indicators be selected purely on simplicity. The computational power of modern software makes the mechanics of calculation an insignificant factor in our ability or inability to construct and plot indicators. The choice of indicator should be made on the basis of the combination and approach which most closely matches your understanding of the market, and which brings out the relationships you think are important. The signature of the nugget you look for is subtly different from other signatures.

Crossed Signals

Averages, in all their forms, help establish where today's price is in relation to prices as they were, on average, in a pre-defined past period. They help build the balance of probability and show the trader if his contemplated entry price is a bargain, or fully priced, when compared to a previous period of price behaviour.

Traders are a suspicious lot. Amongst the rabbit's feet, lucky coffee mugs and winning routines, is a strong feeling that more is always better. Within reason this is true. Confirmation of any indicator result helps 'prove' the initial conclusion. For confirmation many traders plot two moving averages, using the crossovers as trading signals.

By overlaying a longer-term moving average — one that gives very reliable signals — with a shorter-term average — one that gives less reliable signals, but which is more responsive to changes in the market — the trader gets confirmation and, he hopes, the best of both worlds. When the current price is higher than the short-term average, and when the short-term average has crossed over, or turned above, the longer-term average, a buying opportunity is signalled.

The simple strategy identifies a bulge in the balance of probability and, as expected, we can make it more complex in steady degrees. The Moving Average Convergence Divergence (MACD) indicator explores changing relationships between averages.

This impressive-sounding and popular indicator measures the distance between two averages, usually a 12-day and 26-day EMA. The difference between the two values is calculated and plotted as a solid fast MACD line. Then a 9-day EMA of the fast MACD line is calculated and plotted as a dashed signal line.

Briefly, the trading rules for MACD are:

1 Buy when the fast MACD line crosses above the signal line.

2 Sell when the fast MACD line crosses below the signal line.

Building further complexity gives the MACD-Histogram indicator. This takes its name from the vertical histogram bars used to plot the value of the fast MACD line minus the signal line. Figure 9.3 is an example of this indicator histogram plot in a Metastock format.

In screening the database to identify stocks meeting these crossover criteria Metastock users can select the default MACD Buy Signal. Ezy Analyser users choose MACD Crossover. A selection of results of an entire market search for MACD crossovers in the last ten periods are listed in Figure 9.4 in three groups of ten. Out of a universe of 2,638 securities, this scan identified 374 meeting the criteria. This list must be reduced further, either by comparing it with another list, preferably one based on a different group of indicators, such as R-plots, or perhaps the trend-following performance indicators discussed below. Ultimately, we cannot get away from the task of eyeballing the final candidates.

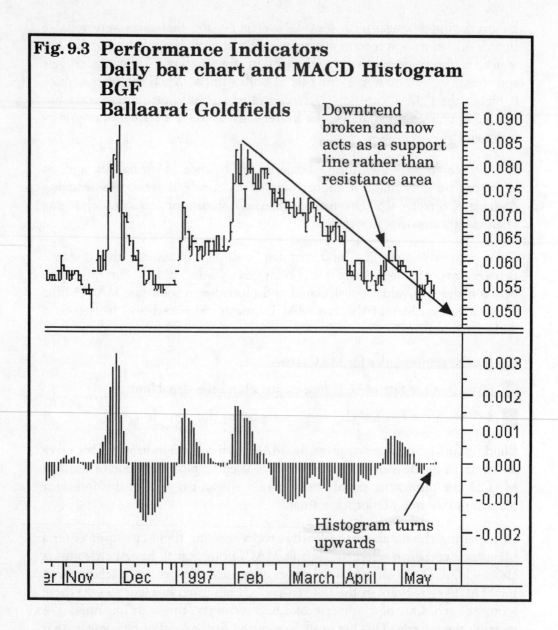

Fig. 9.3 Performance Indicators
Daily bar chart and MACD Histogram
BGF
Ballaarat Goldfields

Downtrend broken and now acts as a support line rather than resistance area

- 0.090
- 0.085
- 0.080
- 0.075
- 0.070
- 0.065
- 0.060
- 0.055
- 0.050

- 0.003
- 0.002
- 0.001
- 0.000
- -0.001
- -0.002

Histogram turns upwards

er | Nov | Dec | 1997 | Feb | March | April | May

Our intention is to show how these groups of performance indicators are used to find specific types of information about market activity and build a list of trading candidates for closer study. Readers who wish to further explore the construction and use of this and other related trend-following performance indicators are referred to Colby and Meyers' *The Encyclopedia of Technical Market Indicators*, or Elder's *Trading For a Living*.

Fig. 9.4

**Performance Indicators
Moving Average Convergence Divergence
(MACD)
Entire ASX market
Ezy Charts Analyser results (first thirty only)**

MACD crossover		MACD crossover		MACD crossover	
1	ABR	1	AJI	1	BAE
2	ABT	2	ALA	2	BAH
3	ACH	3	ALM	3	BGF
4	ADF	4	ALO	4	BHT
5	ADH	5	ANI	5	BKS
6	AFD	6	ARP	6	BLK
7	AGL	7	ASH	7	BMX
8	AGN	8	ASL	8	BNM
9	AGS	9	ATE	9	BOG
10	AIG	10	ATI	10	BRL

The trend-following indicators tell us where we are. From simple beginnings, where we recognise the neighbourhood, we layer levels of complexity until we reach the equivalent of a GPS positioning system. The objective of the search remains the same — find securities where, on balance, the current trend is changing. Effective screening using indicators has clear objectives and a clear understanding of the message each indicator is delivering.

From Zero to One Hundred Per Cent

The remainder of this chapter deals with the second group of indicators, the oscillators.

Knowing the position of today's price relative to a previous range of prices is useful, but the market does not stand still. Good trading moves in the same direction as the market, and at the same, or greater, speed. The momentum of price movements is important, but so too is the speed.

we drive beyond the speed limit we run the risk of making an
ntary contribution to reducing the State debt and this encourages us to
own. Put on a broad-brimmed hat, chain a dog on the back of the utility
ive below the speed limit and some road rage maniac will encourage us
to accelerate to match the flow of traffic. The smooth flow of traffic is
bounded by those who drive too fast and too slow. A driver may oscillate
between these extremes, but the pressure is always to return to a middle speed.

This pressure represents a probability bulge. At extremes of oscillation there
is increased probability that events will swing in the opposite direction. This
observation is at the core of the way oscillator-based indicators are used in
trading and the way we include them in performance-based screening criteria.
Trading presents two problems for oscillators. First, how to measure the
speed limit; and second, how to find the middle or equilibrium point when
extreme speed limits change.

On the road we measure our speed in absolute terms — from zero to 100
kilometres an hour or more. There are no absolute terms in trading so we
measure momentum, or speed, results as a percentage — lower limit, 0% and
upper limit, 100%. In a percentage calculation the equilibrium point is always
50%. In extreme situations these indicators sometimes give readings above
100 and below 0, but this is most unusual.

Within these upper and lower limits, experience, and testing, suggests most
price activity takes place within a very broad band. The software standard
Stochastic indicator is ideal for this measurement. It compares where today's
price closed relative to its highest and lowest trading range over the last 10
trading days. By adding a Slow Period we select an average figure for the high
and low over the last 10 days and compare today's against the average range.
This gives %K slowed by, for instance, 5.

Some Stochastic plots steps straight into complexity by plotting a %D line.
This is an average of the %K line and conceptually no different from any
other 10-day moving average. Except — it is a moving average (%D) of a
smoothed moving average (Slow Period) of an average calculation (%K).

Simple or complex, the Stochastic plot sandwiches these values, expressed as
percentages, between an upper and lower band usually placed at 20% and
80%. The Relative Strength Index (RSI) uses the average upwards price
changes and average downward price changes. This value is compared with
today's price range. The RSI sets speed band levels at 30% and 70%.

Most price activity, or speed, is within an equilibrium range. The Stochastic plots the current calculated position within this range. The upper and lower chart bands define the areas approaching the extremes, rather like the thick line in the high-speed areas on a speedometer. The momentum or velocity of price is also limited within an equilibrium range. The RSI style of performance indicator red-lines the extremities.

In the equilibrium range the buyer's mood almost exactly matches the seller's mood so there is high agreement about current market value. There are fewer trading opportunities in this equilibrium range. All things being equal, prices will return to this state of rest and when activity reaches extremes there is increased probability it will swing back towards, not the other extreme, but the point of equilibrium. Just like the speeding driver, speed slows to within the normal speed limit and his location changes.

Speed Bumps

Oscillator indicators surrender information about speed, but not about location. Activity in the lower extremities is termed oversold. On the balance of probabilities price will move upwards. The indicator suggests an underlying shift in the demand and supply situation.

In trading terms, there are less sellers and more buyers.

An overbought reading, above 80%, suggests the current price will return to normal. This implies prices will steady within their established range before moving out of equilibrium again. In trading terms, there are now more sellers than buyers altering the balance and forcing prices down.

Securities moving towards extremities are candidates for a return to equilibrium, and perhaps, even overshooting towards the opposite extremity. Figure 9.5 lists an Ezy Analyser full market RSI search result of candidates moving into the oversold area in the last ten periods. This full market search of 2,638 securities took around four minutes and found 22 candidates. This list is further refined against stocks which have started to recover from oversold positions and move upwards towards the equilibrium point. This distinctive signature points to possible nuggets.

Fig. 9.5
Performance Indicators
Relative Strength Index(RSI)
Entire ASX market
Ezy Charts Analyser results

RSI oversold and moving up			RSI oversold and moving up	
1	AEV		1	GPA
2	APE		2	GRT
3	BSG		3	HHM
4	CMK		4	HMT
5	CMT		5	K GM
6	CRT		6	LEO
7	CUD		7	MOH
8	EGL		8	NNA
9	ENT		9	PGT
1 0	GGN		1 0	TCL
1 1	GIP		1 1	W ME

Oscillator performance indicators show three bulges in probability and search criteria are adjusted to identify them. With a bulge at each extremity and a very large bulge in the middle, the trader can position all trading candidates on a performance curve. Most securities spend most of their time in the middle area and this suggests a strategy based on fading the trend. This trades from the extremity towards a return to normalcy. Charting this, as shown in Figure 9.6, is the first step in assessing the further viability of the trade. Knowing where we are, and how fast we are travelling, sets the scene for a trade. A database search based on performance indicator results provides this information.

Oscillators revel in complexity. By manipulating the calculation parameters, price element, and time periods, percentage or point change, the user builds more subtle indicators. Some traders look for disagreement, or divergence, as an additional distinctive oscillator signature. When the bar chart price makes new lows and the RSI plot does the opposite, developing a series of new highs moving up from the oversold level, the indicator signals divergence as shown in Figure 9.7. Some traders use this as a leading trend change signal, both at market tops and bottoms, believing it uncovers performance relationships obscured by the bar chart. The road to complexity is easily opened but users are warned of blinding clouds of confusion.

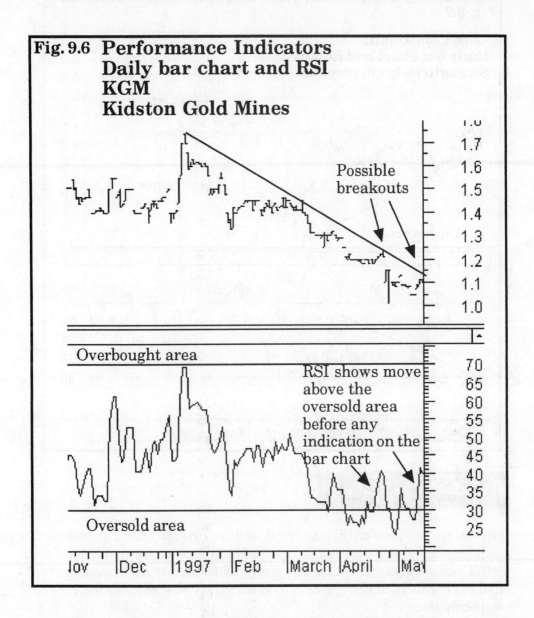

Fig. 9.6 Performance Indicators
Daily bar chart and RSI
KGM
Kidston Gold Mines

Possible breakouts

Overbought area

RSI shows move above the oversold area before any indication on the bar chart

Oversold area

In selecting indicators, the choice between a specialised, flighty thoroughbred, or a robust general duties stockhorse is yours. The market yields winning outcomes for each, but whether you ride them to the finish depends on your trading style. Complexity is not a panacea for profits so do not confuse the search for increasingly subtle signatures with the search for nuggets.

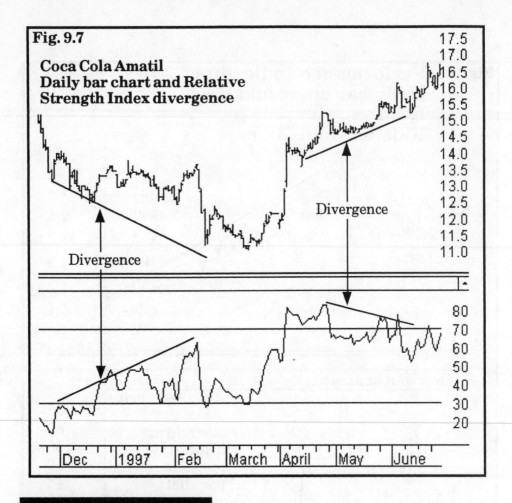

Fig. 9.7

**Coca Cola Amatil
Daily bar chart and Relative
Strength Index divergence**

The Indicator Success Test

Performance searches clarify the trend and its strength. Use them to find candidates for closer analysis, or to confirm initial conclusions based on eyeball observations. The lists provide candidates, but not solutions. We build better lists by applying search tools correctly rather than on the basis of complexity alone.

By comparing a screen display of our chosen indicator, and parameter settings, with a bar chart of the stock being analysed, we assess the effectiveness of our choice. All indicators must pass this test. Past bar chart activity shows the very best trading opportunities. If our selected indicator signals these historical opportunities then it is likely to signal future opportunities.

Traders must get this relationship correct. The indicator reflects decision points already on the bar chart. Indicator signals fit the bar chart, not vice versa. It is a sad trader who moans "The indicator signalled a trendbreak but price continued to fall." Price validates indicator results and the further you move away from market price — the more complex the indicator calculation — the greater the danger of losing touch with the market.

If your chosen indicator does not pick historical turning points it certainly will not select future ones. Any database search built around such an indicator turns up fool's gold.

Juggling Lists

Mining the database using performance indicators to identify particular signature activity is not a substitute for further analysis. Like the previous searches, this search helps to manage our time effectively by eliminating irrelevant price activity. Those candidates passing the test are not necessarily good trades.

Each candidate on the list, as shown above, is finally eyeballed on a chart. This way the nugget is cleaned and inspected to discard any made of fool's gold. The chart gives additional information and the first set of supplementary numbers needed for any trading decision. When other market numbers confirm the balance of probability, the trade is opened, or closed.

Some nuggets are counterfeit so we need some simple tests for real gold before we start converting the nuggets into dollar signs. The following chapters describe these tests.

10

An Assay Test - Looking for Life

In the 18th century suspicious merchants bit gold coins to make sure they weren't made of soft gilded lead. Our first list of trading nuggets must undergo a similar quality test because some potential trades are counterfeit. Sometimes every indicator flashes a buy signal, but the trade goes nowhere or prices do move, but not far enough or fast enough to satisfy our trading objectives. We need to determine if the market sees imminent price action because some breakouts move sideways rather than upwards. We tighten the search focus, looking for signs that the market thinks the stock needs revaluing.

Although it pays to be patient in trading, it is also dangerous to wait too long for a trade to turn in a profit. In assessing the shrinking list of candidates we need a means to assess the probability of price action developing within a reasonable time.

The stochastic and momentum-style indicators point us in this direction, but we need additional confirmation. We get this by exploring some further relationships between moving averages and applying one further observation about the nature of the market.

For this we use a Guppy Multiple Moving Average (MMA) indicator to confirm the market is coiled for action. Like a compressed spring the market sometimes explodes into action and we can be ready for it. Other indicators tell us the direction of movement, but the Guppy MMA tells us it is imminent. This indicator tells us the balance of probability is tipped in our favour because price is about to get a kick along.

This kick does not come out of nowhere. The operation of the market demands that price gets booted under specific circumstances.

Fixed Price

Australians and others are often bewildered in Bali when they discover that shopping really means haggling. 'Fixed price' stores have sprung up to cater to this insecurity. The market stalls and beachfront tourist art markets are a confusing babble of hard bargains. For many, shopping is unpleasant because there is no fixed price.

This is one of two different market approaches. We are used to the fixed price model. When we talk of bargain hunting we usually mean finding the store with the best bar-coded pricing for the goods we want. Shopping for the same basket of groceries at Woolworths may cost less than shopping at Coles, and there may be differences between suburban and country stores. But in every case the price of the goods is marked on the shelf and encoded in the bar code. There is no room for negotiation with the young lady on the checkout.

A bargain hunter searches for the best location offering the best price. Some traders try to use this approach to finding buying opportunities in the stock market but the financial market rarely works this way.

The financial markets are built on the Bali model. There are no fixed prices and buyers and sellers constantly argue with each other about the trading price of every security. We label them bulls and bears as shorthand to describe how optimism attempts to triumph over pessimism. As we show in the next chapter, the market has morning prices and afternoon prices, it has special prices and tourist prices. The one thing is does not have is a fixed price.

This important observation tells us the market is constantly in a state of unstable equilibrium. Like a ball balanced, or resting, on the top of a flagpole, the slightest puff of wind will send it plummeting. The tendency is to move away from the resting point towards another balance point.

In contrast, a stable equilibrium is when the ball is at the bottom of a gully. It takes a fair amount of pressure to push it up the sides. The tendency is always to fall back towards the resting point.

The stock market shows an unstable equilibrium. It has to. If it did not, there would be long-term agreement on pricing and, effectively, no stock market. Without disagreement about prices and value traders are reduced to shopping at Woolworths or Coles, tracking down the best fixed-price offerings.

This pricing instability means that just when prices pause and are apparently stable — when there is a high level of agreement about prices — prices are most likely to change. Nature abhors a vacuum and the financial markets abhor fixed prices. The dynamics driving the market zero in on stable prices because someone inevitably sees an opportunity to do better, or worse, than the current price.

In the same way that fixed-price stores broadly agree on pricing an item, most of the time the market broadly agrees with the valuation of a stock. This does not provide a trading opportunity where we can exploit the difference between our entry and exit prices. But every now and then the market comes into near-perfect agreement about value. This stability cannot last.

It is usually a signal for a violent disagreement and this disagreement is what we trade. Points of temporary stability and agreement imply a greater probability of imminent instability. The MMA indicator discussed below is used to find this point of agreement.

A Boot Up the Market

Stability and stable prices are relative terms. When we talk in this way about the financial market the trader frequently reaches for a moving average to compare today's price with some average of prices in the past. Moving averages in all their forms tell us a great deal about current price in relation to a previous price series, or about the behaviour of price over a selected period.

At this level of analysis we would like to know what the market is thinking about the stock, and if the current price is in tune with that thinking. If the current price is below market thinking, then we have a tougher decision to make because we are pitting our conviction against the common opinion of the market. If current price is above market thinking then we have to decide if the security is overpriced, if it represents a bargain entry price when compared to the potential for the stock, or if this is merely an enthusiastic bubble that will not last.

Essentially, any combination of moving averages is equipped to provide us with information and answers for these questions. Taking it at its most basic, a common grouping compares a 3-day moving average with a 10-day moving average. To recap briefly, the 3-day moving average tells us how today's price is situated in relation to the previous 3-day period, on average. This comparison with today's price tells us if the stock, on a very basic level, is overpriced, or underpriced. The 3-day average gives us a reference point for Coca Cola Amatil, Figure 10.1, but the trend, or price activity it measures, is too short for most trading purposes.

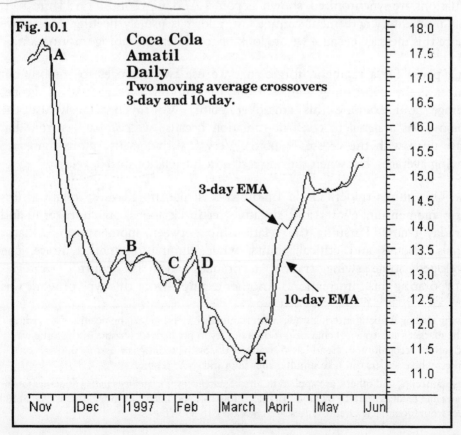

121

Hence we smooth out the sudden bumps and lumps with, say, a 10-day moving average, using Coca Cola Amatil for base data. This gives us an additional reference point so we can more effectively compare the placement of today's price in a context of a more established trend. For those who are involved in investing rather than trading, these figures are often shifted from 3 days to 3 weeks, and from 10 days to 10 weeks. On the other extreme, intraday trading, we could use a 3-minute and a 10-minute tick chart. The principle remains the same in all cases. By using two reference points, plus a known point — today's close — we can triangulate a position.

The trading signals given by most moving average approaches are usually based on crossovers. That is, when the short-term line crosses the long-term line, and when both lines are heading in the same direction, is usually understood as a good indication that prices will continue to move in that direction.

But, additionally, each crossover point also indicates a moment of agreement on prices and this is the aspect we want to draw out. In two time frames two valuations are synchronised, shown as points A, B, C, D and E on Figure 10.1. This momentary agreement cannot last, and it is usually fleeting. Mostly we ignore this message because we are looking for different trading information.

Let's pause for a moment, forget that we use two averages to smooth out whipsaws by confirming signals from the shorter average with a longer average, and examine this crossover point. We subconsciously use the crossover as a signal to confirm valuation because we compare current bar chart price with the crossover point. Very few traders use more than two moving averages, but when they do a significant relationship develops.

The US futures trader, Linda Bradford Raschke, noted these relationships using momentum charts and negative feedback loops on short-term and intraday charts. Pursuing the relationship between momentum, oscillator signals, fractals and critical points, while eliminating market noise, she developed some swing trading techniques and risk control strategies incorporating this information.[1] Another example from this type of work was

---

[1] Swing trading is about entering trades with minimal risk and managing positions according to the market's subsequent behaviour. It does not try to predict an outcome in the same way that pattern recognition or trend-based strategies do. Swing trading is a useful approach to markets where traders can take simultaneous long and short positions.

These concepts, and others, are applied in *Street Smarts: High Probability Trading Strategies for the Futures and Equities Markets*, by Linda Bradford Raschke and Larry Connors. This is available direct from Oceanview Financial Research, fax US 818 353 2099.

used in Chapter 8. Our purpose here is at a less complex level so we use one of these concepts in the context of a basic Exponential Moving Average. Our intention is not to solely manage positions according to the market's subsequent behaviour, as in swing trading, but to use this information to confirm previous analysis of points where there is increased probability — a bulge — of imminent price action.

By plotting a group of six short-term averages — 3, 5, 8, 10, 12 and 15 — the emerging relationships are clearer. Figure 10.2 shows Coca Cola Amatil with this group of moving averages. Here we combine multiple short time frames on a single screen display. It does not include a closing price line.

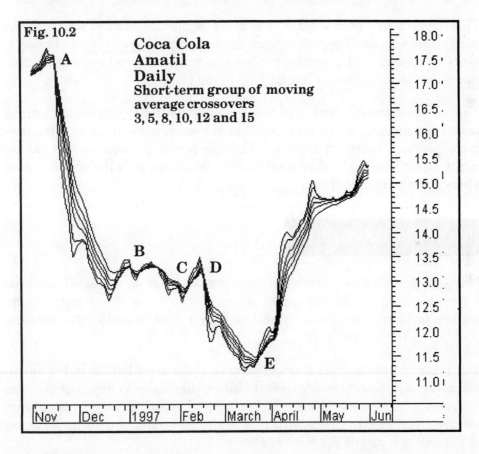

Fig. 10.2

Coca Cola Amatil Daily
Short-term group of moving average crossovers 3, 5, 8, 10, 12 and 15

As expected, each of these different time frames, or moving averages, give us additional useful information about the nature of the price activity. We might expect the crossover points to lean to the right as each point develops a little later, depending on the length of the average used. Instead the crossovers are almost simultaneous, such as points A, D and E. The crossover signals generated by each are roughly in the same place no matter which time scale — 3, 5, 8 etc. — is used. The entire collection of short-term averages all converge and cross within very short time spans at points A, B, C, D and E which are placed in the same locations as the first figure, 10.1.

The moment of price stability captured by two moving averages is confirmed by every other short-term average, at about the same time. The action of the group of moving averages tells us something that the individual averages cannot. This convergence of average calculation across multiple time frames pinpoints important market turning points.

This happens in a time window that is not significantly out of step with the current price action. The convergence does not signal the direction of price. It alerts us to increased potential for price movements because we know that agreement on value cannot last for long in the market.

This combination of short-term averages suggests that at significant turning points the strength of the revaluation of the stock is so strong that it draws every previous valuation together. The short-term averages do not, as we might expect, streak ahead because they are measuring only the revaluation in a very short-term time span.

The Boot on the Other Foot

Using a group of short-term averages, the trader sees an increased potential for price action as the temporary agreement on value disintegrates under market pressure. The investor, with a longer time horizon, also sees the possibilities in this approach.

The investor usually takes a longer view of the market but he still wants to select the significant turning points. Identifying these points, but not the direction of the turn, is assisted by using a group of long-term moving averages. The logic of the construction of the averages and the interpretation of the results is exactly the same as above.

When plotting the averages from an investment perspective we have two choices. The first is to shift to a weekly display, using 10 as the time value. This is automatically read as 10 weeks because we are using a weekly display.

The second choice is to use the daily display. When we do this we must change the weekly time periods into the daily equivalents. So 10 weeks becomes 50 days.

Why 50 days? 10 weeks on a weekly chart means 10 trading weeks of five days each. The daily equivalent is 50 days, not 70 days.

In selecting short-term averages we used a mid-week starting point and then shifted to a full week. In selecting a long-term group we double the last of the short-term group and start with 30 days. Moving one week at a time, we add 35, 40, 45 and 50-day moving averages. I choose to end with a 60-day moving average which I use as a last resort confirmation line.

Traditional market theory lists late entry and exit signals as a penalty attached to long-term averages. They are late because the time scale is too long. We expect any convergence, or coming together, of this average group will be spread over days and weeks.

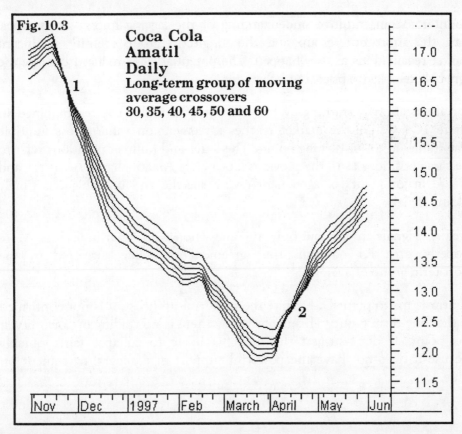

Fig. 10.3

**Coca Cola
Amatil
Daily**
**Long-term group of moving
average crossovers
30, 35, 40, 45, 50 and 60**

Instead there are sudden and decisive shifts in the relationships, mirroring the activity of the short-term group. Staying with Coca Cola Amatil, Figure 10.3 paints the picture clearly. The crossover points are just as dramatic as with Figure 10.2, but now there are only two — points 1 and 2.

This chart message tells us when the market reaches long-term agreement on valuation the long-term averages converge. At this moment of convergence, when the lines crossover, the market undergoes a significant revaluation of the stock leading to a major price change. The investor can use this type of information for investing in the same way as the trader uses the short-term information for trading.

But, surprisingly both charts have an unexpected application for the trader.

Boots and All For the Trader

Counter to our intuitive understanding of the lagging impact of averages, both the short-term group and the long-term group identify significant market revaluations as they happen. The potential lag is reduced because the signal we read is not price, but behaviour.

The signal we read is behaviour not price

The implication is startling. When Figures 10.2 and 10.3 are combined in Figure 10.4 we see the market reaches agreement on value across multiple time frames at major turning points. The letter and number notations refer to the same positions as in the previous Coca Cola Amatil charts. Areas A1 and E2 are major points of agreement giving specific and unambiguous timely trading signals.

Area A1 signals an exit, but only in conjunction with other indicators. More properly, area A1 confirms the agreement on value suggested by the short-term group of averages.

Contrast this to point D. Despite the powerful upthrust, it is not confirmed by the long-term group. This is not to say there is no trading opportunity at this point. It does suggest the move is likely to collapse fairly quickly because it does not have the powerful support of a general agreement on value.

Area E2 signals an entry, but only when the direction of the price move is confirmed by other indicators. Again, more properly, this area shows a high level of agreement on valuation, and therefore an increased probability of violent disagreement. This was suggested a few days earlier as the short-term group of averages combined and drew the long-term group with them. Later we look at rules to turn these areas into more precise signals.

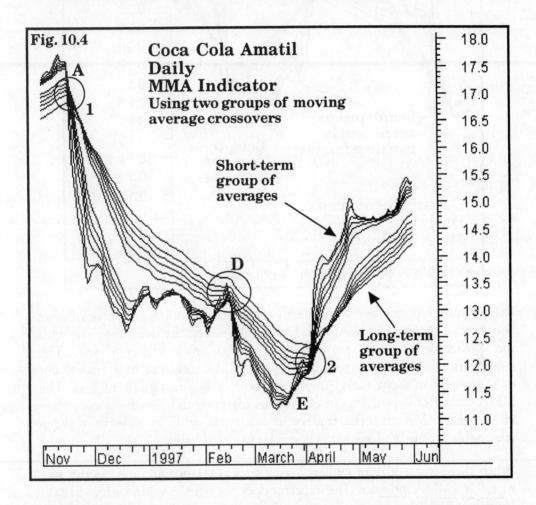

Fig. 10.4

Coca Cola Amatil
Daily
MMA Indicator
Using two groups of moving
average crossovers

Short-term
group of
averages

Long-term
group of
averages

Lasseter had his samples, and we have perfect examples. By comparing a scrappy everyday chart with perfection we improve our use of trading tools. This combination takes place simultaneously in both time frames in Figure 10.5. Here the major signals at points A and B were given in time for traders to jump onto the major price moves.

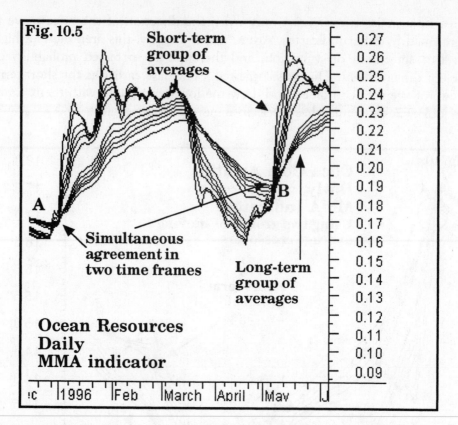

Fig. 10.5

Short-term group of averages

Long-term group of averages

Simultaneous agreement in two time frames

Ocean Resources
Daily
MMA indicator

A   B

0.27
0.26
0.25
0.24
0.23
0.22
0.21
0.20
0.19
0.18
0.17
0.16
0.15
0.14
0.13
0.12
0.11
0.10
0.09

ɛc | 1996 | Feb | March | April | May | J

Real trading has to work with less than perfect examples, which is why we concentrate on Coca Cola Amatil. Figure 10.6 shows the daily bar chart with the MMA letters and numerals transferred from earlier charts. The confirming trading signals generated by the MMA indicator took traders out of a position in Coca Cola Amatil at point A before significant loss. The MMA assay test kept them out of the enticing potential, but disastrous, trade at D. The MMA test put traders into a trade at E in time to make a reasonable profit. We look at trading rules in detail below.

When these two groups of moving averages are combined and used in this way we call it a MMA indicator. The indicator does not signal a value, such as $12.00. Visually it highlights an agreement in valuation across multiple time frames. It is the agreement between both long-term and short-term stockholders and signals a greater than normal probability that the price action will be substantial.

When the market reaches agreement on the value of a security in both time frames then explosive action often follows. Contrary to our intuitive

MMA INDICATOR- Highlights AN Agreement in VALUATION ACToss Multiple TIme FRAmes

understanding, the long-term averages do not lag so far behind the short-term averages that they provide no trading signal. At explosive market points the revaluation of stock, as reflected by price, is so fundamental that every calculation is affected. When each group comes into agreement and when both groups simultaneously cross within a single narrow window of time, then we can be confident the balance of probability is very much on our side in this trade. This trade is going to move, and move soon.

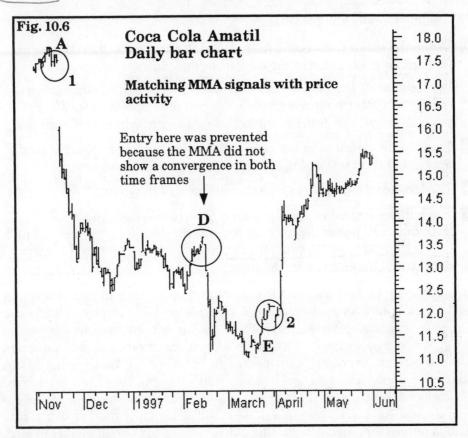

Fig. 10.6

Coca Cola Amatil
Daily bar chart

Matching MMA signals with price activity

Entry here was prevented because the MMA did not show a convergence in both time frames

We have searched our database with other indicators and they have already suggested the direction of the price move. The MMA indicator allows us to put this in a time frame narrowed by the balance of probability.

When we start to look more closely at our small list of trading opportunities this helps select those where action is imminent. The MMA gives a better understanding of how the market is viewing the value of the security. When agreement is high, disagreement is inevitable and we want to be in the market when it moves.

MMA Trading Rules

The MMA indicator develops four main trading rules, but remember it is not a stand-alone indicator. It is most useful as a confirming entry signal, although it can assist with timing exits. The signals should be confirmed with the results of other indicators and price plots.

The trading rules for the MMA are:

1 When the bands from both groups begin to narrow down and converge prepare for price action as the agreement on valuation collapses.

For those using the MMA in a swing trading approach, a combination of long and short positions straddle the potential price action. When prices do surge, the losing position is closed and traders ride the winner.

2 Trade in the direction of the crossover. Go long if the crossover is on the upside. Go short or exit long positions with downside crossovers.

3 The long-term averages confirm the direction of the trend.

4 The bubbles created by the short-term group of averages show the favourable exit points. Judging the top is difficult so look for the leading two or three averages to converge or come together. Confirm this early signal with other indicator readings.

Each of these rules is applied to the exciting run-up in the gold price tracked by the Comex continuous contract for Gold, Figure 10.7. Implementing these rules gives us a way to assay the quality of trading opportunities in this market sector. While others were busy buying gold, gold producers and gold explorers, as the short-term averages group peaked in February the trader using MMA indicator information sold gold stocks into the bubble. Even a delayed application of Rule 2 — go short or exit — to the exit signals took the trader out around the $400 level while others were still debating if the fall was a new trend, a retracement, or the beginning of the next leg of the bull market in gold.

Assay Results

The MMA is only used to fine-tune trading opportunities already selected by other processes. Like the merchant biting every proffered gold coin, we use the MMA to assay the candidates thrown up in early searches. The MMA is not easily defined as a search criteria because the mere crossover of one or two averages does not reveal the synergy displayed on the chart.

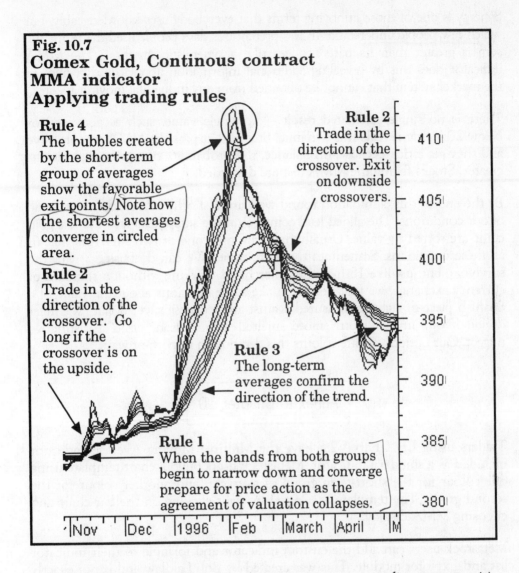

Fig. 10.7
Comex Gold, Continous contract
MMA indicator
Applying trading rules

Rule 4
The bubbles created by the short-term group of averages show the favorable exit points. Note how the shortest averages converge in circled area.

Rule 2
Trade in the direction of the crossover. Go long if the crossover is on the upside.

Rule 2
Trade in the direction of the crossover. Exit on downside crossovers.

Rule 3
The long-term averages confirm the direction of the trend.

Rule 1
When the bands from both groups begin to narrow down and converge prepare for price action as the agreement of valuation collapses.

I use the MMA as one of the final steps in assessing trading opportunities identified as the result of other search methods. You may wish to use it as a prospecting tool applied to your entire database. A series of closely-related custom formulas and subsequent Metastock Explorer search criteria for the MMA are shown in the annex to this chapter. This speeds up the database search by returning a 'yes' — 1 — response for securities. Charts from this list are inspected visually for the synergistic relationship. The significance and degree of the MMA constriction is a judgement call you make as a trader because no formula construction gives a definitive answer.

Synergy is one of those annoying terms that everybody uses knowledgeably, but which few people understand. In less-pretentious days people used the term "the sum is greater than its parts" to describe a synergistic situation. The MMA indicator does this by revealing additional information about the dynamics of the market system that cannot be obtained from any individual moving average.

There is no single calculated result — no single value, such as above 80 or below 20 — that reveals this dynamic. Stocks that pass the MMA test are alive and they get a tick because, on balance, the probability of a price explosion is greater. Stocks failing the MMA test are discarded.

By the end of this elimination round we want a short list of stocks meeting all of our conditions. The gilded lead coins go on the scrap heap and the real gold coins are sorted by value. Usually there are only one or two survivors that fit all these conditions. Sometimes there are none. We can do business with the survivors, but just like 18th-century merchants working without a standard of currency exchange, we first need to make some decisions about the value of a Spanish piece-of-eight as measured against a Portuguese silver dollar. We must decide if our find is worth more smelted into bullion, or as a distinctive nugget. Our outlook on life colours this decision in important ways.

Annex to Chapter 10

Traders using Ezy Chart V2.5 have the Multiple Moving Average Indicator included as a standard indicator. Metastock users build a chart template using one colour for the short-term group of averages, and another colour for the second group. The template is selected by right-clicking on the bar chart and choosing MMA display.

Metastock users can add the custom indicator and formula to their indicator list and Explorer module. This was created by Bob Laidlaw and is not exactly the same as the MMA indicator. He has added a layer of complexity to the MMA, but this is consistent with developing complex and subtle indicators based on simple concepts as discussed in previous chapters.

The seven custom indicators are:

```
MMA 10/45
If(OscP(10,45,E,%)>0,+1,-1)
```

MMA 12/50
If(OscP(12,50,E,%)>0,+1,-1)

MMA 15/60
If(OscP(15,60,E,%)>0,+1,-1)

MMA 3/30
If(OscP(3,30,E,%)>0,+1,-1)

MMA 5/35
If(OscP(5,35,E,%)>0,+1,-1)

MMA 8/40
If(OscP(8,40,E,%)>0,+1,-1)

MMA TOTAL (Note space between MMA 3/30 must be retained)
Fml("MMA 3/30")+Fml("MMA 5/35")+Fml("MMA 8/40")
+Fml("MMA 10/45") +Fml("MMA 12/50")+Fml("MMA 15/60")

The Exploration formula is:

Column A
Close
Column B
Ref(C,-1)
Column C
Ref(C,-2)
Column D
Fml("MMA 3/30")+Fml("MMA 5/35")+Fml("MMA 8/40")
+Fml("MMA 10/45") +Fml("MMA 12/50")+Fml("MMA 15/60")
Column E
Ref(Fml("MMA 3/30")+Fml("MMA 5/35")+Fml("MMA 8/40")
+Fml("MMA 10/45") +Fml("MMA 12/50")+Fml("MMA 15/60"),-1)

Filter source
Formula
When (colD,>,0) AND When (colE,<=,0)

11

TWO SIDES OF
THE SAME COIN

"Know your enemy" is the tactician's adage. Many traders believe the enemy is the person on the other side of the trade. Instead they need only to look in the mirror, not the computer screen, for the answer. The trader is often his own worst enemy, defeating himself before the trading battle starts.

The simple question: *Are you a bull or a bear?* tells us how this happens. With nuggets in hand we must answer this question every day: *Do we buy or sell?*

Intuitively we make a decision and intuitively bring our bias into action. Oblivious to this intuitive bias, we marshall a battery of indicators to support a decision already made subconsciously. It comes as no surprise that the initial good trading opportunities seem to get better — even when they start to go down.

In selecting the way we mine our database for trading opportunities, in choosing the types of indicators we use, in looking for particular types of chart patterns, we act on our bias before we even glance at the day's price data. When the nugget is unearthed we do not thoroughly test for fool's gold. We believe we are good prospectors and often this belief trades us into trouble.

We get into trouble by confusing objective results with subjective conclusions. Every indicator, a stochastic for example, consistently measures the same relationships in exactly the same way. The placement of the last data point is an objective, calculated decision made according to the construction rules. Mathematics alone positions the line. Indicator results are arrived at objectively and this is often claimed as a technical analysis strength.

No such logic restrains the trader so we subjectively interpret the results. If the stochastic falls below the 20% line we believe the security is oversold. Above the 80% we understand the market is overbought. The conclusions are valid because they concur with past behaviour, but our interpretation of the potential for future price action is very subjective. We trade our interpretation so it doesn't pay to be blind to our bias and the ways it appears to shift the balance of probability.

If we do not recognise our bias then as trades fail it is easy to blame our indicators, or our technique. Instead of dealing with the real issue we chase after irrelevant solutions — buying more expensive software or trying different trading techniques. And the real problem remains unsolved.

The solution is in understanding our bias and using it to our advantage. For those with a bearish disposition, the process described below helps with the entry into long positions. For bulls it is particularly important in deciding exits, although it helps in assessing entries as well. This step fits into your personal trading process at the point you identify as your weakest. We have included it here because it plays a part in the entry decision for both bulls and bears.

There's a Bear in There

Many traders believe it is sufficient just to acknowledge one's bullishness or bearishness about the current market in general or market segment in particular. This orientation does help to identify the better opportunities for trading with or against market feeling, and ways to use these market clues are discussed in the following chapter. This is a last process in a trading decision, all too often reached by taking a shortcut around our bias.

Understanding and using our bias involves two steps and determines, *a priori* – before the fact – how we look at a chart. In the first step we learn to recognise our bias. In the second we consistently take it into account when charts are being analysed before a trade so that it does not unfavourably distort the entry or the exit decision.

The exit is no problem when we meet profit objectives. The exit becomes a problem when we think the price will continue to rise. We succumb to temptation and stay with the trade beyond our initial profit objectives. Or when prices falter before our objective is reached. Now we hang on, ignoring the reversal signals and eventually riding with the trade into a loss.

In the best of all possible worlds these situations never arise. In the reality of the market they happen with alarming frequency and we cannot ignore them. We need to develop strategies and tactics to cope with these situations and retain profits. A trade that initially shows a profit but is later abandoned at a loss because you held on hoping it would return to old profit levels is a poor trade – even if the eventual loss is less than 2% of trading equity.

Step 1 – Getting an I.D. on Bias

How do you decide if your bias lies with the bulls or the bears? The two charts below give a simple test and show the impact of a bullish bias on trading analysis built around simple trendlines. In both cases we look for the best entry. In Figure 11.1 we want to continue a profitable trading band strategy. In Figure 11.2 we want the best possible entry for a long position, buying in anticipation of a price rise. These are two sides of the same coin so we see how a bullish bias gets us into trades early and out of them too late.

The security UKN in Figure 11.1 offers an entry opportunity in a rising trend as part of a long-term strategy based on trading bands. Let's explore the reasoning that encourages us to enter at point A and stay in the trade at point B.

1. An established trendline is in place, line F, and the pullback at A is consistent with the price activity in December.

2. A logical stop-loss is around the support/resistance level shown at C. If the entry at A turns out to be incorrect then recent price action sets level C as a confirmation of the error and a good exit point.

3 Pullbacks to the trendline, such as point B, provide additional buying opportunities. This trend is so well established that we can be fairly confident any spikes below it are very temporary.

4 We set conservative profit targets on the upper edge of the parallel trading channel passing through the bulk of trading activity over the past nine months. This is shown in bold. Upper targets are set with reference to the outer trend line although this defined the limits only in the early part of this prolonged uptrend.

Trading summary

An entry at point A or B is consistent with a bullish trading strategy based on trading bands. An exit is not signalled at B. Good stop-loss is provided by the trendline and nearby support levels.

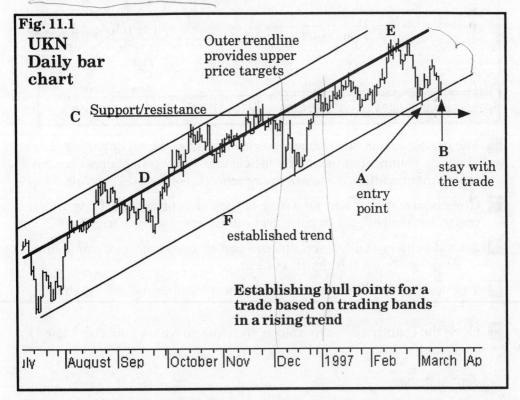

Fig. 11.1
UKN Daily bar chart

Outer trendline provides upper price targets

C Support/resistance

E

A entry point

B stay with the trade

D

F established trend

Establishing bull points for a trade based on trading bands in a rising trend

July | August | Sep | October | Nov | Dec | 1997 | Feb | March | Ap

In the second chart, ILM, Figure 11.2, we look for a bullish breakout to decide if taking a position at point A is worthwhile. Below we assemble all the points in favour of buying this breakout.

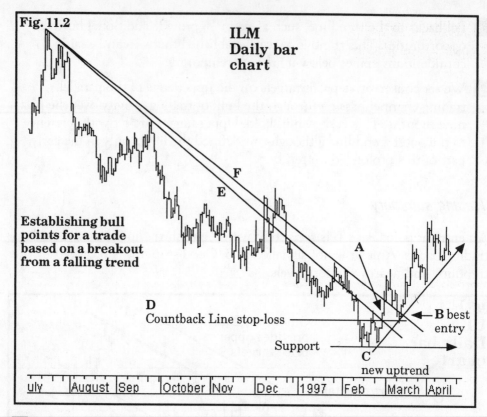

Fig. 11.2

ILM Daily bar chart

Establishing bull points for a trade based on a breakout from a falling trend

F

E

A

D
Countback Line stop-loss ——————

B best entry

Support ——————

C

new uptrend

uly | August | Sep | October | Nov | Dec | 1997 | Feb | March | April

1 The trendline, E, is validly drawn because it touches the maximum number of points. Shifting it further to the right ignores the September peak entirely. In its current position the January price action uses it as a support line.

2 Conservative traders wait for a close to the right of trendline, F. Aggressive traders use the pullback to point B as confirmation of the uptrend.

3 Point B helps establish a new uptrend and we tentatively plot this as line C. Any close below this signals our exit.

4 The stop-loss conditions are set by the short-term resistance level shown as line D.

5 Using the countback line technique, the close above the countback line D confirms the entry.

Trading summary

This is a bullish entry offering, as it turns out, a six-week trade. The entry is confirmed by the countback line and the stop loss is clearly set on old support levels just below our entry point.

Bully for the Bears

In both cases we use a bullish bias to confirm the validity of the trend, to develop our trading tactics and to support our decision to take an early entry, or to stay with the position despite a temporary pullback. The analysis of these charts appears straightforward and is typical of the way we approach chart analysis with our eyes closed.

But there is one major problem.

Both charts are of the ASX All Ordinaries, but Figure 11.2 has been turned upside down using the Metastock Invert Scale function in the Y-Axis Properties menu.

Use stock charts to do this

Bullish bias made us in identify the best possible entry point, A or B, on the inverted chart in Figure 11.2 because we were psychologically prepared to act on the bullish breakout signal.

When the chart is shown the correct way up, this bullish bias becomes a significant disadvantage because it gets us into, and keeps us in, a losing trade, particularly the one shown at point B in Figure 11.1. We suggested this pullback was an entry signal into the old trend, but when the chart is inverted, we suggested it was confirmation of a new trend. We can only have it both ways when we understand the role our bias plays in the way we see a chart.

In Figure 11.1 our bullish bias makes us reluctant to take the objective exit readings from our indicators. We don't draw a downtrend line from the high at E because it doesn't seem consistent with our overall bullish understanding of the previous long-term trend. Yet we draw this in Figure 11.2 as a new upsloping trendline and use it to justify and confirm our entry.

Why the difference? In both cases we are look for evidence to support our bullish and biased belief in rising prices. We add a silver lining to every chart.

The result of our enthusiasm is often disastrous. We stay with established rising trends, delaying our exit and giving up a substantial part, sometimes all, of the profit. Yet, the bull enters early on downtrend breakouts. This maximises the potential of the trade if only we were equipped to take advantage of it. We need to turn our strength into an advantage on both ends of the trade.

We cannot eliminate this bias. The glass tends to be consistently half-full or half-empty. The bias usually helps on one end of the trade — the long side entry if we are bullish, or the short side entry if we are bearish. Modern software gives us the means to turn the tables. This time, with our eyes open, we take the second step with a test for bias.

Step 2 – The Bull and Bear Test

Consider the typical giveaway signs of bullish behaviour and look for a match with yourself. Bulls are surrounded by half-full coffee mugs. They know they are good at picking a breakout from a downtrend, or a price surge from resistance levels, or retracements. As a rule their entries are very good, made near the bottom, exactly on support, or just after the breakout has started. Most of their trades start out as winners. They like to think their judgement is superior, but hard reality would suggest it is their bias that puts a rosy glow on otherwise objective indicator results. This is their strength and they want to build on it.

Visit the bears for a moment. Of course the opposite applies to the group huddled around half-empty coffee mugs. Their entry on the long side tends to be their weak point because they are fearful the downtrend will continue proving the breakout is false, so they enter late.

Bulls are the last to leave the party. Their weakness is the exit. They wait too long, requiring too much confirmation that the trend has changed before selling. They give indicators every benefit of the doubt – on the upside. When the stochastic enters 80% every twitch down is ignored in favour of every twitch up. Their trades start with certainty and end with hope.

Bears, with their half-empty coffee mugs, have no such problems. Terrified of any bad news, they chop the trade immediately and protect profits.

Which are your giveaway signs? It is hard to read them close up, so ask a friend to read them for you. You will never look at a half-cup of coffee, or a chart, in quite the same way again.

The test answers are shown in Figure 11.3. The answers are read from the first column, using a standard chart, or from the second column if we start with an inverted chart. These answers use our bias in the most effective way at both ends of the trade.

We want to use our bullish strength in entries to overcome our weakness in exits. We make a better exit by treating the exit as an entry. The mental gymnastics calls for a sleight of hand and this is assisted by a sleight of chart. The daily bar chart of Roebuck Resources, Figure 11.4, has been inverted. We have one test question about this inverted chart: Is this a long-side entry at point A?

Fig. 11.3

READING INVERTED CHART
TEST RESULTS

TRADING SIGNALS **LONG** SIDE

looking to →	**ENTER LONG**	confirmed by →	**EXIT LONG**	then →	**ENTER LONG**
looking to →	**EXIT LONG**	confirmed by →	**ENTER LONG**	then →	**EXIT LONG**

Normal chart　**Inverted chart**　**Normal chart**

TRADING SIGNALS **SHORT** SIDE

looking to →	**ENTER SHORT**	confirmed by →	**EXIT SHORT**	then →	**ENTER SHORT**
looking to →	**EXIT SHORT**	confirmed by →	**ENTER SHORT**	then →	**EXIT SHORT**

Inverted chart
Normal chart　**Normal chart**

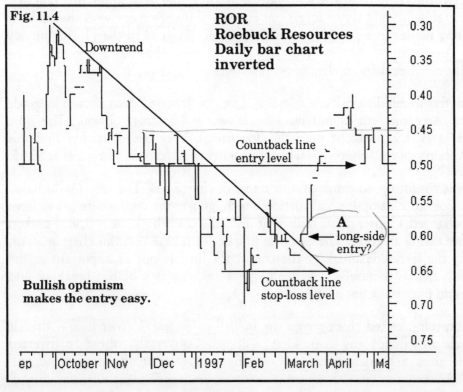

Fig. 11.4

Downtrend

ROR
Roebuck Resources
Daily bar chart
inverted

Countback line
entry level

A
← long-side
entry?

Countback line
stop-loss level

**Bullish optimism
makes the entry easy.**

0.30
0.35
0.40
0.45
0.50
0.55
0.60
0.65
0.70
0.75

ep | October | Nov | Dec | 1997 | Feb | March | April | Ma

INVERTED

If the answer is 'yes' when the chart is shown inverted, then it signals a long side exit from any established open positions. Starting in the middle column, inverted chart, this is consistent with the second rule in the test answer matrix, Figure 11.3. This seems illogical, but closer inspection shows how it helps overcome our bullish bias.

Applying the Test

Inverted charts are difficult to work with at first so change the colour of the bars, using red for down and blue for up. Metastock users can save a template screen of the inverted display, making it easy to flip between the standard and inverted chart displays. Ignore the inverted scale and concentrate on the message delivered by the price bars and trendlines. If your charting software does not offer this facility then download the shareware program Invert.exe from the link on www.guppytraders.com. This temporarily inverts your screen display.

Our assumption in this Roebuck Resources test example is that we have entered the trade from the long side at around $0.45. To apply this bull and bear test we should try to forget our emotional involvement with the trade. If making money in a profitable trade clouds our judgement then losing money is a severe thunderstorm. We treat the inverted chart as a potential long position rather than an already open position.

With this in mind we ask one question: Does the inverted chart show a long-side entry? Accepting our bullish bias, the answer is blindingly obvious. The price close at A is a breakout from the downtrend. Very bullish traders find this indication powerful enough to warrant an entry at $0.55 with a stop loss at $0.65.

This is confusing, so think of it in terms of chart lines. The stop-loss is based on a countback stop-loss calculation which ignores the days where prices have not changed. Conservative bulls wait until the countback entry line is broken before taking an entry. The exact trading decision based on this chart analysis, using the trendline break or the countback line, is not as important as the bullish signals themselves. By many measures, this is a bullish breakout and gives an important test answer.

When the inverted chart passes the bullish entry test – enter long – then it signals an exit for any open long positions. Conversely, where an inverted chart gives a bearish signal – exit long – suggesting the downtrend will continue, then any open long positions should remain open. This simple test keeps bullish traders out of trouble by using the bias behind our interpretation of otherwise objective indicators.

The bull has problems believing in bears. When the bull looks at the Roebuck Resources chart with the scale placed correctly, Figure 11.5, the exit decision required at point A is more difficult to accept.

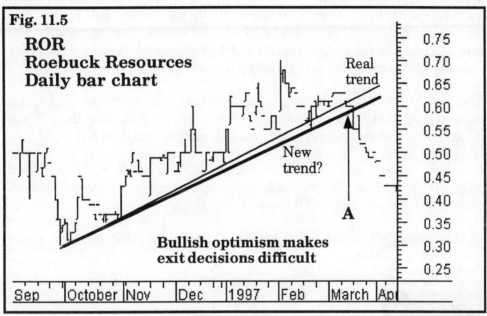

Fig. 11.5

ROR
Roebuck Resources
Daily bar chart

Real trend

New trend?

A

Bullish optimism makes exit decisions difficult

0.75 0.70 0.65 0.60 0.55 0.50 0.45 0.40 0.35 0.30 0.25

Sep | October | Nov | Dec | 1997 | Feb | March | Apl

Correct

The bull too easily convinces himself the close at point A is an aberration, or even more excitingly, a fifth point defining the new trend line shown by the thicker line on the chart. He clicks through mental snapshots of other charts where trends developed in a series of fan lines and gave excellent long-term returns. He should not do this, but his bullish bias does it automatically for him, searching his memory for the most favourable gloss on a deteriorating situation.

Then he turns to the indicators, looking to support the decision he wants so desperately to make. When he made the original entry decision he recognised the time lag inherent in most indicators and he extrapolated their development in a favourable bullish direction. The MACD wasn't really turning up, but it looked like it was about to, so he read this as a positive sign and put a tick against it on his checklist.

Unfortunately, he repeats this using the same indicators to manage the exit. Now the lag extends — it isn't really turning down — and he waits too long for confirmation of the bearish evidence. He becomes an expert in managing losses rather than a profits.

Can we do this with Roebuck Resources? The bull has no difficulty in finding the silver lining. Although not shown here, the stochastic fast line crosses below 80% on March 12, the exact day shown as point A in Figure 11.5. It also did this in late January, but it was a false signal. The bull reasons this most recent crossover might also be false, so he gives it room to breathe. The slow stochastic turns and crosses the fast line three days later by which time the only exit possible is at $0.55, costing the bull money.

The RSI turns sharply through the mid-range 50 level on March 12, accurately signalling the trendbreak. The bull ignores it because the RSI has done this once every six weeks over previous months and then recovered.

In making a decision not to close the trade at point A he carefully and diligently lines up his favourite indicators, takes objective readings, and skews them towards his bullish bias. Do you do the same?

In this sample trade the bull's optimism defeats him, locking him into a deteriorating position.

Profit or Loss

By the time the exit signal is undeniably clear, even to the most convinced bull, the profit has often shrunk to a loss. Then the exit decision is grossly distorted by emotional quibbling where we convince ourselves that a loss at today's prices can be reduced if prices move up to yesterday's close. The lure of saving a few dollars is powerful and it paralyses decision-making. In Chapter 18 we look at ways to minimise this emotional impact.

As soon as the answer to the exit question produces a loss our emotional reactions become much more severe. The loss may mean taking a lesser profit, or even a real loss on the trade. If fear of loss makes it difficult to decide what an indicator really signals, then exercising the discipline necessary to take a loss is even more difficult. The sooner we act, the smaller the loss and the better the chances of action being implemented.

Inverting the chart is only part of the solution in overcoming this reluctance to act. By taking positive action we make our bias work for us in all aspects of our trade management.

This is not just a problem for novice traders. Trading success does not eliminate it. Just ask Jim Paul, author of *What I Learned Losing a Million Dollars* or Nick Leeson, author of *Rogue Trader*. All traders are affected by their bias to a greater or lesser extent. It is very difficult to trade mechanically. There is no absolute solution so we make do with solutions that make us more aware of our trading strengths and weaknesses.

I have spent a lifetime developing my biases. I cannot reasonably expect to overturn them to accommodate just one aspect of my trading decisions — no matter how important. I must learn to live with them and turn them to my advantage. If something as simple as inverting a chart neutralises my bias and makes it work in my favour on both sides of the trade, then I will use it. If you use a consistent method to identify and discount your biases when they adversely effect your ability to enter, or exit a trade, then you will trade better.

We have applied this assay test early in the trading decision. You might find it more appropriately applied to the exit decision, but it is also a useful confirmation of every entry. The nuggets in our final list have been rigorously assayed, passing the inverted test, but before we trade, we look for the pulse of the market to make sure we are trading in the same direction. Although there are good trades available for cool heads in collapsing markets there is a difference between skilled traders and those who are oblivious to the collapse around them.

CHART INVERSION IS BUT ONE
PART of the SOLUTION TO
SAVE A PROFIT

12

INDEX HUNTING

If you remain calm while those around you are losing their heads it may be that you haven't heard the news. In a falling market even the strongest stocks get battered, and rising stars, pulled back with the rest of the market, fail to rise as far or as fast. The nuggets we assayed so carefully may not suit the fashion of the market.

In a rising market, most stocks, even the weak and mediocre, rise in sympathy, so we profitably trade smaller nuggets in addition to the best of our finds. The general market Index, or the Sector Index, tracks market activity in the same way a weather forecast tracks the weather.

Like a weather forecast, the index sets the trading scene for the day, or for a period. Unless we are trading the Share Price Index (SPI) on the Sydney Futures Exchange (SFE), the index acts as a bell-wether for general market behaviour. In *Share Trading* we suggested that a private index is particularly useful in establishing trading conditions for the specific basket of stocks you follow. We also looked at strategies to identify where the smart money is positioned.

This chapter looks at some other ways to use information given by the general market or sector index to decide if our potential trade is consistent with market sentiment, and more importantly, if the trade stands a better probability of success. This assessment uses three steps.

1 Understanding the index message.

2 Trading with index backing.

3 Assessing a security against the index.

Get Me An Index

What language does the index speak? The usefulness of an index is limited by the number of securities included. A broad index like the All Ordinaries, which is taken as a proxy for the entire market, may at times be less representative than a sector index. The performance of a single stock, such as a bank, or BHP, may cause a significant movement in the index. Some so-called broad indexes are composed of just a handful of stocks so the distorting effect is more dramatic.

The All Ords is drawn from a bag of around 328 stocks from 1,193 listed companies. Membership of this index is determined by capitalisation. A company must have capitalisation of 0.02% of the total market's total capitalisation before it is eligible for inclusion in the index. Eligibility rules also include several liquidity criteria.

In contrast, the Dow Jones Industrial Average is the average of 30 stocks, weighted for splits, trading on the NYSE exchange. The S&P 500, not widely quoted in Australia as a measure of US financial markets, is much broader, including 500 stocks weighted by capitalisation. The composition of the S&P 500 Index changes intermittently to reflect market changes. The NASDAQ Composite Index is the most broadly-based US index measuring the performance of 4,985 listed NASDAQ stocks.

In contrast, a sector index such as the ASX Banking Index includes all banking stocks listed on the ASX. Obviously the information drawn from this index is of a more precise nature than the broader indications given by the All Ords or the Dow.

With these caveats in mind, we look more closely at the role indexes play in market decisions in the broader equity market. These conclusions are not relevant for those who trade the indexes directly on various futures exchanges. There, derivative products including the SPI are traded like any other security or futures contract. The conclusions reached by technical analysis apply equally to these derivatives as they do to any other individual security.

Bi-lingual Indexes

Indexes provide us with two approaches to understanding broad market behaviour. They use different language to describe the same processes. The type of index you select determines the way you read the messages. The two index types are:

1 *Representative approaches*

Here the index represents a broad selection of available stocks. This includes the All Ords, the DOW, S&P 500, etc.

2 *Absolute approaches*

The index includes all of the relevant stocks in a sector, or nearly all. These are becoming more specific and include Engineering, Small Ordinaries, All Resources, Infrastructure and Utilities, Midcap 50 and Media, among others.

Representative Approaches

These are the weather forecasts and this is the index message. The representative approach is a strange mixture of normal distribution theory and conservatism. The conservative aspect is present in the criteria for selection — for example, the National Australia Bank or BHP. These are the most active, the most prominent, and generally the better blue chips of the market. This elite selection is representative of the broader market — or so we are told.

It is claimed they are representative because their behaviour will be reflected in the behaviour of all other stocks and understanding how this is true, or false, helps us to make better use of index messages. This belief is drawn from the theory of normal distribution, often shown as a Gaussian or bell curve, which is more fully discussed in *Against the Gods* by Bernstein. Our interest is in how the representative nature of an index translates into trading signals.

In 1877 the mathematician Galton used a simple experiment to graphically demonstrate the operation of normal distribution and the physical construction of a bell curve. This experiment also hinted at another useful trading concept, standard deviation, so it is worth taking a moment to examine this branch of mathematics from a trading perspective.

For his demonstration, Galton filled an hourglass-style device with shotgun pellets and let the small round lead balls fall through a narrow funnel onto a plate below. Small pins were stuck in the neck of the hourglass so the balls were dispersed randomly. The plate was covered with a grid of compartments so as each ball hit the plate it remained in place. The falling balls consistently built a three-dimensional bell curve, higher in the middle and sloping down to each side. The idealised result is illustrated in Figure 12.1. We return to the trading information in this shape a little later.

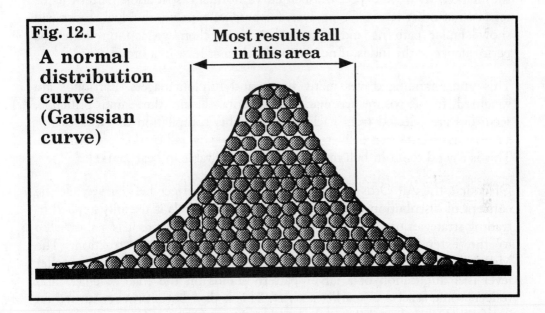

Fig. 12.1

A normal distribution curve (Gaussian curve)

Most results fall in this area

This bell curve shape suggests the normal distribution of, for instance, stocks, where they are sorted on the basis of performance. Most fall into the average category. How do we move from this to selecting a small sample as representative of a wider market?

Galton took another step which traders have been taking ever since. In his second demonstration, he drilled a hole in the bottom of each compartment on the first plate and placed another gridded and compartmentalised plate below it. Now the lead balls could cascade to another level. The extraordinary result was that each new and smaller pile of balls exactly duplicated the bell curve shape of the larger pile. Galton's theoretical objective was quite different from ours so we will leave him on the history shelves.

Traders, and exchanges, have been taking the next step ever since, using a small sample as representative of a wider market. We move from a single pile in the middle of the bottom plate — selected from the peak of the bell curve — and extrapolate the shape and distribution of the lead shot as it first hit the upper plate. We use a small sample to infer the shape and distribution of a larger sample.

If the All Ords Index shows a bell curve normal distribution, and if each stock in the All Ords 'represents' a basket of stocks from various sectors of the market, then we expect the bell curve normal distribution pattern to be repeated at other levels. Going even further, we expect individual stocks will show similar patterns and if we select those then we can duplicate the performance of the index, if not precisely, then at least in a broad sense.

This understanding drives many funds and fund managers. Portfolios are weighted for exposure to market segments. Using the same principle, securities are selected from each segment. This compilation of averages not surprisingly most often delivers returns matching overall market performance. This is a good result in bull markets, but less desirable in bear markets.

Of course the All Ords Index does not build a perfect bell curve, but the concept of distribution duplication at descending levels is usefully applied to trading strategies used by aggressive hedge funds. From here it is a short step to the extensive new trading road currently under construction. The Manderblot screen saver based on fractals where each successively smaller level is a duplication of a larger pattern stands on the edge of chaos and reflects some aspects of market activity. This is distribution theory turned on itself and Deboeck and Peters deal with aspects of this in *Trading on the Edge* and *Fractal Market Analysis*.

We are not taking that short step onto the new road. Instead we will work further with the idea that the index is representative of the broader market as a consequence of normal distribution theory. In trading terms this suggests we search for stocks moving in the same way as the representative index. Our final choices are checked for consistency with the index behaviour.

We have two important choices in considering how to use these broad indexes.

The first is to use the index as a guide to probable crowd and market reactions so we can trade with index backing.

The second is to use the index as a reference point for individual stocks placed on the left of the bell curve towards the incompetent end. This can be limited to securities that make up the index, or widened to include sector index groups or, more broadly still, individual stocks drawn from the entire market. All of these choices are similar in important ways and we discuss them as a group in the next section dealing with absolute approaches. Before doing this we look at how the index is commonly used to trade in the direction of the market trend.

Making Friends with Index Trends

The first choice is a traditional way to incorporate representative index results in specific trading strategies by using them as weather forecasts and treating them with about the same level of reliability. This combines the last two assessment steps — trading with index backing and assessing the security against the index. The All Ords is a broad indicator of past market directions and potential future directions.

In buoyant markets chart patterns and indicators which suggest upwards movements for individual securities are more likely to be accurate because they are consistent with the market. The family of triangles is a good example of this process. The combination of these rules are illustrated in Figure 7.8, Chapter 7.

We visited the triangle family in Chapter 7 so, briefly, an upsloping triangle is an indicator of rising prices. The horizontal upper line of the triangle is formed by a resistance level, as shown at A and B in Figure 12.2, Fosters Brewing weekly chart. (The one-third divisions are again marked '‡') Placing this line is clearer at B than at A. It is the interaction of the uptrend with a resistance level that is important, and markets do not always give perfect examples. The sloping uptrend line creates the triangle in both cases and take place in a generally rising, or bullish, trend. Prices pull back to these upsloping trend line levels after hitting resistance. Buyers are so confident the stock is going to increase in value they refuse to let prices fall to old lows. Afraid of missing out, they bid slightly higher to get ahead of their competition.

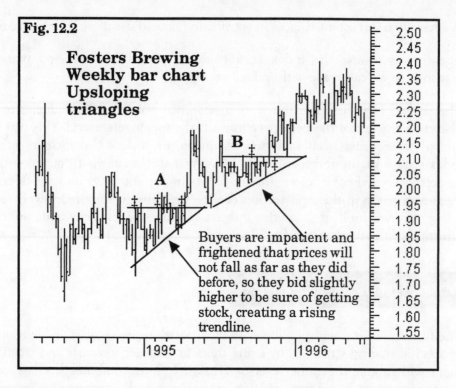

Fig. 12.2

**Fosters Brewing
Weekly bar chart
Upsloping
triangles**

A

B

Buyers are impatient and
frightened that prices will
not fall as far as they did
before, so they bid slightly
higher to be sure of getting
stock, creating a rising
trendline.

1995   1996

Sellers see this action, and hold out, waiting for higher prices before putting their stock on the market. The result is an upsloping trendline. As the tip of the triangle approaches many sellers realise they can get even better prices and the supply of stock dries up. Bidders have to bid higher than the old resistance level and prices typically break out decisively and dramatically rocketing upwards in their search for new levels of stability.

Such, briefly, is the theory and the standard explanation. But remember it comes with no guarantees. The development of an upsloping triangle strongly suggests further upwards price action. In reality the market shows some upsloping triangles that react differently with prices moving sideways, or falling back below the trend once the pattern is completed.

However, in a buoyant market, as indicated by the market or sector index, breakouts from upsloping triangles are more likely to be successful and sustained. Traders use this knowledge to trade in the direction of the market. When everybody is running for the elevator everything that looks like an elevator attracts a crowd.

In a bull market defined by a rising index even the most unlikely chart patterns look like elevators. As noted above, the equilateral triangle is a graphic representation of market indecision but a rising market or sector index casts it in a different light. The weekly chart of Faulding FH&Co in Figure 12.3 shows the way this indecision is bullied into a preferred direction by the market trend. This sinking ship rises briefly with the tide.

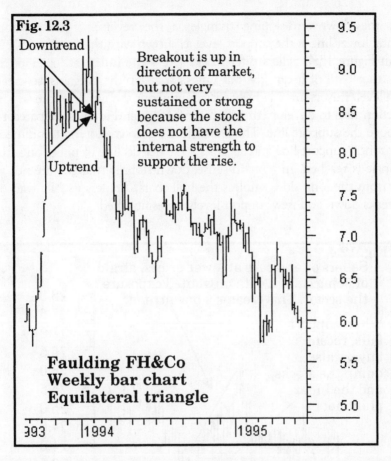

Fig. 12.3

Downtrend

Breakout is up in direction of market, but not very sustained or strong because the stock does not have the internal strength to support the rise.

Uptrend

**Faulding FH&Co
Weekly bar chart
Equilateral triangle**

9.5
9.0
8.5
8.0
7.5
7.0
6.5
6.0
5.5
5.0

1993   1994   1995

Nobody is fully convinced the security is undervalued, or overvalued. Some people think it is a bargain, and bid up to get the stock. Others think it is destined to fall, so they bail out at the best possible price taking a little less then yesterday's price because they are frightened the previous high will not be reached. The result is two sloping trendlines, one going up and one going down. They converge, building an equilateral triangle that once completed, is often followed by price action moving sideways for an extended period. In strong markets the breakout, as with Faulding FH&Co, is in the direction of the index. As a creature of the index, reversals can be sudden and sustained, as shown, because the stock has no internal trading strength as would have been indicated by a stronger chart pattern.

In a buoyant market, there is increased tendency for prices to break upwards. Using the index to identify the temporary, or sustained, direction of the market tells the trader if these weaker chart patterns have an increased probability of moving in a favourable direction.

Finally, the downward-sloping triangle is the reverse of the upslope. The horizontal lower line is the support level as shown with the weekly ASX Building Index in Figure 12.4. Sellers offer stock, across the index, at lower prices in an attempt to get rid of it quickly, but buyers snap up the bargains, so creating the support level. Buyers are relatively confident about the future of the sector, but as price action fails to develop, they lose confidence and are not prepared to bid as high above the support line. The chart shows a down-sloping trendline meeting the horizontal support line and suggests a further decline in prices once the tip of the triangle is reached. In a broad sense, down-sloping triangles are not good for trading from the long side – unless the bull roars. Traders usually wait until the price breaks down and new support levels are established.

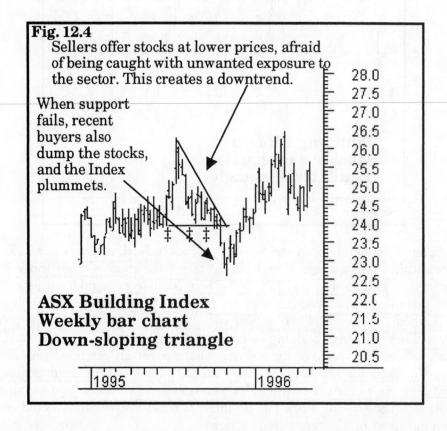

Fig. 12.4
Sellers offer stocks at lower prices, afraid of being caught with unwanted exposure to the sector. This creates a downtrend.

When support fails, recent buyers also dump the stocks, and the Index plummets.

ASX Building Index
Weekly bar chart
Down-sloping triangle

28.0
27.5
27.0
26.5
26.0
25.5
25.0
24.5
24.0
23.5
23.0
22.5
22.0
21.5
21.0
20.5

1995   1996

Using an index in the standard way suggests the stronger sector index trends are more likely to carry the downside triangle upwards. A range of different trading approaches become possible by matching the chart direction with the index direction, or by understanding how the index direction shifts the balance of probability towards a specific outcome.

When the final list of trading candidates is complete we select the best possible opportunities. Generally we will only want to add one or, perhaps, two new positions. Each trading opportunity is a valid one, but the probability of success is increased if the signals are consistent with the index weather forecast.

We used the group of triangles as an example, but the same applies to all chart patterns which are normally considered to be indicative of a bottom, or a top. Most of these reversal patterns are discussed in detail in Elder's *Trading for a Living*, or *Technical Analysis of Stock Trends* by Edwards and Magee. Books dealing with specialised charting methods, such as *Candlepower* by Greg Morris, *Point and Figure Charting* by Aby and *Martin Pring on Market Momentum* by Pring usually devote a section to reversal patterns. No matter which patterns you decide to use, the representative index both measures and helps to create or reinforce market sentiment and can increase the probability of the pattern completing in its usual manner.

The penultimate step prior to committing money to a trade is to verify that the chart pattern, the current orientation of the security, is consistent with the market direction. This is the basis of many trading approaches and is an extension of the old market saying "The trend (of the index) is your friend." But friends do not always point the way to better profits.

Absolutely Mean

We talked of two index types – representative and absolute – and the way these dictate different approaches. The second approach uses the index as a reference point for individual stocks placed on the left of the bell curve. This involves assessing our trading nuggets against the sector index. This enables alternative ways of understanding the index message, trading with index backing and assessing the security against the index.

The absolute index message is subtly different because instead of using a small sample to generalise about the market, such indexes use a small market segment to deliver messages about placement.

Absolute indexes include all stocks and are most commonly sector indexes. The ASX Asia Index and Banking Sector Index include all the banks, and all Asian listed stocks. These are similar to the second plate Galton placed under his hourglass and we expect to see a bell curve of performance in each sector. We briefly return to the problem of normal distribution because it provides the core of a trading strategy for absolute indexes, and also a second way of using representative market index information.

A normal distribution curve, or bell curve, puts most result values in the middle, with fewer results at the extremes of excellence and incompetence. An absolute sector index most often shows this distribution — a few leaders, and few laggards, and a substantial number of also-rans.

This distribution can be based on many criteria, from rate of increase in security price, or capitalisation, to Earnings Per Share or Net Tangible Assets. No matter which criteria are used, the distribution pattern tends to form a bell curve. But this is not a fixed constellation. It is a snapshot of a dynamic system. While the curve remains much the same shape, the relative position of each security changes over time. The leaders become laggards. This is how we understand this index message and the bell curve determines the signals we accept and reject.

Most traders are looking for superior performance and intuitively turn their attention to the securities on the right hand side of the bell curve towards the end defined by excellence. This intuitive reaction is unthinking, and like many unthinking reactions in the market, not particularly profitable. We reason that what is good now will only get better — forever more.

This does not seem such a sound idea when stated baldly, but it forms the basis of thousands of investment decisions. The advice to buy strongly-performing securities has a comfortable ring to it, but this bell curve has a crack called regression to the mean.

Once again we will sidestep the mathematics developed by Galton, Gauss and others and explained more fully in *Against the Gods*, and opt for a trader's application of the concept. It is illustrated by Figure 12.5 which shows the normal distribution bell curve. We have inverted the traditional display, with excellence on the right hand side. From either extremity, incompetence or excellence, the tendency is to slide, or regress, towards the bottom of the curve, the mid-point or the mean.

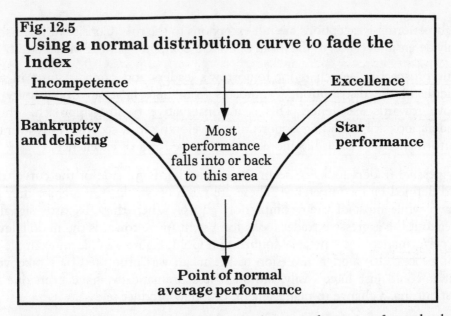

Fig. 12.5
Using a normal distribution curve to fade the Index

Incompetence   Excellence

Bankruptcy and delisting   Most performance falls into or back to this area   **Star performance**

Point of normal average performance

This regression to the mean gives us a way of using information from absolute and also representative indexes, to confirm trading opportunities and know which nugget is best in current circumstances. It builds on the trading concept we used in Chapter 9 for a range of other indicator displays such as Stochastics, and Relative Strength Indicators.

Fading the Index

Where do trading opportunities exist in a bell curve distribution under regression to the mean? In the assessment of the market, how can we trade with index backing? The mathematical rule tells us securities on the extremes will tend towards the middle. Visually this makes more sense on the inverted display in Figure 12.5 above. In some important ways this mirrors the bulge in probability used in Part I.

Those securities on the left — incompetence — will tend to move forward towards the middle. The high-performing securities on the right — excellence — will tend to move back towards the middle. In trading terms, the leaders of today's pack will be overtaken by today's unknowns launching themselves from the middle of the market group.

Obviously there are exceptions, and these provide excellent investment returns, although as the 14% fall in Coca Cola Amatil over a few days in early 1997 shows, good things do come to a sudden halt. These consistently high-performing exceptions are not exceptions to the rule. Consistent leadership only defers a reversion to the mean as the US computer giant IBM can attest.

Our prospecting search is for tomorrow's leaders and often it starts in the middle of the distribution. Candidates from here have an opportunity to move towards excellence. This is a conservative trading approach. These traders look for a trading opportunity developing in a security with average performance because it has more room to move towards excellence.

[handwritten margin note: Conservative Approach]

Aggressive traders look for securities on the left-hand side of the curve, the end defined by incompetence. These are catch-up stocks. On a chart they go down while most of their compatriots go up. When these laggards signal a breakout the aggressive trader looks for a swift move towards the middle level of performance – the mean. Mount Edon Gold, Figure 12.6, is an example of this process. Its sudden reversion to the mean was prompted by a takeover, but it could just have easily, although less dramatically, have been due to cost-cutting, a change in management, or a new product release.

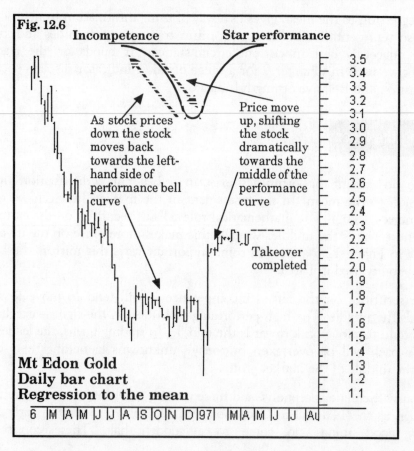

Fig. 12.6

Mt Edon Gold
Daily bar chart
Regression to the mean

The aggressive trader puts the balance of probability on his side because the laggard is moving towards the mean – towards the performance level enjoyed by most securities. The conservative trader is less well positioned because his security is moving away from the mean.

Let us be clear about how we use the bell curve to trade with index backing. Merely buying a security on the left-hand side of the bell curve does not guarantee success any more than taking a position in a stock towards the right-hand side implies a loss. We apply this analysis only to the nuggets exhaustively selected and assayed by other methods. These, by definition of our search, are the best trading opportunities available today. If the security is positioned towards the left of the bell curve we build profit expectations based on this. Stocks moving towards excellence have a harder task, and profit expectations from the trade may be reduced.

This style of index analysis is the first step towards building reasonable expectations that are consistent with our chart analysis. The next section explores these steps in detail. The trading opportunities we have selected by this stage of the process are all valid ones. The one that gets our money is the one that is consistent with our understanding of the probability of its future performance. Although we cannot see a bell curve on a chart, we can trade its inferred behaviour.

Trading the Bell Curve

We use the sector index to decide if our potential trade is consistent with market sentiment and we look for a better probability of success. The third step assesses the security against the absolute index.

The trader infers the relationship between the chosen security and the bell curve, aided by the knowledge that the value of the sector index, or representative index, can be taken as the mean. We build this plot by using the concepts of beta and standard deviation. These values provide an anchor point against which we compare the position of the security we have selected as our potential trade. If we use the day's closing price to build a single index reference line then we have a mobile 'mean' towards which other securities will regress.

In a perfect world our target, the mid-point, would stand still. In the market it keeps moving and is distorted by speed and direction so the bell curve is sometimes slanted to the right by bullishness, towards excellence – or to the left by bearishness, towards incompetence. A bullish bell curve is shown in Figure 12.7. This bias indicates and confirms the market trend, providing the base information used in common investment approaches. From our trading perspective it suggests stocks on the extreme left have been left well behind. These are candidates for delisting, bankruptcy, and financial oblivion. Make sure they don't take your trading capital with them. We look for stocks skewed to the right, matching the orientation of the index.

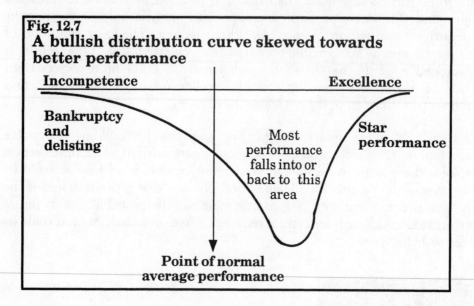

Fig. 12.7
A bullish distribution curve skewed towards better performance

Incompetence — Excellence

Bankruptcy and delisting

Most performance falls into or back to this area

Star performance

Point of normal average performance

The single index line on a chart gives us the mid-point and two ways to confirm our trading opportunities:

1 First, by plotting an individual security against the index to establish its position. This is the beta value. Beta is the amount a security moves in comparision to each move of the index it is compared to. A beta of 1 means for every one cent move in the index the stock also moves one cent. A beta less than 1 identifies the laggards and we put them on the left-hand side of the bell curve. A beta larger than 1 tags the leaders.

Figure 12.8 shows two securities, MIM and PLU, placed parallel to and below the mean as defined by the index close. This Metastock display plots the reference line, All Resources in this example, and compares the performance of two other securities. Performance can also be smoothed using a 30-day Exponential Moving Average (EMA). Ezy Chart users have the Compare Stocks function for the same type of display.

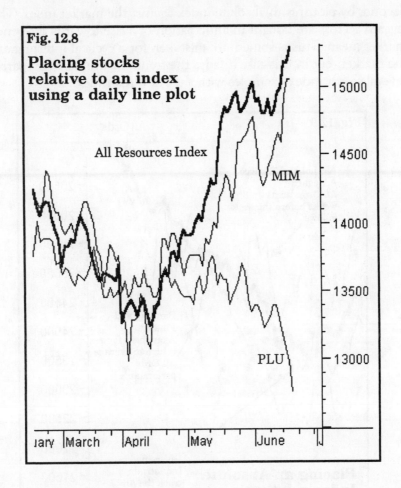

Fig. 12.8

Placing stocks relative to an index using a daily line plot

All Resources Index

MIM

PLU

Your trading approach — moving towards the mean, or moving towards an extremity from the mean — will determine which is the better position on the bell curve for each of your trading candidates.

A trade taken in a security running below the index line is not guaranteed success. Although there is an increased probability price will move upwards towards the midpoint, and if the midpoint is moving forward in a bullish bias, then the upward pressures are much greater — but, it ain't necessarily so. Other genuine fundamental factors may be responsible for the security appearing on the left-hand side of the bell curve. These include bankruptcy, expensive product liability litigation, mining a disappearing resource, or making hub-caps for stagecoaches. It pays to check because not all laggards are potential winners. Many are potential losers so fading the trend from this end is a more aggressive strategy.

2. Second, by plotting an absolute index against the market index. The laggard sectors are bought in anticipation of a rise towards the general market mean. This is sometimes mistaken for a cyclical interpretation of the market, but in this case it fades the trend. Figure 12.9 compares several sector index examples with the All Ords Index.

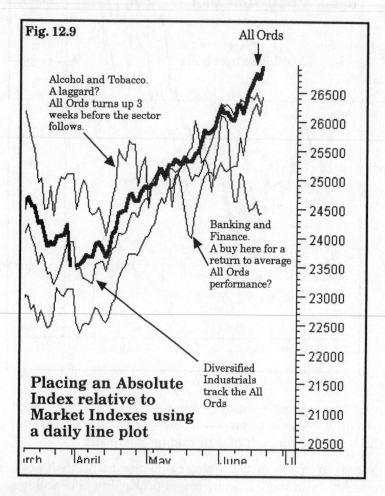

Fig. 12.9

All Ords

Alcohol and Tobacco.
A laggard?
All Ords turns up 3
weeks before the sector
follows.

Banking and
Finance.
A buy here for a
return to average
All Ords
performance?

Diversified
Industrials
track the All
Ords

**Placing an Absolute
Index relative to
Market Indexes using
a daily line plot**

26500
26000
25500
25000
24500
24000
23500
23000
22500
22000
21500
21000
20500

March | April | May | June | Jul

Turning Selected Nuggets Into Profit

The successful traders enter at the beginning of the move — either when the laggard starts to pick up speed, or when one of the pack breaks away to become a leader. Where we want to position our entry decides which trading candidate gets our money.

This is a weather forecast, not a trading signal. It helps establish the balance of probabilities by positioning the sector, or a particular security, in relation to its mid-point. If we accept the security is more likely to move towards, or back to, the mid-point, then we are better equipped to decide the reasonable potential for our proposed trade.

In the final analysis, we are trading an individual security within an environment created by the market. Our initial selection of trading candidates is based on many factors. Our final selections are pruned by confirming the potential for explosive price action, by discounting our bias, and finally by verifying current performance against a representative or absolute index.

Now the trader turns the nuggets to a profit by using a spreadsheet and supplementary numbers from the SEATS screen to confirm our chart analysis, set our buying price, establish profit targets and to build a stop-loss safety net. This gold is ready to go to market.

Part III

SUPPLEMENTARY NUMBERS

13

THIS LITTLE NUGGET
GOES TO MARKET

Finding nuggets is one thing. Selling them is another, and this chapter explores ways to identify the most willing buyers. If our market favours round nuggets rather than square ones, then we need ways to find this preference and shift the balance of probability in our favour. We do this by combining chart analysis and financial calculations.

At the beginning of Part II we stood on the edge of a financial escarpment. The track we used to get to the bottom, the methods we used to locate the best gold-bearing country and the way we assayed each potential trade were different from the methods used by those who chose the more traditional fundamental path. These two paths converge in this section and the steps we take to assess our trade will determine who is the more successful trader.

There are eight steps, too many to apply to every stock in our database. We reserve our judgement, taking these steps towards the end of the prospecting venture when the list is reduced to a very small number of opportunities. On many days there may be no opportunities at all. Later we look at ways to manage open positions.

Private traders have a luxury, and an advantage, not enjoyed by institutional traders. We have the time to make sure every trade is the best trade possible, but too often we squander this advantage. Many traders think once they have identified the trade and completed the analysis covered in Part II and in *Share Trading* that they can ring their broker and start trading. Sometimes this does work, but in the long run additional analysis is required. Spotting the probability is the starting point in the trading process. Calculating the potential for each trade provides supplementary numbers which make, or break, a trade.

Just identifying the trade through sound analysis does not mean we can financially afford to take it. Not all trades are created equal and separating the better winners further reduces the list of trading opportunities.

Our trading objective is to shift the balance of probability in our favour. This involves identifying a developing situation where the balance of probability suggests the market will reverse its current direction, giving us an entry on a breakout. Alternatively, we try to get on board an established trend, but only if the balance of probability suggests the trend will continue.

As discussed in Part I, the basic bar chart is used to broadly identify these balance points, either as a starting point, as in the eyeball search, or as a finishing point after other analysis methods have been used. These include R-plot searches, performance searches using indicator results, or rankings based on accounting or fundamental analysis.

Immediately prior to entering a trade we return to the bar chart because it gives us a basic starting point. The supplementary figures required to confirm our analysis against our financial objectives for the trade are drawn from the bar chart. These financial objectives are more achievable if they are matched with the bulge of probability, both on the entry, and more importantly, on the exit.

This chapter explores these processes. There are eight steps in two groups of four. Each group weeds out the weaker opportunities, gradually reducing our initial extensive list to just a few candidates.

The first group includes steps to establish the break-even point. They are:

- Assessing risk for this trade
- Deciding position size
- Assessing the impact of brokerage
- Considering the tax implications.

The second group tests for time and risk. The steps here are:

- Setting realistic trade objectives
- Estimating time in the market
- Assessing downside risk
- Meeting money management objectives.

Chart patterns, or indicator readings, suggest when the balance is in our favour. We set exit targets based on the bar chart. The temptation is to take a position, hang on, and shoot for some vague notion of profit. This type of open-ended objective is built on hope rather than on good trade management.

To weed out the trades that are not worthwhile we test them with these two questions.

(a) *Does the trade have enough meat on it – enough realistically potential profit – to be worthwhile?* Some trading opportunities are so skinny that trading them is foolish because the potential returns are so small. To decide this we use a combination of chart and financial analysis to put some numbers on probability. The remainder of this chapter deals with this process.

(b) *What are the financial objectives for this trade?* Without objectives we are adrift in a sea of opportunity, constantly battered by fear and enticed by greed. By knowing our financial objectives in advance we steer a course with certainty and make a rational decision about when to end or extend the trade. The calculations involved are covered in Chapter 14.

Of course, knowing when to make a rational decision and actually taking it are two different things. Many people fail the test because they cannot pull the trigger on a losing trade. Nor can they pull the trigger on a winning trade and we look at these problems, and some solutions, in the next section.

We use a bar chart to assess the validity of the trade after our research and before our entry. This has a significant impact on our overall trading success. It is not enough just to be confident the stock you have bought will go up. Nor is it good enough to believe, however sincerely, that the stock has good long-term prospects. The identification of a trading opportunity does not in itself mean the trade is worth taking. In Chapters 7 and 8 we looked at the way the concepts of support and resistance, or price projections and trading bands, help to establish trading targets. This chapter builds on those concepts.

Group One

How Much do We Need to Break-Even?

The first group of four steps helps us decide how much we need from the trade to make it worthwhile. The steps are:

➲ Assessing risk for this trade

➲ Deciding position size

➲ Assessing the impact of brokerage

➲ Considering the tax implications.

Small nuggets are interesting curios so we discard them in favour of larger specimens. Four steps help decide the bare minimum return we are prepared to accept. Any trade not meeting these criteria must be discarded. A high probability of success does not compensate for a low return. It is no good being right if we cannot be profitable at the same time. The trader aims to match his capital with financial objectives and bring them together in a single trade. This defines the level of return you consider acceptable.

Group 1: Step 1: Your assessment of the risk of this particular trade

How long will the trade take to complete? Is this a quick trade, measured in days, or is it a longer-term trade that might take weeks or months to mature? The projected return must meet or beat benchmarks provided by other investment opportunities. The longer the trade is open, the greater the risk the trade will move in a way we have not anticipated because new events are, by definition, unknown.

Trading opportunity is matched with risk and volatility and assessed against time. Greater volatility applies equally to the downside as to the upside. Stable blue chip securities with low volatility, like The Australian Gas Light Company (AGL) shown in Figure 13.1 can yield 17% over 18 weeks. When this trade is compared with a similar security, Lihir Gold (LHG), the difference in return over time is a function of volatility. LHG, Figure 13.2 shows a 21% return in seven weeks.

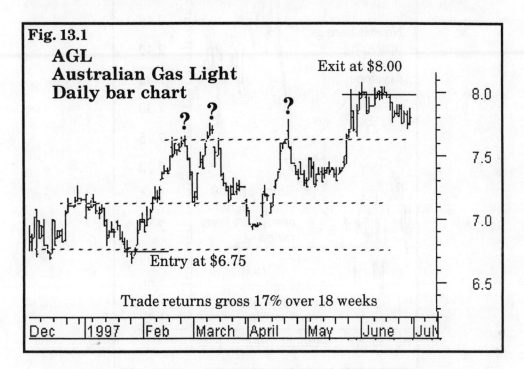

Fig. 13.1
AGL
Australian Gas Light
Daily bar chart

Exit at $8.00
Entry at $6.75
Trade returns gross 17% over 18 weeks

Both stocks are flagged in our search list as trading opportunities. Which is the better trade? The answer depends on your assessment of, and your tolerance for, risk, always remembering we approach the market from a trading perspective. However, as a general rule, when lower returns are matched with lengthy exposure to the market, the trade has increased risk. From an investing perspective this rule is less relevant because the objectives of the 'trade' are different. Steady returns over an extended period are desirable.

Which is a more difficult trade? The LHG trade requires better timing, but its signals are clear and consistent. Using an entry and exit technique based on congestion areas around support levels, or the MMA indicator, multiple trades can be taken from this security as it ranges consistently across a broad trading band.

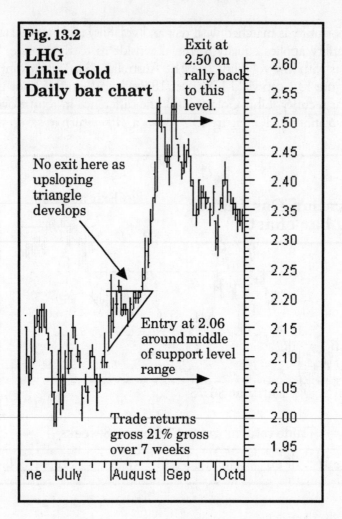

Fig. 13.2
LHG
Lihir Gold
Daily bar chart

Exit at 2.50 on rally back to this level.

No exit here as upsloping triangle develops

Entry at 2.06 around middle of support level range

Trade returns gross 21% gross over 7 weeks

ne | July | August | Sep | Octo

The AGL trade is difficult, with several possible exit points indicated by the question marks in Figure 13.1. The possible early exit points return around 13% and do not offer additional enticing trades. Unlike LHG, once an exit had been made from AGL it was not useful to enter the trade again looking for a return of similar size. Potential returns are reduced to around 10% or even less if a countback line entry technique is used. If trades were taken at the bottom and top of the trading bands, shown as dotted lines in Figure 13.1, returns are 6%.

The trading opportunities turned up as a result of our prospecting process are unequal. The risk/return relationship varies. Past behaviour shown on the charts helps to eliminate the weaker trades. Good chart analysis helps set profit targets, again weeding out the lesser trading opportunities. We look at volatility and using chart analysis in this way in more detail in the next chapter.

Group 1: Step 2: How much trading capital do we commit to the trade?

The market may not let you spend as much as you would like, while at other times it absorbs your capital without a hiccup. This liquidity and depth of market eliminates some trading tactics and favours others.

Depth describes the way orders are arrayed above and below the current bid and ask. A deep market where the last sale was at $18.50 will have sellers at $18.51, $18.52, $18.54, $18.55, etc. all the way through to perhaps $20.00. Each higher level is only a cent or so above the previous level. On the buying side, each lower level is only a cent or so below the previous level.

A shallow market might see a seller at $0.30 and the next seller at $0.36, then $0.37, followed by a gap to $0.40 etc. Buyers and sellers are not required to neatly line up in one cent increments so it is not always possible to buy or sell stock at exactly the price we nominate.

A liquid market describes the number of shares on offer at each price level. Highly liquid markets tend to have good depth, as in the $18.51 example above. In addition there are often three or four, or eight or ten, or more, sellers at each level. The total number of shares on offer at each level is substantial. An illiquid market is most often associated with shallow markets. A single seller at $0.30 might only have 20,000 shares to sell. Buyers wanting to buy 60,000 shares must either wait, or bid higher to collect their preferred number of shares.

Some very liquid positions encourage scalping — large positions for small returns. With smaller stocks, large positions cannot be executed because there is just not enough stock available so smaller positions come with higher execution risk. These factors determine trading tactics, and in turn, decide which stocks will be retained in our trading list.

A highly liquid security like BHP can be traded with confidence for scalping returns. With a significant number of buyers and sellers at almost every level there is enough depth in the market for BHP for traders to take large positions. Using a countback line entry as shown in Figure 13.3, an entry at $17.40 with a countback line exit at $18.40 returns 5.7% gross. Under normal circumstances such margins are too thin.

In this case the margin is profitable because we place large buy and sell orders confident they will be filled. On many days BHP turnover is around four million shares or more. The market has depth and liquidity. At the entry price of $17.40 this represents daily turnover of around $69,600,000. A $30,000 buying order does not stand out and is easily absorbed by the market.

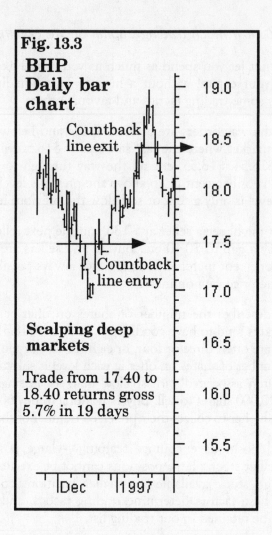

Fig. 13.3

**BHP
Daily bar
chart**

Countback
line exit

Countback
line entry

**Scalping deep
markets**

Trade from 17.40 to
18.40 returns gross
5.7% in 19 days

19.0

18.5

18.0

17.5

17.0

16.5

16.0

15.5

Dec   1997

With this liquidity the figures stack up attractively. Buying and selling 50,000 BHP shares still goes almost unnoticed in a market of this depth. A trade of this size using the entry and exit points as shown in Figure 13.3 for $878,700 would return $32,100 profit. This is a nett 3.65% return after brokerage. Generally we would want to do better from a trade, but it is still a handy dollar amount for 19 days of market exposure.

Position size does make a difference, but only if the market has sufficient depth to accept your order without a hiccup. Scalping opportunities are reduced with smaller stocks because the average order size is smaller and although the percentage returns are the same, the dollar value scarcely buys lunch. The average order size is easily obtained from the depth of market information discussed in Chapter 15. It can also be worked out by looking at average daily turnover. Your intended position size is unlikely to equal the average daily turnover of BHP, but with smaller stocks this can be a real concern. With $30,000 to commit to a trade in a small speculative stock we run the risk of becoming the market.

Group 1: Step 3: The impact of brokerage

Brokerage is a cost of doing business. It is inevitable and, in most cases, unavoidable. The exceptions include rights issues and takeover offers. Obviously traders like to avoid paying unnecessarily high brokerage rates, but there are times when this is not possible. No matter what brokerage is paid, if the rate of brokerage makes a trade unprofitable, then the trade is not worth it. Do not blame the brokerage. A trade should be substantial enough to support the normal costs of doing business, and still return a healthy profit.

Factor in brokerage. This has a significant impact. If we are paying brokerage at 2.5% then effectively we need at least 5% return to break even — 2.5% on each side of the trade, the entry and the exit. Not all trades will offer this. If we are trading larger position sizes, and paying perhaps 0.5% brokerage, then we still require a least a 1% price increase before we start making money.

Group 1: Step 4: Tax

This is not a uniquely Australian problem, but the structure of our taxation system encourages traders to place undue emphasis on this factor. Tax is always an annoyance, but it should not be a major consideration in making a trade. The primary purpose of trading is to make money — not to reduce a taxation liability.

The full-time private trader uses his trading skills to generate his primary income stream. This is his strength and these trading skills are quite different from those skills practised by tax accountants. In the same way that a businessman concentrates on improving his business rather than worrying about the tax effect of each transaction, the trader should do likewise.

From a trading perspective what is important is making a successful trade. If success leads to a tax liability then the appropriate person to deal with that is a CPA or tax accountant. Taxation advice will assist the trader to structure his business in a manner which is the most tax-effective. Taxation advice should not be designed to structure each transaction, or trade, to be most tax-effective, as at times this will be counter to the very objectives of trading. Such advice is more applicable to investment positions where ill-timed decisions can have major tax implications.

The crux of the problem is the choice between capital gains tax or income tax generated on trading profits. The solution depends on many factors, including the annual turnover of positions, the contribution trading income makes to total income stream and trading history. It is a complex field best left to the professional tax advisers and accountants. Consult with them but do not be driven by tax considerations alone. Trade well and be prepared to pay the price, or tax, of success.

The trader, by definition, is active in the market holding positions for short periods. Market timing is of the essence. If the trader falls victim to the Australian preoccupation of basing his business around taxation minimisation rather than on making a profit, then trading activity is crippled by artificial restraints preventing timely exits based on market movements. When the market signals 'out' then the trader exits. The cost of ignoring the signal is often much greater than the taxation consequences of acting on it.

The way you take these first four steps sets an initial target for the minimum acceptable return from each trade — the break-even point. This is one of the important numbers in your trading universe. It tells you the break-even point for every trade.

If you need a minimum 5% from a trade to break even then potential trading opportunities are discarded if they do not meet these minimum requirements. If you do not have these minimum requirements then you enter trades with your eyes closed. No matter how good your fundamental or chart analysis is, unless you know your break-even point, then the trade has no starting point and no direction. The methods we use to create our list of trading candidates do not tell us anything about profitability until we assess them against our break-even point.

Break-Even

A spreadsheet calculation provides an example of how a break-even point is calculated. Figure 13.4 shows a sample trade with National Australia Bank (NAB) at $19.34. With brokerage set at 2.5%, a level that is not unusual for full-service brokers, the price must reach $21.32 before the trade starts to break even. Brokerage is a two-way charge. Brokerage on the purchase is $483.50. Brokerage on the sale depends on sale value. For convenience and ease of comparison between these two examples, we treat it here as the same on both entry and exit, incurring another $483.50 for total brokerage of $967.

Fig. 13.4

BROKERAGE	
Av. brokerage rate	2.500
EQUITY DETAILS	
Equity name	NAB
Number of shares	1,000
Purchase price	19.34
Net cost	19,340.00
Av. brokerage	967.00
Full cost	20,307.00
Break-even price	**21.32**

For this trade to succeed the price must increase by nearly two dollars ($1.98) just to remain in the game and not lose money.

In contrast, when brokerage is reduced to 1%, and every other factor left the same, the breakeven point is reduced to $20.12 as shown in Figure 13.5. Now the same trade needs to add only 78¢ to break even. This is 60% less than the breakeven figure calculated with 2.5% brokerage.

Fig. 13.5

BROKERAGE	
Av. brokerage rate	1.000
EQUITY DETAILS	
Equity name	NAB
Number of shares	1,000
Purchase price	19.34
Net cost	19,340.00
Av. brokerage	386.80
Full cost	19,726.80
Break-even price	**20.12**

Brokerage has been used as the variable in these examples. Position size — the amount you allocate to each trade — is a variable, as are stamp duty and the rate of riskless return in a Cash Management Account (CMA). Make this calculation as complex as you wish, but one way or another, a calculation must be made. Establishing the breakeven point in any trade is the first step in a business calculation of potential profit.

Gross is Good but Net is Better

The first group of steps looks confusing so many traders skip them — and so skip the next group. Traders do have a tremendous capacity for self delusion. Profit is temptation so the danger in the first search pass is the bewitching attraction of gross returns rather than the lower net figures. It is so easy to see the entry on support and the exit at resistance. The calculations are completed on a scrap of paper — support at $1.00, resistance at $1.50. Profit equals 50%. The cash register rings obscuring rational thought.

These are initial calculations and do provide a further means of ranking the trading opportunities, but they need to be examined more carefully. Using the start figure calculations shown in Figure 13.6 — entry $0.031, exit $0.050 — the gross return of $15,000, or 61% is much more attractive than the net return. We should avoid the temptation to dwell on these. Gross returns should be reduced to net figures, and then ranked. Getting net figures means:

➲ Assessing risk for this trade

➲ Deciding position size

➲ Including brokerage

➲ Including tax.

When each group of steps is completed we weed out the break-even and skinny trades. We move from good trades to better ones, and finally to the best trading opportunities on the day.

Before the better trades are selected they are assessed against the final group of four steps.

Group Two

Time and Risk

The first group of steps give us one number — the break-even point. Before we commit cash to a trade we take another four steps to calculate the potential profit based on and closely matched with chart analysis, and the stop-loss level, again based on and matched with chart analysis. The second group of steps builds a profit and loss statement by understanding the relationship between time and risk by:

➲ Setting realistic trade objectives

➲ Estimating time in the market

➲ Assessing downside risk

➲ Meeting money management objectives.

Group 2: Step 1: The ability to achieve the trade objectives

The size of the market for our selected security may make taking a large position impossible. If the stock is tightly held we might not be able to buy enough of it to make it worthwhile. When prices dip to our entry level we need to buy more than just a fraction out of our intended parcel of shares.

Pelsart Mining (PRN) is a penny dreadful with a profitable habit of bouncing from negative price dips to established resistance levels. The trading tactic is to buy at $0.031, just above the lowest level of the dipping spike, and to sell as it hits resistance at $0.05. The calculations are shown in Figure 13.6 on the left-hand side, Pelsart Planned. The proposed trade offered a 56.5% return and with 300,000 shares this translated into $5,336. Brokerage on the selling side is calculated at actual cost in this instance.

The trade was perfectly analysed and prices behaved as anticipated. From these perspectives all trading targets were achieved, but only if 300,000 shares are purchased.

These calculations collapse in the face of market reality. Pelsart Actual, right-hand column in Figure 13.6 shows what happens when only 10,000 shares were available for purchase at this price. Faced with minimum brokerage on the purchase and the sale, return is reduced to 25% because brokerage is much higher as a proportion of total costs. In percentage terms the return is acceptable, but when the dollars are counted out – all 90 of them – it seems barely enough to compensate for the potential risk.

Fig. 13.6

PRELIMINARY DETAILS		
Av brokerage rate	**1.500** Minimum brokerage	**$50**

EQUITY DETAILS		
Equity name	**Pelsart Planned**	**Pelsart Actual**
Number of shares	**300,000**	**10,000**
Purchase price	**0.031**	**0.031**
Net cost	9,300.00	310
Av Brokerage	139.50	50
Full cost	**9,439.50**	**360**

REWARD PARAMETERS		
Sell price (inc brokerage)	**0.050**	**0.050**
Gross return	15,000.00	500
Av Brokerage	225.000	50
Net return	14,775.00	450
Clear $$$$	**5,336**	**90**
%%% Return full cost/net return	**56.52**	**25**

The liquidity of the market may work against us so all spreadsheet calculations are compared with past market conditions and verified against the current market. The Pelsart trading example above was valid in assuming 300,000 shares would be available for purchase. Average daily volume had been around these levels and the price spikes to support at $0.031 at the centre of the trading strategy had shown good volume in the past.

The trader should have verified these assumptions against current market conditions when the order was executed. These supplementary numbers would have told him only a few shares were on offer at $0.031 and that the next parcel of shares was for sale nearly one cent higher at $0.04. A quick look at these numbers allows the trader to recalculate the financial viability of the trade and abandon it if necessary. Using these supplementary figures in this way is discussed in more detail in Chapter 15.

Group 2: Step 2: Time in the market required to reach the profit target

In options trading time decay degrades the value of the option as the expiry date draws closer. The margin for hope is reduced. With only a few days to expiry the final option price is known and the market is not interested in bidding beyond this known value. When an option has months to run to expiry the market allows a larger margin for hope.

Equity trading does not include an expiry date, but time decay is a factor because longer market exposure increases risk. The relationship is shown in typical form in Figure 13.7.

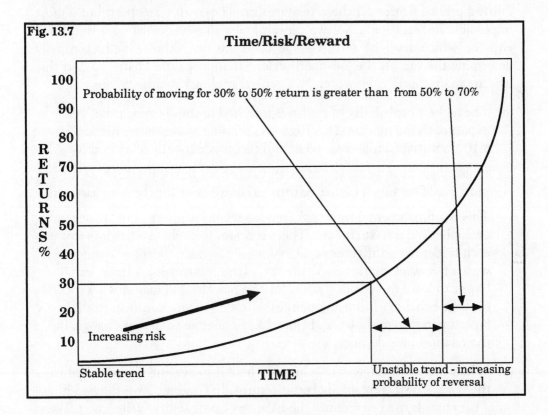

Fig. 13.7

Time/Risk/Reward

Probability of moving for 30% to 50% return is greater than from 50% to 70%

RETURNS %

Increasing risk

Stable trend   **TIME**   Unstable trend - increasing probability of reversal

Risk increases with time. On a daily basis the probability of the market moving more than a few percentage points against us is small. Over several days, on a cumulative basis, this risk increases. The further we move along a price trend, logically, the closer we must be to the end of it. The longer we are in the market, the greater the probability the current trend will reverse, diminishing open profits with falling prices.

We find it difficult to tell when the trend will, or has, ended. We cannot put a time line on the curve, but we do know the typical shape of the curve. We use this information to protect current profits rather than by trading increased risk along the curve for incremental returns.

Although the left-hand scale caps returns at 100% this is not always the case. Returns may be well above this, but the shape of the time and risk curve remains the same. The risk of a trend reversal increases with time. Additionally, the pursuit of incrementally higher returns is inversely related to the probability of achieving them.

Putting precise figures on these relationships is easy in retrospect, but almost impossible in real time, since we cannot know in advance when a trend will end, or which level of return – 50%, 100% or 300% – will eventually determine the cap on the left-hand scale. Attempts to use Figure 13.7 in this way are inappropriate. However, two general trading conclusions are valid.

(a) The highest probability of return is matched to the shortest time exposure to the market. This suggests spending a year in the market for a 10% return is a high-risk event and inconsistent with good trading.

It also suggests if we do spend extended periods in the market that we must shoot for much higher returns to compensate for the increased risk.

This is a fundamental time/risk/reward relationship we apply to several examples in the next chapter. There is no set formula for deciding this as each trader has a different capacity for risk. Some traders feel comfortable with a five-week market exposure for a 10% return while others are happy to leave the position open for five months. No matter where you set your benchmark starting point, the trade will still conform to the typical parameters shown in Figure 13.7. The time scale may change, but the relationships do not.

(b) When the profit targets are achieved, there is increasing risk attached to the pursuit of incrementally better returns. In Chapter 3 we showed how a bar chart is used to identify the balance of probability. When we make an entry these points set our profit targets. Using Figure 13.7 we may have set 50% return as consistent with our profit targets based on the balance of probability.

When prices reach this level what should we do if they appear to be going higher? It is hard to take a profit and close your eyes to the growing pile of missed profit left on the table as prices continue to rise. If our initial analysis is correct, then prices will pause at around our exit level. We are not shooting for the very top because we want to leave some potential profit for the person who buys from us. Chasing this additional profit gives an incremental return while dramatically increasing risk of a trend reversal. The probability of success is reduced because it requires prices to move beyond the level reflecting the balance of probability we identified before the trade was opened.

Sometimes prices do move consistently above our profit targets. If our initial analysis was poor, or flawed, then this is one consequence. The trader looks at the trade again, making perhaps a new entry, adjusting the time scale on Figure 13.7 as required. Alternatively, the trader can retire content with the achievement of his financial objectives in this trade.

Time in a trade is balanced against the return and the estimated risk. Generally more time exposure should be rewarded with better returns. In the final stages of analysis the time/risk/reward ratio is matched with all the previous analysis to identify the very best trading opportunity.

Group 2: Step 3: Downside risk

If the trade fails, how much do we reasonably stand to lose and is this consistent with our stop-loss strategy? The interaction of this calculation with other factors is complex. For the moment we will note its importance. In the next chapter we look at how it is calculated in a way consistent with the balance of probability and incorporated into a full trading analysis.

Group 2: Step 4: Matching your money management objectives

Does the trade and intended position size meet your capital allocation requirements? Establishing and using these objectives are discussed more fully in *Share Trading* and we assume you are familiar with these concepts. The consequences of this decision are often difficult. If taking the very best trading opportunity means your portfolio is overweighted in speculative stocks, the impact may be dramatically different from your expectations.

Establishing a portfolio balance and deciding how you will deal with profits and capital allocation between classes of stock has as much impact on trading success as the actual trade. Even the best trading opportunities are passed up if they distort money management objectives and outcomes. The money management models discussed in *Share Trading* explore these consequences in detail so here we only mention them in passing.

This Little Nugget Goes to Market

We started this journey equipped with a pair of dice and a bulge in the balance of probability. From the top of the escarpment the path looked as if it finished at the point where we found trades that looked good on the chart. As we travelled down the path we looked for market confirmation of our analysis. Armed with this information, our trading list was reduced. Every twist in the path takes us to another checkpoint, reducing our list further because we want these trades to look good on the numbers. Not every nugget is good gold.

Many traders fail to complete this journey. Baffled by many checkpoints they launch into a trade before they reach the journey's end. For those who have travelled with us this far the prospects of success are enhanced, but not yet complete. Before trading we gather all this information together, setting precise financial objectives for the trade and matching them with market reality on the day.

14

PINNING A NUMBER

ON RISK

At the very core of trading is the aggressive management of risk. It is too easy to forget this as the search for trading opportunities consumes our attention. The final selection is designed to tilt the balance of probability on our side but the advantage is squandered by poor risk management invariably accompanied by poor trading discipline. Improving both comes from planning.

Forget this core business and the market reminds you very quickly. Profit is not enough because loss is inevitable and loss is the generic risk in all trading activity. With certainty we can assign a number to some aspects of risk, but not to reward because it is always uncertain. Trading discipline is applied risk control. Without it, a string of winning trades is easily destroyed by a single losing position. Traders with the trading discipline to cut losers and ride winners avoid these losses by defining risk before the trade is opened.

Trading discipline supplies the answer to the question posed in the previous chapter: *What are the financial objectives for this trade?*

This discipline comes from sound trade planning constructed with reference to risk. Without planning we are adrift in a sea of opportunity, constantly battered by fear and enticed by greed. Pre-set financial objectives help us steer a course with greater certainty by pinning a number, by quantifying, trade risk. So armed we are better equipped to make rational decisions about when to end or extend the trade.

These calculated and inferred figures are vital supplementary numbers required to finish the search to identify and exploit trading opportunities. We use known numbers, drawn from the chart, to infer the value of other risk variables. The numbers selected define our trade risk and are a function of three elements:

⮑ Element 1: *The Fear of Loss*

Good traders respect loss and use this fear to build sensible trading tactics based on specific financial calculations. Poor traders are terrified of loss. As a frightened child closes their eyes against the dangers of the night, so the poor trader skips these calculations, and pays a substantial penalty.

⮑ Element 2: *Profit Objectives*

Good traders chase carefully-defined financial returns. We prefer to use charting techniques to establish these returns, but others use a range of benchmarks. Poor traders rely on satisfying a growing sense of greed. Sometimes they win, but often they ride from the top to the bottom always chasing the most recent high in the decline – promising whichever trading Deity they believe in that "I will get out on the rally."

⮑ Element 3: *Timing Financial Objectives*

Time is the third, and most difficult, risk variable. Financial objectives bring together time and profit objectives. Good traders look for returns commensurate with the length of time exposure to the market. Poor traders become investors hoping to ride through the downturns and back into profitability by extending their time in the market. This is a valid approach in its place, but it is not a trading approach.

These elements come together in a single spreadsheet with three calculation groups. For clarity in this chapter we split the calculation groups into separate sheets. In examining these three elements we will use a plain trading example.

Diversified Mineral Resources (DMR) is a fairly unexciting miner with a well-established non-trending chart pattern.

Establishing financial objectives involves building a trading plan. This does not have to be complex. Many plans look deceptively simple, such as the summary of the DMR trading plan below.

> Stop-loss — $0.095 for $2,000 maximum
>
> Entry conditions — on support
>
> Exit conditions — at resistance or reassess after 6 weeks
>
> Financial objectives — 21% over 4 to 6 weeks.

Determining the figures included in the plan requires more work than such simplicity suggests. Developing this plan, and others like it, is the subject of this chapter. This is an intensive process demanding time. When applied to a small number of trading opportunities we give planning the time it deserves. When applied to an even smaller number of open positions, we give them the trade management they demand.

The starting point is a weekly bar chart for the selected security. The DMR weekly bar chart, Figure 14.1, has been selected because the chart analysis is not complicated and the simple trading strategy is built around support and resistance — buy at $0.105 and sell at $0.13 for a 24% return. These levels provide two of the three base figures for every subsequent calculation.

The third figure is a function of long-term support, total trading equity and position size brought together in a stop-loss calculation.

We choose this stock because understanding its chart pattern does not add additional layers of complexity. It is easy to concentrate on the important factors of loss, profit and time. With more complex trading strategies and chart patterns the calculations do not grow substantially more difficult, although selecting the appropriate starting figures may be more time-consuming.

Additionally, DMR has an advantage of illustrating how simple chart concepts are profitable. The four indicated trades in 12 months, each returning 24%, are a handy consistent addition to any trading portfolio.

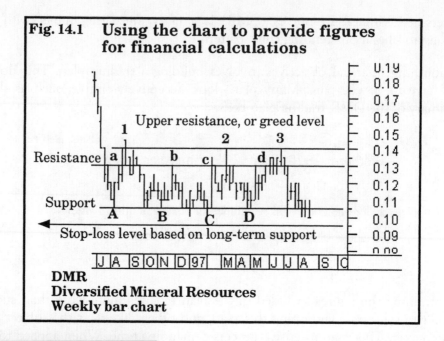

Fig. 14.1 Using the chart to provide figures for financial calculations

DMR
Diversified Mineral Resources
Weekly bar chart

Element 1: Fear of Loss

Taking a loss is difficult when you have a plan, but it is virtually impossible when you do not have any plan. Planning involves the entry, the potential exit to limit losses and the potential exit to realise profits. Private traders spend a lot of time on the entry, and too little time on the profitable exit. As for the stop-loss, we tend to pick a fuzzy figure at random and call it a stop-loss.

Trading is an emotional process, particularly when we are asked to take a loss, and we cannot eliminate this emotion. Successful trading requires us to sideline emotion in an open trade because rising prices galvanise us, while falling prices paralyse. As private traders we have to overcome these emotional responses ourselves because no-one else will do it for us. There is no floor supervisor to step in and close a losing position. We beat this emotional blackmail by planning the trade ahead of time before the position is opened. We do this using the chart to set objectives, and to decide if those objectives match our money management requirements.

From this we develop a plan for taking small losses. The strategies employed to prevent losses from growing can be complex, or they can be simple, but the objective is always the same — to limit the loss. Good trading accepts the inevitability of a loss — not the inevitability of a profit. Using a spreadsheet to overcome the fear of loss is the first part of this process.

Planning for a Portfolio Bereavement

The fattest spreadsheet trading opportunities are not always the healthiest. Although these initial calculations provide a means of ranking the trading opportunities, they need to be examined more carefully for defects on the downside. We do not know which way this security will move, and although we have taken care to shift the balance of probability to our side, we know this does not guarantee certainty.

If the stop-loss points do not match our criteria, then this nugget, no matter how good the potential upside, is no longer a trading candidate.

The first base figure is our intended entry price, in this case $0.105. As prices tumble towards our chosen entry level in the DMR example we must concentrate on the dreadful possibility we might be wrong in taking an entry at $0.105.

If we are wrong, and the price continues to fall, at what point do we recognise our error, or do we wait until it is totally beyond doubt? We need to build a big sign saying "WRONG WAY GO BACK", and the chart helps set the third base figure.

This is a central problem for every private trader. It is not enough just to trade well. The private trader must also know something about money management and trade risk. There are many options when it comes to money management, and some are discussed in detail in *Share Trading*. The one I prefer is the 2% rule. You may use something different, but you should go through a similar process of calculating the trade risk and setting your responses in a way consistent with your money management before you enter the trade.

Measuring Loss

How do we measure loss — against the cost of each position, or against the cost of the total portfolio? The 2% rule is one answer and it says no single trade should put at risk more than 2% of your total trading equity. Loss is measured against the total portfolio. This is not a complex rule and as it, or a rule like it, is central to any stop-loss strategy we will quickly refresh its main points.

First, trading equity. This is the total amount of capital we intend to use for trading. Active traders aim to have this entire amount exposed to the market in open positions most of the time. When we calculate 2%, we use the total of our intended trading capital rather than the total currently committed to the market. When we add profits to our trading pile, then the 2% calculation changes. It also changes when we take losses.

The rule does not mean, if we have $100,000 in trading capital that we must allocate only $2,000, or 2% to each position.

It does mean that when the position is 'marked to market', if loss is equal to $2,000 then we must exit the trade. This stop-loss strategy works best when the stop-loss point coincides with both the dollar value and a logical point indicated on the chart. The logical stop-loss level is shown in Figure 14.1 and is based on long-term support. Later our calculations match this level with other financial considerations. Most importantly, note that I do not exit when DMR shows a 2% loss from the entry point as price falls by 2% to $0.103.

Fig. 14.2

OVERCOMING FEAR OF LOSS		
Av. brokerage rate	**1.20**	
Total trade equity	**100,000**	
ENTRY DETAILS		
Equity name	**DMR PLANNED**	**DMR ACTUAL**
Number of shares	**180,000**	**100,000**
Purchase price	**0.105**	**0.105**
Net cost	18,900.00	10,500.00
Av. brokerage	226.80	50.00
Full cost	**19,126.80**	**10,550.00**
RISK PARAMETERS		
Equity risk @ 2%	2,000.00	2,000.00
Risk on this trade	**2,000.00**	**1,100.00**
Stop-loss exit price based on full cost	0.095	0.095
Break-even price	0.108	0.107

By combining chart information with spreadsheet calculations, as shown in Figure 14.2, the trader sets the parameters of the trades. He has three known figures – the preferred entry price; the dollar value of 2% of equity; the price value of the stop-loss point. These figures allow him to infer the values of others to set appropriate financial objectives. Bringing these together in a single calculation includes three components – the chart, a spreadsheet and a matching process.

Component 1: The chart

Basic chart analysis is used to establish support areas. The DMR bar chart indicates solid support at $0.105. The next nearest support level is at $0.095. Although not shown on this chart extract, this level acted as resistance in 1994, 1995 and 1996. If prices do fall past $0.105 they are likely to pause around $0.095. This is a straightforward application of the trading approach discussed in earlier sections. These levels show where the balance of probability hides.

Component 2: The spreadsheet

We use this to calculate the dollar value of our total trading equity. To make calculations easy to follow we use $100,000 as Total Trade Equity with brokerage at 1.2%. Using the 2% rule this equals a maximum of $2,000 we may risk on any single trade. This value is entered in the cell opposite the label: Equity Risk @2%. This value changes as our trading equity increases when profits are added, or as equity decreases when losses are taken.

Component 3: The challenge – match position size with risk

Here we bring together long-term support and total trading equity to calculate position size consistent with stop-loss conditions.

The 2% rule puts a figure on risk – $2,000 – and a price value on support – $0.095. The price value is calculated from the chart based on the support level. These two known figures are the reference point for all further calculations. Here we choose to limit the dollar risk to $2,000 and this is entered into the cell Risk On This Trade. We could select a different figure but we will obey the 2% rule for this example.

Our task is to get the cell Stop-Loss Exit Price Based On Full Cost to read $0.095. For traders who use a spreadsheet to compensate for lack of mathematical dexterity this process is based on a juggling act where position size — Number Of Shares — is manipulated until the $0.095 target is achieved.

We skip the juggling and show the solution. The maximum position size is 180,000 shares for a total cost, including brokerage, of $19,126.80 as the column DMR PLANNED shows in Figure 14.2. These results are always the starting point for further calculations.

However, risk is a function of position size. It is further reduced when position size is reduced. This is sometimes deliberately manipulated to suit our current circumstances. The maximum position size, for instance, might be inconsistent with our portfolio allocation strategy, creating a mismatch between time and risk as discussed below. More frequently, traders do not always have access to the maximum cash amount. Not having enough cash exactly when you need it is a trading reality.

By reducing the position size as shown in the last column of Figure 14.2, DMR ACTUAL, the overall risk is reduced. This is why the spreadsheet shows two cells. The upper cell Equity Risk @2% is calculated automatically from total equity size. The lower cell forces the trader to make a conscious decision to accept, or lower this risk factor.

With 100,000 shares costing $10,550, the calculation reveals prices could fall to $0.086 before $2,000 of trading equity is lost. This does not mean we now exit at $0.086. The stop-loss figure derived from the chart and based on support is still valid. Using it, the dollar risk on this trade is reduced to $1,100 making this a safer trade by reducing the impact of failure on our total trading equity. We do not expand our risk level beyond the logical stop-loss points indicated on the chart.

These calculations acknowledge we have very little real control in the market — the odds are against us. All we control is the entry, the exit and our position size and we use the balance of probability to match these events with market conditions. The market controls every other aspect of the trade. Of the three we do control, it is the exit that allows us to manhandle risk.

Element 2: Profit Objectives

Calculating profit objectives is a pleasant task and as most traders are familiar with it, we will cover this briefly. Calculating profit is independent of setting financial objectives although the novice trader usually confuses the two. Financial objectives determine how the profit contributes to overall portfolio risk. Calculating back-of-the-envelope profits is a dangerous task if not balanced against more structured calculations.

The question, "How much profit is enough?", has a definite answer. In the same way that the chart, and associated spreadsheet calculations, help to set a stop-loss, they are also used to set profit objectives based on past price action.

The DMR PLANNED column in Figure 14.3 outlines the process using the chart in Figure 14.1 as the starting point. The trading strategy provides the price figures for profit calculations. In this case an exit at $0.13 based on resistance returns 21%. Greed beckons at $0.14 and the results are shown in the last column DMR GREED. The 30% return looks enticing but at what additional risk? Ways to make this judgement call are considered below.

Fig. 14.3

CALCULATING PROFITS		
Av. brokerage rate	1.20	
Total trade equity	100,000	
ENTRY DETAILS		
Equity name	**DMR PLANNED**	**DMR GREED**
Number of shares	180,000	100,000
Purchase price	0.105	0.105
Net cost	18,900.00	10,500.00
Av. brokerage	226.80	50.00
Full cost	19,126.80	10,550.00
REWARD PARAMETERS		
Sell price (inc. brokerage)	0.13	0.14
Gross return	23,400.00	14,000.00
Av. brokerage	281	168.00
Net return	23,119.00	13,832.00
Clear $$$$	3,992	3,282.00
%%% Return full cost/net return	20.87	31.11
%%% Impact on total trading equity	3.99	3.28

There are other ways of establishing profit objectives based on exit prices. These might range from using a set of moving average crossovers, or when the Stochastic turns above 85%, to exiting on a 10% return or when the current close is below the countback line. Had this trade been based on any of these other strategies the figure entered in the cell opposite Sell Price (Inc Brokerage) would be different. It may be more difficult to calculate or estimate but this is not an excuse for not having a figure. No matter which exit conditions you choose you should add, and later adjust if necessary, the exit price. This is the final base figure required to manhandle trading risk. Without it you are fully exposed to the emotional turbulence of the market.

It does matter how you decide on this profit figure. The one indicator measure to avoid is Higher Opening Prices Everyday, or HOPE. The market leaves no room for wishful thinking. The profit objective must be realistic.

Realism comes from chart information, either past price action or anticipated price action based on a consistent analysis of current price behaviour. Realism requires, and good trading demands, a clearly defined set of exit conditions preferably defined with a figure.

The gross figures we jotted down, after deciding all trades are not created equal, provide an intuitive ranking. It is natural to lust after bigger profits and unless we are careful, these trades will always receive the benefit of the doubt. Traders must be particularly vigilant in realistically assessing the upside potential because this impacts on the achievement of our financial objectives.

In ranking these outcomes, and in making decisions about financial objectives for the DMR example, the 21% figure is preferred. It is realistically consistent with the third variable — time.

Element 3: Timing Financial Objectives

Selecting profit objectives is a process combined with estimating the reality of time in the market. For clarity we have separated these processes to consider more carefully the impact of time, as measured by volatility, in the final ranking and selection of trades.

A good trade meets its financial objectives. The worst objective of all is to maximise profit. Riding the price rise to the very top involves increasing risk as discussed at the end of the last chapter. Good traders understand the relationship between time and risk so they balance reward in a way designed to achieve their preferred financial objectives.

Profit plays a vital role in these calculations. The primary obstacle to sound financial planning in a trade is unrealistic profit expectations, either because we think the stock will give us more than it is able, or because we feel if it continues to make a profit then this is enough without having to calculate it. Either way is fatal because without a better way to measure achievement the trades start to manage us.

Taking a loss is easy when compared to turning your back on a profit. Watching a stock go onto new highs after your exit is the hardest aspect of trading. Nevertheless we must put a cap on greed because greed keeps us in excellent positions that turn into losers. The price goes up and we hold on, giddy with excitement and unrealised profits. When it turns, we cannot believe it, and we refuse to sell, hoping to regain our lost profit. We hang on because we have no realistic financial objectives.

Volatility

The first step in developing financial objectives for the trade is to eliminate unrealistic expectations. Trading volatility provides the measure. This is obvious when you pause to think. There is no point in trying to take a 100% return from a staid bluechip like BHP because it is unlikely to happen. With a skyrocketing chart of a speculative miner, why take a 10% return when a lot more is on offer? On the other hand, there is no point in buying a stock at $0.07, and refusing to sell it at $0.16 because "This is going to be a $2.00 stock."

Unrealistic expectations disappear when we identify the trading volatility of the stock we are dealing with. Essentially we identify three groups or classes of stock, based on trading volatility. We use the term in a specific way, defining it as the distance between the year high and the year low combined with the frequency and ease of movement between these extremes.

Volatility is usually associated with daily price ranges and has two more common understandings in the market so it is important to explain the differences.

The first compares daily ranges to select those with increasing or decreasing volatility. In addition to the indicators discussed in Part II, the Chaikin volatility indicator compares the spread between the high and low prices using two moving averages. The first plots the difference between the daily high and low prices and then calculates the rate of change in the average as a percentage. This indicator is standard with Metastock and the default uses 10 periods for each calculation.

It does not serve our purpose of defining trading volatility because the indicator measures volatility as a function of wider price swings during the day rather than total behaviour over a year or more.

The second is implied volatility, a concept used in pricing options and warrants. It is an inferred figure derived from the actual option price and the actual security price. Essentially, implied volatility arises when two different financial products are compared. Sheldon Natenberg covers these issues in *Option Volatility and Pricing Strategies*. Metastock users have the opportunity to play with the calculations in the OptionScope module.

For our purposes implied volatility is not useful. Later we want to compare and rank several trading candidates but they are not related in the same way as a security and its option. Implied volatility does not give us a way to measure the internal historical ranging behaviour of a single stock. Chaikin concentrates on a single stock, but the time frame is too short and cannot be meaningfully extended to encompass the variety of ranging activity in a year.

Trading Volatility

Trading volatility is a long-term estimated figure used in the calculation of risk by defining profit. It establishes the range of reasonable return and allows us to draw comparative conclusions about the frequency of these returns. Trading volatility is the return realistically achievable, given the trader is likely to enter late, above the absolute low, and exit early, below the absolute top.

The concept is simple, but its application is inelegant. It requires judgement rather than mathematical precision so it is difficult to program as search criteria. The technique is used to select stocks for the trader's private index as discussed in *Share Trading*. It is a time-consuming process and impractical to apply on a daily basis to every chart in the database. Because trading volatility supplies the vital 'estimated' figures used in final trading calculations it is more efficient to apply it only to the very last candidates examined as trading opportunities.

In classifying these stocks we use low trading volatility, mid-range trading volatility, and high trading volatility. Trading volatility is determined by the annual trading range, from peak to trough, and by the frequency of these moves. Some equities give multiple trading opportunities of about the same range many times a year. DMR is an example. Others offer these opportunities infrequently and this is an important time factor in the risk calculation.

Low trading volatility describes those stocks consistently yielding realistic trading returns around 10%. The range of reasonable returns varies from sector to sector. It is difficult, for instance, to find a bank with high trading volatility. In the resources sector reasonable returns are along these lines:

Low trading volatility — 10% — usually includes most blue chips

Mid-range trading volatility — 20% to 50% — often stocks in the mid-cap grouping, the so-called green chips

High trading volatility — 50% to 100% plus — usually stocks with low capitalisation

The actual tradeable moves may be greater, but on average these classes of stock, based on trading volatility, offer price movements in these ranges.

Deciding which class of stock each of the selected trading opportunities belongs to determines if our profit levels are within reasonable expectations. Without this decision it is impossible to set financial objectives and the trading plan is incomplete.

Setting financial objectives is based on the spreadsheet calculations and chart analysis, but ultimately it is a judgement call. Judgement does not mean we make a decision on the day when profits look good. This is a perfectly sound plan in theory, but in practice we rationalise, we quibble, we hang on, and ultimately, all too often, hand back substantial chunks of the profit. When we reach judgement day we often discover we do not really have a plan beyond avarice.

Plotting Trading Volatility

Judgement calls are made before the trade is opened and are based on chart analysis. The first set of estimated figures is drawn from here. The upper parameters of the judgement call with DMR are set by the resistance level at

$0.13. This offers a gross 24% return. The profit calculations in Figure 14.3 brought this closer to reality by including brokerage, indicating a 21% return.

The final judgement is based on the weekly bar chart. Our example is chosen for charting simplicity so the placement of the trading band using support and resistance is clear-cut. Similar bands are drawn on every chart of our trading candidates. Like a trendline, the lines are placed to encompass a significant section of the price extremes. Unlike a trendline, our objective is to identify those areas where a trade entry or exit is most realistically possible. This is rarely at the extremities.

The Fosters Brewing (FBG) weekly bar chart in Figure 14.4 shows the difference in the two plots. The upper and lower thin lines are correctly-plotted trendlines. They touch the maximum number of extreme price moves defining the limits of trending activity. The thicker lines define trading volatility showing the best fit to identify the four realistically achievable trades. Each is marked by arrows and returns about 10%. In contrast, only a single trade based on the trendline extremities was possible in the same period. This is shown as X-X.

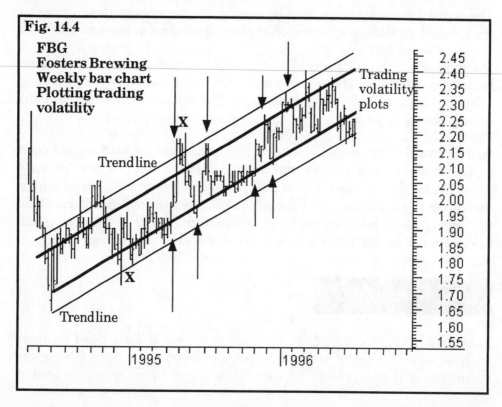

How many times in a year is it reasonably possible to take a trade between the lower and upper sections of the trading band? The answer not only shows the trading opportunities, but also the trading volatility.

The DMR chart in Figure 14.1 shows how these comparison figures are obtained for DMR PLANNED. The entry is at $0.105 and exit at $0.13. The first trading opportunity marked by A-a developed over three weeks. These are 'at best' estimates derived from the latest possible entry and the earliest possible exit. The second, B-b, at best, took four weeks. The third and fourth, C-c and D-d, again at best, took two weeks. These trades potentially return 21% over an average 2.75 week period. For our example we stay with this average, but understand this is deceptively clear-cut.

The time spans must match reality. The time of exit is accurate on the chart and in trading terms when advance sell orders are placed at the target level. Timing the entry is not as precise, so additional time is added to reflect the reality of market timing. On average if you were taking these trades, would you have entered one day, several days, or weeks, before the upleg began? The answer depends on your trading style. Applied consistently it lengthens the average time span for the trade.

Using the 'at best' solution for each trade, the calculations provide a measure of comparison. They do not tell us how long each trade will take in the real market.

The time in the market for DMR PLANNED compares sharply with the DMR GREED calculations which beckon with a 30% profit. These are shown as A-1, C-2 and D-3. The chart puts these better returns into perspective. Although the first trade was initially achievable in a three-week period, the next best was six weeks, followed by nine weeks. This is an average of six weeks required to attain a 30% return, or more than double the average time exposure for DMR PLANNED.

In other words, for an additional 9% the trader is exposed to the market for 3.25 additional weeks. In actual trading terms the result is less favourable. Using 180,000 shares at $0.105 for each of the four trades, DMR PLANNED clears $15,968. Again, using 180,000 shares at $0.105 for each of three trades, DMR GREED clears $17,313 or 8.4% more after brokerage is included. This type of information is easily plotted on the typical time/risk/reward curve in Figure 13.7. These types of comparisons are a useful way of ranking candidates based on trading volatility and they should only be used for this purpose.

Support and resistance levels lend themselves to precise numbering, as does the dollar value of the 2% rule. Putting an absolute figure on trading volatility in the past is achievable, although the precision belies the imprecision of the market. Putting an absolute figure on trading volatility in the future has no better status than an informed guess. The inferred figure is only useful in our calculation of risk because it facilitates comparison and ranking. It does not imply precision.

Hard Numbers

In this final sequence of calculations the inferred risk is a product of time and trading volatility. We will build a spreadsheet formula to deliver a hard reward/time number. Smaller is better, but ultimately this is a judgement call.

Trading volatility is a function of reward and time. Dividing reward by time, expressed as days, produces a single figure used for ranking purposes. The DMR PLANNED reward/time number is 1.1 (19 days/21% return). The DMR GREED number is 1.4 (42 days/30% return). The DMR PLANNED gives a better reward/time result, suggesting this is a better trading strategy based on a more realistic estimation of profit objectives.

Referring back to the Fosters Brewing chart, Figure 14.4, the same calculations also provide hard numbers. Only one trade was possible based on the trading band extremities − X to X. It took 112 days for a 19% return. This gives a reward/time number of 5.8. Trades made using the trading volatility plots shown as thick trendlines produced four trades. Each returned around 10%. The reward/time result is 10.5 (105 days/10% return).

These are hard numbers but they are based on estimated figures derived from subjective judgement about when you would enter and exit an historical trade based on chart plots. The objective is to maximise profits in a way consistent with risk as measured by time exposed to the market. Obviously by narrowing the trading volatility bands we reduce the time − but we also reduce the percentage profit to a meaningless level.

The basis of estimation must be consistent across all examples. Do not mix weekly with daily charts. The results do provide a basis for ranking trade opportunities, but do not confuse this with trading reality. Ultimately this is a judgement call and your trading discipline determines if the call heralds your trading apocalypse.

As a trader you must decide if exposure to the market for twice the time — six vs three weeks with DMR — for a 9% difference in return represents an adequate balance between risk and reward. Your judgement as a trader balances the return against the time and the probability of achieving it considering the class of stock. Trading takes skill as well as sound analysis.

The DMR trade is on the lower end of mid-range trading volatility, but the short time factor reduces risk and makes it attractive. Our profit objective — 21% — is reasonably achievable in a four to six week period. Although the averages said three weeks we suspect a longer period is closer to market reality. This mix sets our financial objective for this trade.

The DMR sell order placed at $0.13, point d on the chart, was filled, satisfying the financial objectives within two weeks. You might think the objectives were too limited. That is OK. This example shows how to set precise exit conditions. Your challenge is to develop exit conditions compatible with your trading style and which lock in consistent profits.

Trading Plan Summary

Good trading is the achievement of financial objectives. These objectives might be limited or extensive, but any trade meeting those objectives is a good trade.

Prices may continue to rise after our exit, but by taking profits at a predefined level in accordance with financial objectives we manage the trade without emotional interference. We are not managed by this trade because we know the objectives before we open the position. Under certain conditions using depth of market information discussed in the next chapter, we might stay with the trade beyond our initial exit point.

Staying with the trade calls for a repeat of the trading calculation to set new financial objectives as rigorous as the first because the only market 'gimme' is a loss. Trading plans do not need to be complex. Four or five lines written on the chart gives more detail than the plans used, or unused, by many traders. When I open a position I print out the chart and write these details on it. The chart and notes are pinned next to my computer for daily reference.

The trading plan for DMR fits easily into a chart margin. As shown at the start of the chapter, it looks like this:

> Stop-loss — $0.095 for $2,000 maximum
>
> Entry conditions — on support
>
> Exit conditions — at resistance or reassess after 6 weeks
>
> Financial objectives — 21% over 4 to 6 weeks

Fig. 14.5

CALCULATING ENTRY, RISK AND REWARD	
Av. brokerage rate	1.20
Total trade equity	100,000
ENTRY DETAILS	
Equity name	DMR
Number of shares	180,000
Purchase price	0.105
Net cost	18,900.00
Av. brokerage	226.80
Full cost	19,126.80
RISK PARAMETERS	
Equity risk @ 2%	2,000.00
Risk on this trade	2,000.00
Stop-loss exit price based on full cost	0.095
Break-even price	0.108
REWARD PARAMETERS	
Sell price (inc brokerage)	0.13
Gross return	23,400.00
Av. brokerage	281
Net return	23,119.20
Clear $$$$	3,992
%%% Return full cost/net return	20.87
%%% Impact on total trading equity	3.99

Each figure, calculated and inferred, provides a ready reference for risk. When each open position is monitored daily these are the figures which count. The full trading calculations combined in a single spreadsheet to show entry, risk, and reward are contained in Figure 14.5. Using this information we are prepared to take action at specific levels. By taking control of our entry and exit we manhandle risk.

Last Standing, Best Dressed

Trading is the active management of risk and our calculations give us a way to rank risk, even if in the final analysis some judgement is involved. When risk inflicts damage on our open position we are better equipped to manhandle it, keeping it at bay and giving us time to make a dignified exit.

Which trading opportunity gets our money? In selecting it is useful to compare the summary trading plans developed for each identified stock. The final selection depends on many factors, but having followed this process in this book the one factor not lacking is adequate planning and analysis.

By applying this rigorous set of financial criteria to the final candidates on our list we further reduce the nuggets to just a few. Whether we take the trading opportunity or not will depend on our cash position. Not every day will turn up a trading opportunity meeting all of our criteria. Not every opportunity will be traded, but by the end of this process the trader knows which ones are most probable, most financially rewarding and he has a clear plan of action for all eventualities.

A well-planned trade does not manage itself. The open position must be monitored each day and the next chapter looks at how depth of market information helps make the entry and the exit more effective.

15

USING DEPTH
OF MARKET

Setting financial targets and objectives is a wasted exercise unless matched with financial reality on the day. Many times the match is perfect. When the match is imperfect our previous analysis allows us to assess the best fit. Based on previous calculations – the trading plan notes – we know immediately how far we can afford to chase our preferred price. Depth of market information hands the private trader tools to hone this trading edge.

Depth of market gives a glimpse of future intentions by permitting us to verify conclusions based on our chart analysis. It is a link with market reality, both prior to the entry and at the exit. This information is readily available in Australia. In US markets the information is considered to be commercially confidential. It is available, but usually only at considerable cost. It is an important advantage for Australian private traders, and better traders make full use of this to level the playing field.

Depth of market information is different from the current bid and ask provided in the newspapers and by some Internet providers. This shows the price at which the last trade was completed and the current bid and ask above and below the traded price. The bid is the amount the current buyer is prepared to pay. The ask is the amount the seller is asking for his stock. In the US this is called the offer. A trade takes place when the buyer and the seller agree on price.

This bid and ask information is basic to understanding the current state of the market for the security you are trading. Many Internet providers, such as Parklane and the Ozemail Stockwatch service, supply this basic information and the examples below are based on the Parklane format. The information is also available from your broker and is very useful because it gives us immediate clues about the enthusiasm of the market.

The bid and ask details for YDN shown in Figure 15.1 show an active market. The buyer's bid is the same as the last traded price, and the seller's ask is only one tick above it. Six buyers are chasing one seller. The spread of 1¢ is as close as possible under the ASX trading rules for stocks trading at this value. Compared to the previous close, prices are up by 4¢.

Compare this quickly with the same screen for GDC in Figure 15.2. Here five sellers are offering stock at the same price as the last trade, but the single buyer will only pay 2¢ below the last traded price. The spread between the bid and ask is 2¢ on a stock that has already fallen 5¢ from the previous close.

Fig. 15.1
Using the bid and ask to track buying pressure

ASX Code	**YDN**	
Last Sale	19-Aug-97 10.54	
Last Sale @	**1.62**	
Change since close		**0.04**

Today	Buyers	**6@1.62**
	Sellers	**1@1.63**
	Open	**1.59**
	High	**1.62**
	Low	**1.59**
	Volume	**1,187,846**
Yesterday	Close	**1.58**
	Volume	**2,976,119**

Fig. 15.2
Using the bid and ask to track selling pressure

ASX Code	GDC	
Last Sale	19-AUG-97 10.42	
Last Sale @	0.027	
Change since close		-0.05

Today	Buyers	1@0.25
	Sellers	5@0.27
	Open	0.27
	High	0.27
	Low	0.27
	Volume	1,000
Yesterday	Close	0.32
	Volume	70,000

With just this basic analysis we know many buyers are chasing YDN, pushing the price up as sellers hold out for better prices. This is upward buying pressure. In contrast, GDC has lots of sellers and very few buyers, creating downward selling pressure. This information alone has an impact on our trading decision.

If we hold stock it is a good day to sell YDN as prices move towards our sell point. If we want stock, then GDC offers better opportunities. With so many sellers of GDC stock it is better to wait for even lower prices if we are a buyer. On the other side of the transaction, if we want YDN stock, and the price is within our target calculations, then it is advisable to bid a cent higher to meet the ask. As a seller of GDC it would be wise to meet the bid if we were protecting a stop-loss position.

We will move beyond these simple conclusions to more complex ones built on this base information. These two examples tell us more than just how much we would have to pay to obtain either of these stocks. We could meet the ask in each example, but the consequences would be different. From a trading perspective this helps us to fine-tune our entry, or exit, positions. Before moving on to consider the way traders use full depth of market information we look at ways to make better use of bid and ask screens.

Part-time traders find it difficult to access these screens during the day so ask your broker to provide the same information over the phone. Understanding how to read it and use it will improve your trading.

Reading the Screen

Returning to Figure 15.1, we note there are six buyers but only one seller. This tells us there is more buying pressure than selling pressure. More buyers are chasing fewer sellers.

As this is a snapshot screen, it shows the balance of the market orders at just one time — 10.54 a.m. on August 19. Orders meeting the ask — those entered at market — are instantly matched and traded and do not appear in the order line. If we placed a new order to buy at $1.63 this screen would not show Buyers 1@1.63 and Seller 1@1.63. The screen would show the last sale @ 1.63. The 6 Buyers at 1.62 would remain in place and the next seller, perhaps at 1.64, would be added.

This screen does not show the sequence of trades, but this information about the unexecuted bid and ask orders is useful. With only one seller at $1.63 we know we can get stock by raising our bid by 1 cent from $1.62. We know if we take all the stock on offer at $1.63 then the next seller is likely to be at the same price, or a few cents higher.

This buying decision is driven by fear. If nobody is offering stock at lower prices, then an entry at $1.63 is cheap compared with the other asking prices in the market above $1.63. In this type of market it is almost certain one of the six buyers, afraid of missing out, will bid higher to be sure of getting stock. He may be beaten to it by another trader who meets the ask. The fear of missing out in a rising stock encourages traders to jump the line and bid up.

Potential sellers are also driven by greed. After checking the market price they are more likely to hold out for higher prices at $1.63 or above, knowing if the worst happened they could always sell to any of the six buyers at $1.62.

This is the logic of the market. Buyer and seller must agree on price and when all the stock available at a particular price level has been purchased then the price will move in the direction of the most frightened participant. With YDN fear rides beside the buyers. After all, if you had YDN would you sell it at $1.63 knowing there are six buyers chasing you and the price has already increased 4¢ since yesterday's close? Often we do not have to sell, so surfing ahead of buying pressure is very profitable.

Of course, the logic applies in reverse, as shown with the GDC screen in Figure 15.2. Here five sellers chase one buyer for a stock that gapped down 5¢

on the open. The potential buyer waits, confident a seller will weaken, lowering his price just to get rid of the stock. This selling decision is driven by fear. Many of the sellers are worried the buying will dry up, and if it does, they will be left holding stock. In this situation, somebody gets frightened first, and they lower their asking price to meet the bid.

For buyers, patience is likely to be rewarded as sellers become increasingly desperate. The difference in the spread, 2¢, as well as the uneven number of orders on each side of the bid and ask provides the information to support this conclusion.

Unfortunately, this snapshot of the emotional balance of the market at this single point in time can be misleading. The battle between those closest to the last traded price might not necessarily be representative of the overall campaign. For the position trader, the battle is interesting, but we really look for a wider campaign perspective.

What is particularly useful is not just the number of buyers and sellers at the level nearest to the last traded price, but the number of buyers and sellers at levels below and above the last traded price. When this is supplied with full and detailed volume information we have a gold-mine of market advantage. Not only do we make better judgements about the potential course of trades today, but we also use this information to confirm our chart analysis.

Mining Deep Markets

Armed with financial calculations and a clear knowledge of how much we are prepared to pay, or sell for, we do battle with the market. The bid information about GDC is useful, but what is below and above the current bid and ask? Are these orders a temporary phenomena, or are they indicative of a wider selling campaign? To find the answer we need full depth of market information. The most obvious advantage of this information is that it prevents us buying at $0.25 when the next buyer is at $0.23 or less. Depth of market allows us to fine-tune our trading — and also to occasionally outsmart ourselves.

The full depth of market information is shown in Figures 15.3 and 15.4. This is the screen behind the market information shown in Figures 15.1 and 15.2. This type of information is available from Parklane and other Internet-based providers. Some brokerage firms, such as Todd Partners, now provide clients with this access in real time updated screens. The same information is available on any SEATs screen and your broker should be able to read it to you, or fax a copy on request. The screen layouts are much the same as these examples.

The depth of market information gives details of each bid and ask at each price level. It also lists the number, the size and position of orders in line at each level. The buy orders closest to the Buy column are the first orders in line at each level and will be executed in this exact sequence. Orders remain in place until filled or withdrawn. Sell orders closest to the sell column are the first executed.

This new information represents only the potential for price action because not all these orders will be filled during the day. As prices move in one direction or another, the gaps in price levels may be filled with new orders. Someone may choose to place a new buy order at $1.57, for instance. During the day the number of orders at any level may swell as people join the rush. They also fall away as traders cancel their market orders, and perhaps place them at new levels, or leave the market entirely.

And of course, the most important caveat of all, what you see here is not what you will see in one hour's time, or in two days' time. But all this said, these figures provide a remarkably useful guide for trading activity, and they support chart analysis in some very interesting ways considered below.

Many traders and investors use standing, or good till cancelled, orders and this gives a unique character to the Australian market. Orders at specific price levels are lodged early and remain in place for extended periods. Unless instructed otherwise, many brokers leave orders in place for three days before they automatically expire. These semi-permanent orders provide an outline of the structure of the market and help us to identify the bulges in the balance of probability.

Going Up

In mining this depth of market information the first nugget is the number of buyers and sellers. The second nugget is the order volume. It's all very well to know there are six buyers and one seller for YDN but having decided our trading opportunity lies in an entry with YDN then additional volume information helps fine-tune the entry.

Fig. 15.3

Depth of market, buying pressure, typical example

YDN Last sale 1.62

		Qty	BUY	SELL	Qty		
6,300	3,050	250,000	1.62	1.63	3,097		
*0	30,000	27,741		1.64	16,900	30,000	
		100,000	1.61	1.65	25,000		
	100,000	100,000	1.60	1.67	12,000	50,000	
		200,000	1.59	1.68	2,200	25,000	3,300
100,000	1,900	5,000	1.58	1.71	2,537	8,520	10,000
		1,000			5,000	2,000	5,000
23,111	100,000	3,000	1.56		19,000	10,000	2,000
	*0	6,000	1.55		13,500	5,000	25,000
		4,000	1.54		4,000	10,329	7,300
		2,000	1.52		5,000	3,500	4,500
4,000	20,000	2,000	1.51		10,000	4,500	3,300
					4,000	6,000	700
				1.72	25,000	6,000	
				1.73	25,000		
				1.75	5,000	10,000	20,000

The six buyers want at least 317,091 shares. The order marked *0 is for an undisclosed quantity. The seller has only 3,097 to sell. Unless many more sellers come into the market at current prices then buyers will not be satisfied at this current level. Most will miss out on stock. This in itself suggests rising prices as buyers outbid each other to chase scarce stock.

Moving down the depth of market screen gives additional advantages by showing the buyers and sellers at each level. Traders looking to buy YDN draw seven conclusions from Figure 15.3:

(a) There are consistently large orders at every level below $1.62 down to $1.51.

(b) Some of these buyers are certain to become fearful and move their bid prices up towards the last traded price. This will swell the buying orders at higher levels.

(c) Only two price slots — $1.57 and $1.53 — do not have buy orders. An order placed in either of these gaps would be first in line and first filled if prices fell to this level.

(d) Placing a new order at $1.61, or $1.59, puts us second in line. This is only useful should prices fall to this level.

(e) To get to the front of every line we need to meet the ask at $1.63.

(f) If we want more than 3,097 shares then we may have to bid to $1.64 to get our entire order filled.

(g) The selling activity at $1.71 comes from many small orders. This suggests small traders rather than institutions. The larger order size on the buying side suggests large traders and experienced market participants. This conclusion is based on the assumption that size tends to equal experience. As Elder writes in *Trading for a Living*, "Big money didn't get big by being stupid."

Let's take a closer look at how this works to give traders an advantage. Assume the first buyer in line at $1.62 desperately wants 250,000 shares, for whatever the reason. It may be that 250,000 rounds out his existing portfolio, or it may represent a dollar value he is prepared to commit to the market. If this is the case then the size of his order, 250,000 shares, will decrease as the price increases.

To fill his order in this market on current figures he must pay at least $1.64. A more likely outcome is that he will take out the existing sell orders between $1.63 and $1.68, including some orders at $1.71 to ensure he gets the number of shares he wants. His alternative is to wait until more sellers come into the market at $1.63, which is unlikely when prices are rising.

What will this buyer do? In a market where there are many other buyers he is going to have to bid up or run the risk of missing out entirely. During the day he is likely to move his bid price up. When we compare today's depth of market information with yesterday's it is quite common to see the same orders move up the bidding scale over several days.

Sellers and potential sellers watch this action and use it to fine-tune their tactics.

Traders chasing this stock and looking to enter a new buy order will meet the ask at $1.63 knowing three things:

(a) The large buying orders at $1.62 provide a floor for prices, making our purchase safer.

(b) By meeting the ask we go straight to the head of the line and get a position in the stock.

(c) Prices have already risen by 4¢, and the large orders, if they are to be filled, will push the bidding higher.

Using this information confirms the shift of the balance of probability in the trader's favour on this day. If every other analytical tool screams buy at $1.61 this depth of market information tells us it is unlikely we will get stock at this price. If our financial analysis allows us to chase price to $1.65 then we shift the day's balance of probability in our favour by meeting the ask.

Traders looking to sell existing YDN stock have the opportunity to get a better exit. As prices move up many sellers back away, lifting their asking prices a few ticks above the current trade. With plenty of buyers chasing them they can afford to be coy. The large order flow blocks further price rises at $1.71, but any sell order placed at $1.66, $1.69 or $1.70 is first in line. These points represent better selling opportunities — but only if they also lock in profits based on previous financial calculations.

Had these calculations indicated $1.71 as the best sell point then it is now too late to place the order. With over 170,000 on offer at this level even an enthusiastic market is going to have a little trouble swallowing the volume. A better exit is at $1.70 in front of the selling pressure. This is selling into strength and guarantees order execution.

Going Down

Essentially the same types of trading conclusions are drawn from Figure 15.4, but in reverse. The selling order overhang of 64,143 tells buyers they can get their desired number of shares any time, just by bidding a cent or two higher. There is no pressure on the buyers to bid up. Prices have dropped 5¢ since yesterday's close and the volume on offer is nearly the same — 64,143 compared to 70,000 sold yesterday.

Fig. 15.4
Depth of market, selling pressure, typical example

GDC Last sale 0.027							
		Qty	BUY	SELL	Qty		
		30,000	0.25	0.27	15,000	16,000	10,000
		15,000	0.23		19,143	4,000	
		48,626	0.20	0.28	4,000	19,885	144
15,000	19,885	10,000	0.17		3,000	6,970	1,620
	10,000	30,000		0.29	10,000	4,000	1,080
					19,000	16,000	3,000

By waiting, there is a good chance the sellers will lower their price. With so many shares on offer the supply obviously outstrips the demand. Buyers don't need to jump ahead in the line because there is so much scrip on offer that nobody is in a hurry.

The seller looks pessimistically at Figure 15.4. Unless he is very close to the front of the order line at $0.27 there is a low probability of getting out. With at least fifteen traders behind him stretching back to $0.29 it is certain one of them will act decisively to cut their losses by meeting the bid at $0.25. Then the entire sell order structure is likely to cascade towards $0.25.

With such heavy selling in place it is difficult to ask $0.26 and have it filled, even though this new order goes to the front of a new line. When prices are falling it is difficult to entice buyers to bid up by lowering the ask to the mid-point between the current bid and ask. Better not to quibble when the depth of market looks like this. Meet the bid and get out at, or just beyond, your stop-loss points.

The buyer sees Figure 15.4 in an entirely different light. For the trader placing a new order the danger is the buyer at $0.25 will see the market depth, pull his order out, and re-insert it somewhere between $0.23 and $0.17. When markets fall, buyers retreat in front of the selling pressure, realising they do not have to pay as much as they originally estimated. An initial buy order, first in line, could be comfortably placed at $0.18, and monitored closely.

This bid increases only if more buyers flood in at higher levels, or if sellers refuse to lower their ask. This is a waiting game where the buyer holds the upper hand. Depth of market information allows the trader to see how best to implement his trading decision on the day.

Cryptic Notations

The most exciting notation to appear on the depth of market screen is *0 — meaning undisclosed. There are a number of reasons for a buyer or seller to request his order be placed as *0, but the most common is because he does not wish to give away the size. Such orders are often very large — so large that they will have a significant impact on the operation of the market. As a buyer, if there is a *0 order below me I am comfortable because I know this will often act as a cushion against falling prices if it is confirmed by chart analysis.

As a seller, I am less comfortable with an *0 order below my intended exit point. Such an order suggests the market is going to have a hard time gobbling up all the shares on offer at lower levels before reaching my sell target. Such *0 orders do not invalidate my sell, but they do tell me patience had better be a profitable virtue.

Undisclosed orders do not have to be large. Traders use *0 for many reasons, including a desire for anonymity if they are using more than one broker. It is unwise to assume an *0 order is large without any supporting evidence, such as the proximity to a support or resistance level noted previously on a chart. This is discussed below.

Mining deep markets gives an advantage that bid and ask information alone cannot match. Access to this type of screen, either as a snapshot or in real time updated live feed, more than pays for the costs of Internet access.

Too Few, Too Late

Although an entry at a specified price level may be very desirable on every level of analysis, it must be assessed against daily reality by looking at the number of sellers and buyers at that level. An ideal TARGET TRADE is shown in Figure 15.5, with entry at $2.15 on good support. Exit is planned at $2.60 for an 18% return.

Often when price drops to the support level only a few shares change hands. We may have wanted 10,000, but only picked up 100 before the price reversed and climbed.

Now we have an uncomfortable dilemma, shown in the right-hand column of Figure 15.5 headed ACTUAL TRADE. One hundred shares is not enough to make the trade worthwhile. On one hand this is a satisfactory result because our analysis has proven correct with prices falling to the selected level. On the other hand we cannot profit from this because we hold too few shares to make the trade viable.

With only 100 shares, the financial status of the trade is destroyed. The break-even point, assisted by minimum brokerage for such a small trade, blows out from $2.20 to $2.68 — above the original planned exit price. To get an 18% return we look for sales at $3.65. This is highly unlikely.

Fig. 15.5

TARGET TRADE VS REALITY		
Av. brokerage rate	1.20	
Total trade equity	100,000	
EQUITY DETAILS		
Equity name	TARGET TRADE	ACTUAL TRADE
Number of shares	10,000	100
Purchase price	2.15	2.15
Net cost	21,500.00	215.00
Av. brokerage	258.00	50.00
Full cost	21,758.00	265.00
RISK PARAMETERS		
Equity risk @ 2%	2,000.00	2,000.00
Risk on this trade	1,800.00	1,800.00
Stop-loss exit price based on full cost	2.00	-17.35
Break-even price	2.20	2.68
REWARD PARAMETERS		
Sell price (inc brokerage)	2.60	3.65
Gross return	26,000.00	365.00
Av. brokerage	312.000	50.00
Net return	25,688.00	315.00
Clear $$$$	3,930	50.00
%%% Return full cost/net return	18.06	18.87
%%% Impact on total trading equity	3.93	0.05

Our choices are to stay with the trade and unload the 100 shares perhaps months later at break-even. Or we chase the price, building the position to an economic size while at the same time shifting the goalposts. Every parcel bought at a higher price lifts the break-even level. If we still want the original 18% return then our preferred exit price moves upwards and beyond the price targets initially based on the better balance of probability. When this happens the probability of success diminishes as we buy deeper and deeper into the mire.

At these times it is preferable to exit the position as rapidly as possible, take the loss, and reallocate the capital to better trading opportunities.

There are two ways to avoid this uncomfortable dilemma. The first, already discussed above, is front-running the order stream by placing orders ahead of size to ensure our order is filled as discussed above. Effectively this places our buy order just above current support and our sell just below current resistance.

The second way makes use of the average order size to ensure our orders are filled.

Making the Market

A better use of depth of market information helps the trader to avoid this embarrassing situation where he is both right and ruined. We make even better use when we turn away from the screen and grab the latest company report, the *Register of Australian Mining*, the *AFR Shareholder* or similar publications.

We look for the number of shareholders. A small company, Bendigo Mining, might have 2,398. Ashton Mining, on the upper edge of the mid-sized range has 10,984 compared with 70,499 shareholders for MIM. Add to this the number of shares controlled by the top 20 shareholders and we develop a three-dimensional market picture. The top 20 hold 70% of Bendigo Mining, 82% of Ashton, and 69% of MIM. The top 20 shareholders are often funds and institutions with investment-style holdings. Most of the time these shares are not for sale. We get to trade the rest and this determines appropriate order size against which we evaluate the screen information.

The volume, or order size, information allows us to assess the probability of our order being filled. We plan our exposure to the stock based on the average order size within the context of shares available for trading. If our order is too large the market will not be able to digest it. Instead of working with the market, we run the danger of becoming the market, creating new support or resistance levels just by the very size of our orders.

We avoid this by taking the average size of orders at and near our preferred entry price. This average order size should match the capital we plan to commit to this trade. If we cannot get a position with the size we want, then although the trade may be worthwhile by all our other chart and financial criteria, it may be physically impossible to execute in the market.

If average order size over the past five or six weeks is 100,000 then this sets our maximum order size. The proposed trade must be financially successful within these parameters. That is, if the trade cannot meet our financial criteria based on an order size of 100,000 or less, then it must be rejected. This figure is inserted into the Number of Shares cell on the trading calculation sheet and financial objectives adjusted accordingly.

In deciding the order size we use depth of market information to establish the number of buyers at the support level, or our entry level, and the number of shares they want. A single buyer who wants 60,000 destroys our chances of getting 1,000 at the same price if we are last in line where average turnover is 1,000 a day. The same applies when there are many small orders in front of us.

Larger than average orders can be filled, but they take time. Stocks test and retest support levels. This process defines these levels. Although individual volumes at these points may be small, they are often sufficient to nibble away at a larger buy or sell order over time. I have completed several trades where my large sell order was taken out 100 to 200 shares at a time, day after day. This is difficult trading but if selling is consistent then the trader may feel more comfortable in taking the risk of having his order filled over several days, or sometimes even weeks.

By matching our order size with the average order size we increase our chances of being filled. When there is a problem in having an order filled the trader must factor this into his risk assessment when it comes to evaluating the potential for the trade.

Validating Chart Analysis

Depth of market information provides valuable tactical intelligence, but just as importantly, it provides a way to validate chart analysis. The core of our stop-loss strategy is that they ought to coincide with logical chart support levels. This is not a theoretical exercise. It should be validated using actual buy and sell order behaviour.

Validation is a three-step process, starting with basic chart analysis.

Normandy Mining (NDY) is the basis of this example. With smaller stocks, the features are more marked. With larger stocks high liquidity and order flow blur the certainty, but in all cases the correlations illustrated below do exist. These correlations give validity to our chart analysis in particular, and to market charting approaches in general.

The first step is chart-based. Experienced traders will quickly note the two salient features of the NDY daily bar chart in Figure 15.6. Apparently tenuous support is at $1.45, but this is also a long-term support level in 1995 and 1996. Fairly substantial resistance is indicated at $1.64/$1.65.

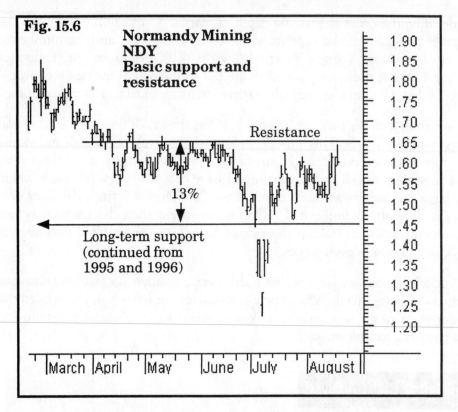

Fig. 15.6

Normandy Mining
NDY
Basic support and
resistance

Resistance

13%

Long-term support
(continued from
1995 and 1996)

March April May June July August

This is by no means sophisticated analysis, although it indicates a 13% return between the bands. As traders we might want to explore the behaviour of NDY at greater depth using the tools discussed in previous sections. However, in setting potential profit targets and stop-loss points, we invariably return to support and resistance levels in one form or another.

The second step in validating this chart analysis is to look at the depth of market. This comes with some fine print which we consider later. This validation is possible because under SEATS, unexecuted orders remain in place across multiple trading sessions. We do use the snapshot figures for tactical purposes, but this consistency over time means major orders tend to remain in place until executed. Like a dotted centreline on a road at night, they outline the shape of the curve.

Order flow is uneven, as shown in Figure 15.7. Some price levels have more individual orders, or order volume than others. These order bulges tend to coincide with the support levels identified on the NDY chart. The first major bulge in the depth of market buy figures is at $1.45. Where orders extend over several rows, as with $1.45, the bulge is obvious. It is less so when a single big order takes less screen space.

Fig. 15.7   Verifying depth of market and chart analysis

NDY Last sale 1.62							
		Qty	BUY	SELL	Qty		
	40,000	10,000	1.61	1.62	5,000	3,800	
	87,018	40,000	1.60	1.63	2,064	70,000	10,000
		200,000	1.59		90,000	30,000	17,000
100,000	1,900	5,000	1.58	1.64	5,899	30,000	10,000
23,111	100,000	3,000	1.56		15,000	12,000	50,000
		4,000	1.54		34,000	15,000	4,500
		2,000	1.52	1.65	10,000	2,537	8,520
	4,000	2,000	1.51		5,000	5,000	2,000
30,000	2,000	3,500	1.48		2,000	19,000	10,000
6,000	10,000	14,000	1.46		25,000	13,500	5,000
2,000	10,000	3,000	1.45		7,300	4,000	10,329
50,600	3,500	14,000			4,500	5,000	3,500
2,500	10,000	5,000			3,300	10,000	4,500
2,500	30,000	3,500			700	4,000	6,000
5,000	50,000	30,000			7,000	50,000	3,800
		1,000			8,000	42,000	
				1.66	25,000	4,000	

As the third step it is convenient to display this information in a consolidated format as a bar chart, shown in Figure 15.8. The Internet provider Parklane provides a similar format and it is a particularly useful way of matching chart confirmation.

Using either display format the trader calculates the average order size from $1.61 down to $1.46 at 32,739. The orders in place at $1.45 total 222,600. This massive block of buy orders, if left in place, provides firm support should NDY prices retreat.

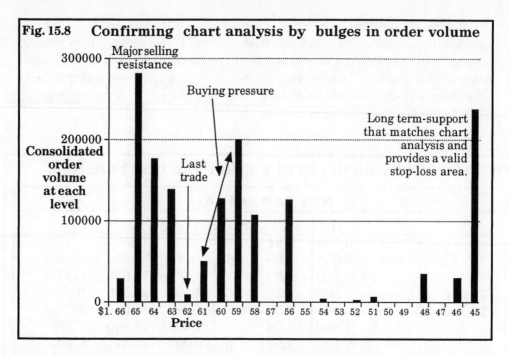

Fig. 15.8 **Confirming chart analysis by bulges in order volume**

This is the support level identified on the bar chart in Figure 15.6 and the large number of orders here are exactly where we expect them to be. This validates our chart understanding, and the placement of the support lines on the bar chart.

This is not just a coincidence in this hand-picked perfect example. It is a correlation repeated frequently across the market and it consistently provides the trader with important confirming evidence.

For the trader who had already taken a position in NDY and based his stop-loss on the support level at $1.45, this depth of market information confirms his risk control strategy. If prices do fall to this level, then the number of buyers gives the trader a better chance of making an exit at his preferred stop-loss level. This is as close to safety in the market as the trader gets.

Upside Instability

Alas, the mother lode of information delivered by the depth of market screen thins out on the upper side. The same techniques can be used to establish and confirm resistance levels but they do not work as well. With NDY we anticipated substantial resistance around $1.64/$1.65 and would expect this to be shown with an increased order flow. This is confirmed with 29 sellers at $1.65. Smart traders have begun to cluster at $1.64, just ahead of the main resistance level.

Superficially, our analysis is verified. However, when people become sellers rather than buyers they take a different approach to value. Writing in *Against the Gods*, Bernstein discusses an example of the endowment effect of ownership. Students were given a coffee mug to keep. Later they were asked to set the lowest price they would be willing to accept for the mug. Another group of students were shown the same mugs and asked to nominate the highest they were prepared to pay. On average, mug owners wanted $5.25 while potential buyers would pay no more than $2.25.

The same endowment effect takes place in the market and makes using depth of market for resistance level calculations less certain. What we bought today for $1.45 we will not sell for $1.45. We buy in expectation of profit, so from the very first moment of ownership, we add a margin for this to the future resale price. This is reasonable, but we become unreasonable as the price increases, holding out for a higher price. This reaction is driven by what we think we can get.

For our purposes as traders this means the resistance levels indicated on the depth of market information are much more fluid than the support levels. Greed keeps moving the bar upwards. Fear pushes it downwards. Significant price points are established in the market, and they often persist, but there is many a slip betwixt the ask and the sale.

Freeze Frame Caution

The market is full of annoying fine print and depth of market information is no exception. Always remember it represents a snapshot of market emotions at a particular point in time. Markets change, and sometimes they change rapidly. Orders can be withdrawn, or re-entered at higher or lower prices. This is the dynamic of the market, jumping onto the bull and off the bear. Intra-day traders use real-time depth of market information to initiate the trading process.

Position traders are less active in the market, making their initial trading decision after the market closes and after the end of day data has been collected. Position traders turn to depth of market information to confirm chart analysis, or to fine-tune an entry or exit. When we use this information it is at the end of the process.

From all this daily, hourly and by-the-minute froth and bubble in the market, certain points of ongoing stability emerge. Frequently they coincide with major points established by chart analysis. When depth of market information does so, it acts as additional confirmation. When it does not support chart analysis, then the charts may need to be re-examined. In the trading world, the market rules. When depth of market is used as a confirming indicator it provides a valuable adjunct to trading decisions.

Ready access to full depth of market information is a distinctly Australian advantage. Just as learning to read a bar chart is a most valuable skill, learning to mine the depth of market information pays trading dividends. Depth of market gives us a glimpse of future intentions so we have the opportunity to match financial targets with market reality.

16

A LEVER TO LIFT

THE WORLD

A rchimedes reputedly said *"Give me a lever and but one firm spot on which to stand and I will move the earth."* When he retired and became a trader he changed this to "Give me a warrant and but one firm analysis on which to stand and I will lift my profit."

Our selected trading candidates provide more than adequate returns, but we have an additional choice before entering the market. A select number of stocks have warrants available for trading. If they appear on our trading list we can choose to put a rocket under our chart analysis, taking leveraged returns from both rising and falling prices. Many equity traders use the speculative end of the market — the gold juniors in particular — to take advantage of leverage. Here prices are low and it is comparatively easily to lift them on a gust of market enthusiasm, or crash them with a whisper. In *Share Trading* we looked at some useful trading and money management techniques designed to give us safe access to this leverage. Here we buy warrants to take advantage of leverage.

In this chapter we briefly investigate warrants as a derivative product delivering similar leverage but without the purely speculative element because they are based upon more stable, and usually more staid, market performers. New warrants are issued regularly and are currently (November 1997) based on about 40 stocks.

The warrant tracks the underlying share, but unlike the share, has a defined life span. It is very generous of warrant issuers to offer us an opportunity for leveraged entry into these stocks so it is important to understand their motivation. There is a home for charity, but it is not normally under the portals of the Exchange.

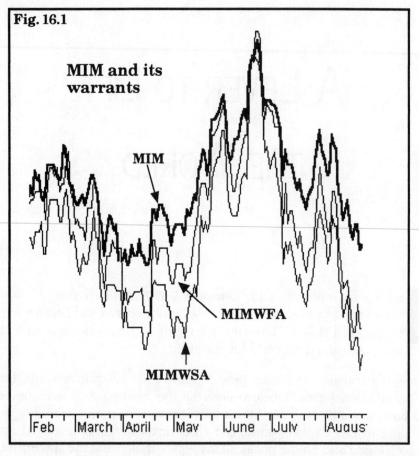

Fig. 16.1

MIM and its warrants

MIM

MIMWFA

MIMWSA

Feb | March | April | May | June | July | August

What interests us here is the way call and put warrants give leverage, rather than any of the other more sophisticated ways of trading them. We want to use our chart analysis as a trigger. While the warrant is 'long dated' with an expiry nine months or more away, it is traded almost in the same way as its underlying stock. Often it rises and falls in unison as shown in Figure 16.1. Here the line chart of closing prices for MIM is placed over the closing price line chart of two of its associated call warrants, MIMWFA and MIMWSA. The scale is deliberately removed to emphasise price unity.

Before surrendering totally to greed please note that our trading decisions are based on the MIM chart, not on the warrant charts.

The trading advantages discussed below use trading leverage rather than the opportunities offered by exercising the warrant to take up the underlying shares. This is not intended to be a full discussion of warrants and readers looking for wider information will find it in the ASX publication *Understanding Warrants*. Should you decide to trade warrants your broker will require you to sign an acknowledgement that you have read and understood this publication. There are also frequent articles about warrants in *Shares* magazine.

Leverage attracts our interest and taking advantage of this observation requires a greater understanding of warrants. Before considering MIM further we will cover some old ground littered with fundamental definitions, important because they determine trading tactics. Readers familiar with warrants should skip to the section Leverage At Last.

On a Promise

Warrants are a growing class of financial products including investment, endowment and capital plus varieties. In this chapter we only deal with call and put warrants. A warrant, like its close cousin an option, is a financial derivative or manufactured product which owes its existence to an underlying security. A warrant has three components:

1 *The exercise price and entitlement on exercise*

This is the price and number of shares the issuer agrees to supply for the warrant. Entitlement varies, with some warrants converting into a single share while others convert to half or quarter of a share so check carefully. Index-based warrants are settled in cash. American-style warrants can be exercised at any time up to the expiry date. European-style are only exercised on expiry.

2 *The premium*

The upfront price we pay for the warrant. Bid and ask prices are quoted on the brokers SEATs screen and are available through Internet providers such as Park Lane. End of day information is listed in *The Australian* and other newspapers.

3 *The expiry date*

Like a carton of milk, this product is unusable after the expiry date.

An important difference between warrants and options is the length of time to expiry. Both derivatives have 'use by' dates and although these can be rolled over it is a more complex strategy than we want to consider here. Chris Temby looks at these approaches in *Trading Stock Options and Warrants*. Long-dated warrants give more time for our plans to come to fruition.

Warrants use a different market structure and are traded on the SEATs screen. Buyers and sellers obtain the same information from depth of market screens as for ordinary shares and their orders directly set the bid and ask. Options were traded on the floor and it was notoriously difficult to get consistently good fills. Options trading has moved to a SEATs-like screen-based trading with automatic matching and this will increase the transparency of options trading.

With these definitions in mind we take a closer look at how they impact on a trading example. We use MIM and its long-dated warrant, MIMWSA.

The exercise price and entitlement

In trading warrants ultimately we buy the issuer's promise to deliver shares at the previously-agreed exercise price. Although we buy and sell as individuals, the derivative product is backed by the issuer's promise. If the MIM warrant has an exercise price of $1.65 then when we pay $1.65 we get the number of shares specified in the warrant. If MIM is trading at $2.10 this is to our advantage.

The premium

Buy a warrant and we buy the right to buy, or sell, the underlying shares. The amount paid for this right is the 'premium' and is usually a fraction of the full price of the shares. On April 14 this right in the MIMWSA warrant was available for $0.23 – the premium – as shown on Figure 16.2. With an exercise price of $1.65 these MIM shares need to reach $1.88 to break even.

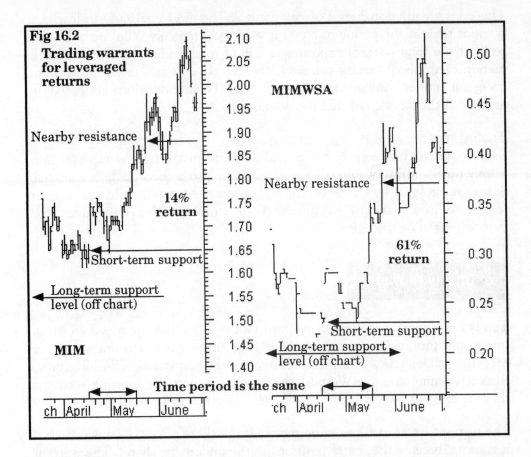

Fig 16.2
Trading warrants for leveraged returns

Nearby resistance

MIMWSA

14% return

Short-term support

Nearby resistance

Long-term support level (off chart)

61% return

MIM

Short-term support

Long-term support level (off chart)

Time period is the same

ch | April | May | June

ch | April | May | June

The 'premium' is a single calculated figure determined on the basis of share price, time to expiry, the terms of issue, the volatility of the underlying shares and other factors. This is not an exact science and traders assign individual values to each of these factors. In the final analysis this translates into a single traded market price encapsulating all these variables. Our choice is either to work out these calculations for ourselves, or just take the 'premium' quoted.

Buy an MIM warrant and we buy the right to demand the warrant provider to supply us with real MIM shares at a previously-agreed value. In return, the warrant provider guarantees to give them to us at the agreed price, no matter what the current market price.

Holding the warrant does not impose an obligation to buy or sell the shares any more than renting a holiday house obligates us to buy it at a later date. Warrants cost us money when we fail to exercise them — to swap them for shares — by the due date. We lose our premium.

This adds an additional level of risk control. The most you stand to lose in a warrant trade is the premium amount you paid originally. You might choose to limit the total warrant exposure to 2% of total trading equity. With this margin established warrant prices are free to move in greater ranges without triggering money management stop-loss exits. Trading decisions are based on analysis of the stock chart, not the warrant chart.

Trading warrants takes the first step across a narrow bridge spanning a financial chasm between the equity and derivative markets. We step over into a sometimes murky swamp of derivative trading so a good guide is essential. Some are explored by Chris Temby and others are listed later in the chapter for those who want to go further with more complex derivatives and derivative trading strategies.

Not Charity I'll Warrant

The warrant market is created by third parties — a select approved group of major institutions permitted to issue warrants. These currently include Macquarie, Deutsche, and ANZ banks, and BT Australia, SBC Warburg, Robert Fleming and NatWest Markets among others. By offering warrants they lay off their own risk by hedging their exposure to the market.

The warrant issuer can lose more money if the share price goes down than if it goes up, because they carry positions in the underlying shares. The warrant is a covered write, although not on a one-for-one basis as they are written only for a proportion of the shares actually held by the issuer.

Think of this as similar to owning a holiday home. During the year it is unused so you rent it out. The ownership of the asset does not change, but you are putting it out to work. An institution may hold a substantial block of shares which, apart from dividends yield, effectively do nothing between purchase and sale. By renting out some of these shares through the issue of warrants the institution puts them to work.

The added bonus is that many warrants expire 'out of the money' and worthless. The institution is not called upon to supply the underlying shares but keeps the premium as a reward for the service it offered. It is a little like keeping the deposit when the couple from Bathurst cancel their two-week booking for your holiday home.

The issue of warrants and options is not done for altruistic purposes. The issuer intends to make a profit, so when trading these derivatives you should remember their cut reduces your profit.

Calling All Puts

Enticing non-linear returns turn our heads, particularly as warrants also provide a way to short the market.

Warrants trade in two varieties — calls and puts. This archaic language comes from the Dutch tulip markets and dates back to the first major speculative boom and bust in 1630. Drawing this language from the period of the Dutch Tulip Mania offers a salutary lesson in itself, but as it is still the language of derivative markets we need to understand it and the way it offers leverage.[1]

A *call* is where we ask the issuer to deliver stock to us at the previously-agreed price. This is a long trading tactic. The exercise price is below the market price, enabling us to convert the warrant to shares, and then sell the shares immediately at a profit.

When we deliver stock to the issuer we *put*, or sell, it to him at the agreed price. Effectively we short the market by demanding the issuer convert our warrants into shares at a higher than current market price.

This is the conventional way to approach warrants, and although useful, does not give the leverage we prize. Leverage does not come from exercising the warrant, but from trading the premium itself.

The difference between a call and put depends on if we are collecting stock — a call — or delivering stock — a put. These often confusing terms hide a powerful leveraged approach to the market. Understanding the outlines of these approaches allows the trader to explore several different ways of making the best use of the chart analysis and selection processes described in earlier sections.

Just as analysis moves from the simple to the complex, so too do the variety of trading alternatives — from equities, to warrants, to options and futures.

---

[1] Readers wishing to understand this mania can turn to standard accounts, *Extraordinary Popular Delusions and the Madness of Crowds*, Charles Mackay, and *The Edge of Chaos*, Benice Cohen or for a more personal perspective look at *The Black Tulip* by Alexander Dumas.

Each bundles leverage and risk together in different ways, most of which are beyond the scope of this chapter. *Options as a Strategic Investment* by Lawrence McMillan, *Option Volatility and Pricing* by Sheldon Natenberg and *The New Option Secret - Volatility* from David Capalan are good starting points.

The Long and Short of Bull and Bear Markets

Our search for trading opportunities has been implicitly based on long side trading — buying low and selling high. This strategy suits bull markets but is applied with greater difficulty to bear markets; it is most familiar to Australian equity traders. Long traders buy low and wait for the price to go up before selling. When these trades move in the same direction as the market, this is a very successful strategy. If the market moves down there is no absolute pressure to sell. Unless the stock is delisted the trader is unlikely to lose all the capital he placed in the stock. This lack of urgency encourages less-skilled traders to remain in losing positions for a very long time.

If we believe the market, or the stock, is going up then call warrants are most suitable. If we believe the market is going down then put warrants provide a way to short the market.

For all intents and purposes it is not possible to short fully-paid ordinary shares in Australia,[2] but without an understanding of the process we cannot take advantage of put warrants. All of the search criteria for finding equity bottoms, discussed in previous sections, are just as easily applied to finding equity tops. This positions the trader to take advantage of trading opportunities to short the market — via warrants.

In an equity market where short selling is permitted, such as the US, traders sell stock borrowed from a third party at current high market prices. Later they plan to buy the shares back and deliver them to the person they borrowed them from. When the market does fall this is also a very successful trading strategy.

If the market moves in the opposite direction they must buy back the shares at higher prices — effectively taking a loss. This 'covers the shorts' and must be done quickly because potential losses are unlimited. Short trading requires excellent discipline and quick footwork. Because the shorted borrowed stock

---

[2] The Senate Standing Committee on Finance is currently investigating the possibility of creating a 'short' market for selected ordinary shares.

must be delivered by a due date the trader cannot wait indefinitely for the market to fall again. Time imposes constraints in equity trading from the short side and in trading put warrants.

Traders buy put warrants to take advantage of the price retreat. Put warrants provide an effective hedge against falling markets in a way that ordinary shares cannot. Warrants overcome most of these equity short-selling disadvantages by limiting dollar risk to the premium paid. The put warrant contract gives the buyer the right to sell a fixed quantity of the underlying security at a stated price. If this is not profitable, then the buyer is under no obligation to complete the sale, and the warrant expires. His loss is limited to the amount he paid — the premium.

Within these basic bull and bear market manoeuvres a range of more sophisticated approaches is available. Aggressive traders who feel stocks are overvalued will attempt to go short hoping to profit from the fall. This is most evident in index-linked trading, such as the SPI contract on the Sydney Futures Exchange. The decision to short a sector index, a market index, or an individual stock is based on the type of chart analysis we covered in earlier chapters.

Time Waits for No Trade

Time decay hurts, and eventually kills with unnerving rapidity. Our strategy is to trade MIM based on its chart activity while using a call warrant as the trading tool. While the warrant has a long time to expiry this is a safe strategy. As the time to expiry draws closer we are hit by time decay. To avoid being killed we must understand this impact.

Buy a call warrant and we buy hope with a time stamp. This trading clock includes an alarm. With one year to expiry we have room to dream, to ride out the dips while looking for the next rally. Our best-laid plans have time to mature, but the clock is ticking quietly. We do not have the luxury of converting this trade to a buy and hold investment.

Six months before the alarm rings there is less room for hope because we have a clearer view of where prices are heading. If the MIM chart is in sustained downtrend we must realistically assess the possibility of recovery. Anyone who is thinking of buying our MIMWSA warrant makes the same calculations. With less time the margin for hope is reduced. The clock ticks louder, reminding all market players.

With perhaps a month to go an 'out of the money' warrant offers very little hope of success. The clock deafens all but the most optimistic. Few traders want to buy something they know will be worthless in a few weeks time. When the alarm goes off – when the warrant expires – those still holding the warrant are left with a certificate attesting to financial foolishness.

Einstein's theory of relativity compresses time, but not as quickly as warrants heading into expiry. As the time for expiry draws near there is less room for hope to lift warrant prices back 'into the money'. Time decay destroys prices, weakening and then breaking the leveraged link between the underlying stock and the warrant. No hard calender numbers exist for this. We cannot arbitrarily say time decay always becomes a problem three weeks from expiry.

The two charts, MIM and MIMWSA in this example, give us important clues to a solution. When the warrant price, MIMWSA, fails to react in the same way to changes in the MIM price, then the link is weakening. In a formal sense this is measured by the delta. This shows the amount the warrant's price will change if the underlying security's price changes by 1. This takes us beyond the leverage strategy we explore here, but when the extent of leverage changes use it as a warning sign that time decay has become significant.

Time decay in all its complexity is discussed in *Trading Stock Options and Warrants*. The success of our leveraged approach rests on avoiding adverse time decay and trading only in the period prior to this. Our exit conditions for warrants include a date as well as financial stop-loss and profit conditions.

Leverage at Last

Look back at Figure 16.1 to remind yourself of the simple observation that long-dated warrants move largely in unison with the underlying share. Remind yourself as well that speculative shares in junior gold explorers offer leverage and problematical liquidity. Bring these two reminders together and you are better placed to see the role warrant trading plays in managing risk while chasing gains of speculative proportions.

MIM is typical of these opportunities, and the left-hand chart in Figure 16.2 shows a bar chart of the underlying security. We use April 14 as our proposed entry point. Without being too complex, and taking advantage of hindsight, this bar chart suggests the following:

(a) Long-term support around $1.55. This is not shown on this chart extract.

(b) Short-term support at $1.65, and buying opportunity.

(c) First profit targets around $1.88 based on nearby resistance.

(d) With the advantage of hindsight, this target was reached on May 26.

This chart provides the basic trigger point for the trading decision. Compare this same time frame with the MIMWSA warrant in the right-hand chart, Figure 16.2. Here we only look for confirmation. The trade is initiated by the MIM analysis. Again a straightforward analysis suggests:

(a) Long-term support around $0.20 matching lowest lows.

(b) Short-term support at $0.23, and buying opportunity.

(c) First profit targets around $0.37 based on nearby resistance.

(d) With the advantage of hindsight, this target was reached on May 26.

The two charts are similar, both yielding to the same style of analysis. This is the first observation of interest, but not surprising. This is a long-dated warrant so please remember the time decay warning. As the warrant expiry date draws closer the warrant chart will place greater weight on time decay factors and less weight on the more typical market reactions.

The second observation pinpoints the leverage and is noted on each chart. The same behaviour in the same time frame delivers massively different returns. This is a substantial trading lever.

In the first chart example an entry at $1.65 and an exit at $1.88 returned 14%.

In the second example, MIMWSA, the warrant entry was at $0.23 and the exit at $0.37. This delivers a 61% return into our trading pockets. This is over four times the return generated by the same move in MIM.

The bar chart analysis swings the balance of probability in our favour but this trading tactic builds a more attractive reward/time outcome. This trading approach builds on all the analysis done to date, but uses the leverage power offered by derivative-style trading to reduce risk and boost returns.

This is a very specific approach to warrant trading using the internal dynamics of the warrant to our advantage. There is no intention of converting the warrant to shares, a strategy suited to other investment styles, but producing poor returns from a trading perspective. Had we done this, the warrant could have been exercised at $1.88 (warrant exercise price, plus premium). A later sale at the very peak of $2.10 represents only 12% return, which although acceptable, does not really put the power of leverage to work.

Adding this leverage works effectively with long-dated warrants before the effects of time decay are felt. There is no intention to trade into the trade time decay period. This calls for quite different methods of analysis, usually relying on high end mathematics with shorthand names like the Black-Scholes Option Pricing Method, or Barone-Adessi-Whaley and Cox/Ross/Rubinstein. This is a valid and exciting field of trading, but quite different from the trading styles discussed in this book. We surrender the field willingly to Chris Tate, *Understanding Options Trading in Australia* and Chris Temby, *Trading Stock Options and Warrants*. We recommend a thorough study of these books should you decide to exploit the option-like trading opportunities offered by warrants as they move towards expiry.

The Bridge and the Chasm

By the end of the last chapter we had identified the very best of our trading nuggets and traded them most efficiently in the market by making the best use of trade planning and market information. The sharemarket is connected to the derivatives market. Many of the techniques, principles and analytical approaches appropriate to the sharemarket apply to these derivative markets and this builds a bridge spanning a financial chasm to connect the two markets. Sometimes our trading nuggets cluster at the other end of the bridge. Here we could trade staid stocks with ho-hum returns and put a rocket under them. This tactic takes us beyond share trading to the edge of a new market.

But there are three important differences that threaten to cast the unwary trader off the narrow bridge and into the chasm. The first is time decay. The second is the way risk mutates, sometimes benignly, as with warrants where risk is limited to the premium. At other times it is malignant, where futures carry unlimited upside and downside risk. The third is trading discipline — particularly on exercising stop loss. Momentary lapses are annoying in the sharemarket, and quickly fatal in the derivatives arena.

The lure of speculative returns is strong and the issuers of warrants know this. Archimedes called for a firm spot to place a lever to shift the world. When you call for a warrant lever make sure the shifting world does not push you off the bridge.

Part IV

FAILURE
IS A
HANDMAIDEN
TO SUCCESS

17

OVER-TRADING

You would think after all this sound analysis, after all the chart examination, and after running the numbers, that trading success is guaranteed. The market failure rate suggests otherwise. This guarantee is not worth the paper it is written on because traders routinely commit financial suicide, often through over-trading, in response to instincts they don't fully understand.

Look in a mirror. It shows the traders' greatest trading enemy — ourselves — but most of us look instead to the computer screen for the culprit. In this section we want to look at some of the more creative excuses for failure — over-trading, inability to take losses, knowing when the market is wrong and gambling. I recognise many of them because I write from my own experience. Learning to look in the mirror is an important step towards trading success.

In this chapter we examine the relationship between how hard we work and how well we are rewarded. Our instinct to look busy — to over-trade —

often costs us a great deal. After losing a million dollars Jim Paul decided the most effective trading approach "if implemented properly, is actually quite boring waiting for your buy and sell criteria to materialise." As private traders it is better to reach the same conclusion as Jim Paul without losing a million dollars. To save money we must learn to recognise when we are over-trading — usually because our wallet allows us — rather than trading with our brains.

Assessing our performance to decide if we are over-trading is made difficult by our accepted understanding of success. For most successful people there is a strong connection between how hard they work and the extent of their reward. Long hours, high levels of stress and frenetic office environments are tolerated because they deliver high pay, relaxing holidays and an upmarket lifestyle. Those who have this also have success. Those who do not have this obviously do not have success.

Success is a relative term. Those who are truly successful apparently no longer have to work. It seems as if there are hurdles placed at an important point in the work/reward equation. Once over the hurdle, the rewards come without apparent effort. These retirees from the shackles of work are admired and we wish to emulate them — either through hard work or luck.

Although these are generalisations, they play an important part in the way we see ourselves and our relationship with reward. In the centuries since Martin Luther hammered his 95 theses to the church door in Wittenberg, the protestant work ethic has gathered an ecumenical following. Trading alters this work/reward relationship in some very important ways because it has the potential to break the nexus between reward and effort. When this happens many novice traders feel uncomfortable and this impacts on their trading, turning success into honest failure.

Trading offers the opportunity of successful non-work and the markets continually lure hopeful novice traders with the hint of reward without too much effort. For the full-time private trader, understanding and adjusting the relationship between work and reward to a personally comfortable level is an important challenge. Incorrectly handled adjustment leads to over-trading and potentially to a retreat from the market. The challenge is also issued to part-time traders, and this tendency to trade with their wallet rather than their brain keeps many of them on the periphery of the market, trapped in a cycle of trading washout and recovery.

Reward Without Effort

There are very few ways to come into riches and wealth without working that are applauded by the general community. Speculative trading is not one of them. Instant millionaires created by Tattslotto, betting on the horses, or by successful gambling in one of the many casinos, are accepted. People are envious, but not scornful. These windfall gains are the result of luck and we feel it could happen to anyone, including ourselves.

This is not wealth without work. It is wealth by luck. The return is not expected to be dependent upon effort because this is a single event. If the win is substantial we retire and live a life similar to those really successful retirees. If the windfall is smaller, we return to work smug in the knowledge that life's little luxuries are no longer out of reach.

Win $30,000 in the lottery and people congratulate you, but make $30,000 in the market and people are suspicious. The difference in reactions is important because it affects the way we approach trading.

To people outside the stock market the private trader appears to have an easy life, working a few hours a day and making substantial returns. The traders of fiction, often loosely based on flamboyant personalities such as Michael Milken or J. P. Morgan, make enormous returns for apparently little work. Professional traders employed by the institutions take home salaries and commissions of telephone-number proportions and all they do is play with computers.

These public perceptions of traders are facile and inaccurate. They do not look beyond the surface gloss to see the amount of research, or analysis, or intellectual effort and emotional discipline required in the trading process. But these opinions cannot be ignored because the novice private trader brings these perceptions to trading, and later to his trading success.

These opinions are reinforced if the novice has some early successes. In return for a few hours of work in his spare time the market might pay him thousands of dollars. For workers whose wages look more like post codes than telephone numbers this return represents substantial money. And it is paid for by so few hours of work — if you can call it work. A bit of extra reading in the financial pages, listening carefully to the hot tip from a friend or broker, or perhaps just a lucky guess in a bull market. Hardly work dictated by a boss, supervised by a clock and assessed against the number of voluntary and unpaid overtime hours.

At this early stage the novice trades in a way that is very close to gambling in many aspects. It is like an expensive lottery ticket, and sometimes the process is not much different. Real problems emerge when the novice decides to becomes more actively involved. Taking a real lottery ticket for a few dollars each week is one thing. Taking new positions in the market is an act of a completely different order. Not only is it much more expensive, but it is also based on the assumption that consistent rewards can be gained in return for less work than our peers.

The prospect of large rewards for very little work is the initial appeal of the market for many traders.

Reward With Little Effort

Is this possible, and if it is, then how is this possible? In answering these questions it is more helpful to start at the end and work backwards. How much time does the full-time trader spend in front of the screen? How many trades are completed in a year? These answers translate into hours worked.

By way of example let's consider an apparently modest ambition. We have $20,000 and we complete one trade every two weeks for 52 weeks. Each trade returns 5% or $1,000. By year end this represents $26,000, assuming only the original trading capital is used and profits are placed on deposit. This is a 130% return for the year. The trader starts with $20,000 and ends with $46,000.

Please understand this example looks easy, but reality has a habit of being more difficult. Readers should compare this with more realistic trading returns shown in Figure 17.2. Brokerage, slippage and transaction costs all eat into the 5%. Market liquidity has a significant impact on the trader's ability to execute the entry and exit at the desired price. To have 26 trades all moving in the desired direction represents very astute trading. Taking smaller returns, around 5%, may seem more modestly achievable than chasing larger 20% returns, but in practice it is still very difficult.

While continuing to keep an eye on reality, we will pursue this simple example to develop an approximate guide to the number of hours required each week. If an average of one trade a fortnight is sufficient to return a reasonable income, then how many hours does the trader need to sit in front of the screen?

```
┌─────────────────────────────────────────────────────────────┐
│  Fig. 17.1  TRADING TIME                                     │
│             An example of daily tasks and time              │
│                                                             │
│  Identify trade opportunities              1 hour           │
│  • Database scan                    20                       │
│  • Eyeball verification, bar chart  15                       │
│  • Indicator verification           25                       │
│                                                             │
│  Analysis of opportunities                 1 hour           │
│  • Check for bias                   15                       │
│  • Assess stop-loss conditions      15                       │
│  • Assess profit targets            15                       │
│  • Rank by time/risk                15                       │
│                                                             │
│  Trade management of open positions  1 hour                 │
│  • Watch depth of market on entry   15                       │
│  • Place and execute buy order      5                        │
│  • Enter details in order log, print out                     │
│      chart with summary trading plan 5                       │
│  • With open positions, each day verify                      │
│      orginal trading conditions are intact 15                │
│  • Place and execute sell order     5                        │
│  • Enter details in trading records                          │
│      and file contract notes        15                       │
│                                                             │
└─────────────────────────────────────────────────────────────┘
```

The private trader does not have to trade every day. Unlike his institutional counterpart he waits until the best trading opportunities come along when the balance of probabilities is firmly lined up in his favour. In this example, we must make a decision once every two weeks. Our institutional cousins do not have this luxury.

Previous sections considered the processes involved in entering a position, including identifying the opportunity using visual scans, or electronic scans of market data. Trading opportunities are evaluated using fundamental, technical, or financial factors. The entry, the open position and the exit are all actively managed to meet financial objectives.

Although the time involved looks daunting, with experience the process is less so. If we have a number of open positions, these processes are all taking place simultaneously as we compare and reject multiple securities. For this example we want to separate these processes to estimate the time required for a single opportunity each fortnight.

Identifying the trading opportunity is the least time-consuming aspect of trading, particularly if our chosen market is relatively small. Identifying the single trading opportunity takes, we estimate, an hour a day on average.

241

Analysing the trading opportunity is much more time-consuming. Perhaps five to ten hours might be spent in analysis. This may include company research, reading balance sheets and assessing the fundamentals. Technical traders will spend much of this time applying and assessing various technical indicators and analysing the price charts. If we take ten hours of analysis per position, then this translates into one hour a day on average over a ten-day working fortnight.

The final trading step is managing the entry. Sometimes the entry is very quick, particularly if we meet the asking price. At other times, such as with an ambush approach, the entry may take more time to be executed. All order details are entered in a trading log for future reference. Once a position is opened the appropriate chart is printed and the summary trading plan attached.

Once the entry is made the trade is monitored daily. This may be as simple as checking the current trading activity, waiting for the sell criteria to be met. Those using Internet access to real-time or snapshot prices do this in seconds. Others ring their broker, and if pleasantries are kept to a minimum, the task is completed in minutes. In slow markets traders check end of day data via the newspaper or data downloads.

Monitoring the open position takes a few minutes each day. Closing a position should be as easy, with the addition of a simple phone call to the broker to place the sell order. Trading records are updated and contract notes filed, both for portfolio management and for taxation purposes. Even with multiple open positions, an hour a day should be enough. Again these are hypothetical figures, and actual hours may be more or less for individual traders.

Adding up the score card as shown in Figure 17.1 we record 3 hours a day — 1 hour for identification, 1 for analysis, 1 for management. For successful traders this is highly-paid work. In return for a 15-hour week they are rewarded with a handsome income. This also makes trading a very appealing way to supplement income from our day job. With just a few open positions, an hour or so each evening with added weekend work makes trading possible. The old trade union chant of 'Eight hours work, eight hours rest and eight hours play' doesn't seem relevant. Just as importantly, the middle-management executive refrain of 'Sixty hours a week with time for your family only when you retire' seems equally inappropriate.

Fig. 17.2
Example of position trading activity over 12 months
Nominal trading equity is $100,000. Profits are swept into a CMA account. Position size was set at around $20,000. 30 trades were completed. Each one was open for an average of 28 days. Losing trades took losses that were usually equal to 2% of the nominal trading equity. Winning trades were closed out when the initial trading conditions were met, even though the price may have continued upwards.

Stock	Date opened	Date closed	Days open	Amount	$$Profit	%%Profit	W/L
LEG	29 Jul 1996	9 Sep 1996	42	$20,000	$2,775	26	WIN
ZPR	29 Jul 1996	18 Nov 1996	112	$20,000	$6,880	34	WIN
PRA	29 Jul 1996	12 Aug 1996	14	$20,000	-$780	-3.9	LOSS
CTR	29 Jul 1996	19 Aug 1996	21	$20,000	$230	1	WIN
LHG	12 Aug 1996	2 Sep 1996	21	$20,072	$3,330	16.5	WIN
NCM	19 Aug 1996	2 Sep 1996	14	$20,064	$334	1.6	WIN
DMR	26 Aug 1996	7 Oct 1996	42	$19,500	-$2,250	-11	LOSS
WRF	9 Sep 1996	16 Sep 1996	7	$20,150	$3,199	15	WIN
FIM	23 Sep 1996	7 Oct 1996	14	$20,040	-$2,505	-12.5	LOSS
TRY	7 Oct 1996	28 Oct 1996	21	$19,780	$1,840	9	WIN
VPE	7 Oct 1996	25 Nov 1996	49	$20,090	-$1,230	-6	LOSS
KGR	18 Nov 1996	25 Nov 1996	7	$20,700	$1,150	5.5	WIN
WSL	25 Nov 1996	16 Dec 1996	21	$19,916	$364	1.8	WIN
CXR	25 Nov 1996	20 Jan 1997	56	$20,400	$10,200	50	WIN
ADN	16 Dec 1996	13 Jan 1997	28	$20,075	$4,125	20.5	WIN
OCN	13 Jan 1997	24 Mar 1997	70	$20,800	$800	3.8	WIN
MEG	27 Jan 1997	31 Mar 1997	63	$20,250	$8,910	44	WIN
GGR	27 Jan 1997	10 Feb 1997	14	$20,160	-$1,440	-7	LOSS
LVG	3 Feb 1997	31 Mar 1997	56	$20,400	-$1,200	-6	LOSS
PRN	17 Feb 1997	24 Feb 1997	7	$20,150	$6,500	32	WIN
SCN	10 Mar 1997	17 Mar 1997	7	$20,060	$12,980	64	WIN
ZPR	7 Apr 1997	14 Apr 1997	7	$20,000	-$2,000	-10	LOSS
AHG	7 Apr 1997	5 May 1997	28	$20,540	$650	3	WIN
CRO	21 Apr 1997	12 May 1997	21	$20,020	$910	4.5	WIN
TAI	3 Apr 1997	28 Apr 1997	25	$20,150	$5,090	24.6	WIN
NBH	5 May 1997	26 May 1997	21	$19,964	$2,346	16.7	WIN
ASH	12 May 1997	19 May 1997	7	$20,900	$1,900	10	WIN
CFR	26 May 1997	23 Jun 1997	28	$20,025	-$2,225	-11	LOSS
IRO	26 May 1997	2 Jun 1997	7	$20,000	$6,250	31	WIN
LYG	2 Jun 1997	23 Jun 1997	21	$20,125	-$605	-3	LOSS
SUMMARY:			Av. days open	$ traded	Year profit	% return	22win/8loss
CLOSED	**TRADES**		**28**	**$604,331**	**$66,528**	**66.52**	**73% win**

If a single trading position requires 15 hours, then logically two positions call for 30 hours and three for 45 hours. Fortunately, such lineal logic does not apply. In reality trading opportunities tend to clump together. A single search may turn up several good opportunities, and then nothing for days. These multiple opportunities are considered together and, within reason, chart analysis is applied as quickly to one as it is to several. Our example, although artificial, is quite close to the actual time involved although it fails to show how some weeks are very busy and others exceedingly dull. The open and close dates for each trade in Figure 17.2 show how trading activity tends to clump.

Such highly-paid hourly work is a substantial part of the trading dream. Achieving it would not seem to create a problem. Nor would it if it were not for guilt. If greed and fear dominate the market, then guilt is the shadow prowling beneath the surface of every private trader's success.

So Much Money for So Little Work

Having achieved this goal, some traders, perhaps many more of us than we would like to admit, feel uncomfortable. The roots of our discomfort lie in our long-held beliefs about work and reward. The protestant work ethic has certainly gathered a large ecumenical following and we are not exempt.

For most private traders the path to trading has seen dalliance turn to commitment, part-time becomes full-time, and then trading becomes serious. Every would-be trader reaches a turning point where a process used to supplement his income becomes a mainstay of his income. It comes at different stages in the trading process but once it is taken, our understanding of the relationship between work and reward is challenged. How we deal with this challenge will decide if we trade with our brain, or with our wallet. Our long-term success depends on this decision.

The challenge is accepting that reward is possible without stress, or sweat, or long hours. If we cannot accept this then, as a private trader, we are doomed to a life of make-believe work. Despite the computer revolution promise of shorter working hours, more leisure and less paperwork, most of us feel 40 hours a week is about right. This sets the parameters against which we often instinctively match the level of work required for a particular reward.

Now what happens if substantial reward, as suggested above, can be reached by working far less hours? This is not a trivial question. Trading turns our understanding of reward and effort upside down.

Homework

For full-time private traders the response is complicated further by a shift to a home-based office environment. Workers shifting to home-based businesses experience the same difficulty in adjusting to new conditions. Old habits die hard.

The habits are so persuasive that some people get in the car each morning, drive around the block and return to their home office in the same way they used to drive to work. More significantly, the home-based businessman, and private trader, must now accept the responsibility for creating, initiating and completing an appropriate workload.

The tele-office worker is exempt from this uncertainty because although he has the freedom to largely organise his own working hours, he is still driven by an external agenda decided by his employer. A set amount of work has to be completed, and in return he gets a set reward.

The self-employed businessman working from home finds the adjustment comparatively easy if clamouring clients are part of the business. Each project has a deadline, and the businessman re-creates an environment of workplace stress through externally-imposed agendas. Coincidentally this equates stress, long hours and sweat with the level of reward.

External agendas are not automatic for the private trader. We have no clients demanding projects be completed in time. Time management is entirely our own, particularly if we are position trading and not tied to the screen all day. Ours is an entirely undisciplined environment where work activities appear to be almost optional. We have one master and it is ourselves.

Unusual questions have to be resolved. If I have no clients to visit, then do I have to wear a tie to work? Why do I have to go to work today? What are the consequences of turning up late for work when I set my own hours? These bring up some worrying questions about standards, self-discipline, self-direction and guilt.

Your partner expects to see you glued to the screen and at least sweating over the market rather than finding you relaxed with a book in hand and a cup of coffee. It is no good explaining there is nothing you can do while waiting for the market to push prices up. If your partner works at a regular job it requires considerable understanding to appreciate the stress you experience during the trading day. It is a mistake to underestimate the impact of guilt on your behaviour.

Not surprisingly, the entire situation can be extremely uncomfortable and we react in one of three ways. We fail as free agents and surrender to wage slavery, or we create our own work discipline. A third reaction is a break-up of the relationship with our partner.

Make-Believe Work

Unfortunately it is sometimes difficult to distinguish between failure and creating our own work discipline. Working harder is a common discipline response because by doing so we justify the rewards. For full-time private traders this can lead to costly over-trading.

As suggested above, trading can involve as little as three hours a day and, without the distraction of a day job, we have the choice of deciding where those hours will fall — in a single clump, spread over the day, or deferred today in favour of a longer working day tomorrow. What do we do with the remaining five hours previously allocated to work? Potentially we have 25 hours a week of additional leisure time. With careful structuring the private trader can lead the life he has dreamed of, living and trading from anywhere in the world as his own boss.

Instead, typically we create more work related to what we are already doing. Some of it is useful study and development while some is over-trading disguised as necessary work. One way or another the amount of work seems to expand to fill almost exactly the number of hours we have available. Traders are not immune from this rule of modern management. Depending on how driven we want to feel, we can add more work to these hours, creating an artificial level of stress. This is when we start trading with our wallet.

The trader extends his activities by taking on new market segments or derivative markets such as options and warrants, by taking many new positions financed by trading profits, by additional capital borrowed from other sources, or by margin borrowing. No matter which combination he chooses the effect is the same. He creates more activity to fill the empty hours and to justify the reward.

Top Australian trader Gary Smith notes, "People with intensive work ethics have to stare at the screen all day to reassure themselves that they have worked hard."

The trader may respond in this way because he cannot accept that the level of reward is commensurate with the amount of work he puts in. This terribly destructive response is driven by guilt based on our intuitive understanding of the work/reward relationship.

This problem applies to full-time and part time-traders. Both try to match the level of work with the increasing level of reward. Either the work increases, or the reward decreases. Over-trading, or trading with your wallet, usually decreases the reward in a subconsciously very satisfying way.

The reaction is destructive because we create the conditions of failure through overwork, through stressed and faulty decision-making. In the desire to be busy and to be seen as busy, we make haste and we make mistakes. We console ourselves that they are an inevitable part of the ups and downs of work and as seasoned traders we accept these mistakes.

A destructive feedback loop is constructed. Mistakes do mean we must work harder. We trade to win, and to win all the time. Losing is a sign of failure, so we drive ourselves harder when we make mistakes. We trade to fill in time without regard to financial objectives. With grim determination we unwittingly build a treadmill to replicate the conditions we used to work under in the corporate office.

Without realising it, we do our best to make this new trading business into hard work because then, with sweat on our brow and a clear conscience, we accept the rewards — guilt free. We believe we are creating a working environment governed by self-discipline. Instead, we set up the conditions of failure because we are trading with our wallet.

Trading With Your Wallet

It is trading success that lets us quit our day job. It is this success that takes us back to our day job if we do not break the destructive cycle of over-trading made possible, paradoxically, by a few trading victories. This is how the cycle develops:

> Our behaviour is driven by an uncomfortable feeling about easy money. We feel we have to trade because we have fallen into the trap that says busy hours are necessary to justify our reward. When the wallet is full, or replenished by a trade, we look desperately for new trading opportunities. To keep the hours busy we empty our wallet buying new positions as soon as the capital is available. If we fail completely, if the wallet is emptied and not refilled, then we retire from the field, exhausted but with trading honour intact. Nobody can say we didn't try to make a good effort of it. Just look at the hours we put in.

This is a danger faced almost solely by the private trader. Over-trading sneaks up disguised by the very success the trader seeks.

For the institutional professionals it may never come to this because they work in an office environment where the relationship between work and reward is clearly established and supported by peer group practices.

A Test for Over-Trading

The essential defining feature of over-trading is not an absolute number of trades but the motivation behind each trade. Later we discuss how trading can slip into characteristic behaviour patterns more closely associated with gambling, or more seriously, pathological gambling. Over-trading driven by a desire to experience the thrill of risk-taking rather than sound money management is one of the features of a gambling approach.

Over-trading takes a step in this direction when trading positions are opened primarily because the trader feels the need to do something other than wait patiently for the best opportunities to arise. This temptation is always present because somewhere in the market good money is being made every day. We suspect if we were more fully exposed, more fully committed, then we too could take part in the great accumulation of wealth. This temptation is particularly strong in bull markets. Rather than miss out, novice traders rush into every reasonable opportunity they can afford. Trades are no longer based on good money management or risk control.

Different markets and different trading approaches dictate a range of trading activity. The day trader takes on more positions than an investor. A position trader completes less trades than an active commodities trader. In assessing the tendency for over-trading the primary test is money management. The test has four questions:

1 Is each trade clearly based on sound financial analysis?

2 Is each trade part of an overall money management objective based on matching position size with risk?

3 Does each trade have clear financial objectives which determine the exit conditions?

4 Does each trade only use capital allocated from previous trades?

Ask these questions of each new trade. If the answers are all affirmative then the trade is well-considered and part of a strategic market approach. If two or more questions are honestly answered "No" then the danger of over-trading is real. A "No" answer suggests trading decisions are emotionally driven and this often draws on a need to justify the rewards.

The typical answers below to the test questions above suggest over-trading. This trader clearly relies more on the size of his wallet rather than his brain.

1 Trade is quickly assessed on the basis of gross returns, or the current low with the highest high over the last year.

2 Position size is determined by how much cash is currently available for trading.

3 Exit is loosely based on previous highs or gut feelings. Some positions are closed early to free up cash for new more attractive positions.

4 Money from other sources, such as the day job, is constantly added so new position sizes can be increased.

Over-trading is a relative concept without absolute measures. As a guide, the trades shown in Figure 17.2 are typical of those taken by a position trader over a single year. These trades were taken in a notional portfolio developed on a weekly basis in real time. They give some idea of the frequency of trading and the spread of activity over time.

Trading with our brains means we are aware of our tendency to create work to fill the time available. It means we accept that significant rewards do flow from work that does not involve long hours, stress or sweat. It means the private trader appropriately values his intellectual and analytical contribution to the process of trading and accepts his rewards as commensurate with this. He understands no additional work is required to justify his income so his wallet stays in his pocket.

The work of a private trader is as hard and as honest as the next man's. You do not need blisters on your hands, nor stress leave, to prove it. Most important of all, you do not need an empty wallet and a file filled with contract notes to measure your success.

18

NERVES OF STEEL -
OR CHICKEN WIRE?

The destitute prospector who once mined a fortune in gold and, like the Australian government, threw it away, is a recurrent figure in literature. Destitution as a reaction to wealth is driven by emotional instability. Exposure to large sums of money is a heady experience which magnifys emotional reactions. As the prospectors found in *The Treasure of the Sierra Madre*, wealth changes people and for some there is an almost irresistible urge to return to the time before wealth. This sounds unbelievable to those aspiring to riches, but the consistent destruction of market fortunes suggests it happens more frequently than we imagine.

Our reactions to our search results and the implications of the supplementary numbers discussed in Part III ultimately determine our success or failure. Every journey starts with a single step and we start with the wrong foot when we let a little loss grow into a large one. This is a process we want to examine more closely in this chapter.

All good traders use a stop-loss calculation, but few traders consistently act on their stop-loss points, showing the best plans in the world are useless if we freeze at the point of decision. An effective stop-loss strategy matches the theoretical calculated stop-loss point with our psychological makeup.

Market myth proposes an excellent three-step trader's training course. First the student is required to put $100 on a busy city footpath and wait until a passerby picks it up. When the student is able to watch this happen without wincing and without tears he proceeds to the next step in the training course. The second stage is a repeat of the first — only this time using $1,000. This stage is successfully completed when complete nonchalance is achieved. The third step involves $10,000. The student must repeat this successfully, throwing money away without tears or fears, for several consecutive days.

Successful completion of the course entitles students to start trading.

I jest, the course is mythical, but the intent of the exercise is quite serious. All traders lose money, and they often lose it on a regular basis. The key difference is that successful traders lose only small amounts of capital. They do this by using stop-loss methods and limiting losses to a small percentage or portion of their total trading capital.

This all sounds very sensible and straightforward. In practice it is much harder. Try the novice training course above, but using only $50. Unless you are particularly dedicated to developing trading attitudes you will find the process very difficult because we do not know in advance if our trading nerves are made of steel or of chicken wire. Most of us have an inherent inability to deliberately lose money, and this has a serious impact on our ability to trade and on our ability to set realistic stop-loss points. Many of us are quite comfortable with debt and with frivolous wasteful expenditure consuming the weekly pay cheque. But this is not the same as taking a loss.

Taking a Loss

Market lore suggests you should: "Never trade with more than you can afford to lose." This well-intentioned advice misses the point by assuming our total trading capital is at risk. Better advice is: "Never set risk levels at more than you can afford to lose." Taking a loss is an integral part of trading and rationally we know money lost in trading is not really thrown away. Emotionally, it just seems that way.

In trading shares, particularly on electronic exchanges, we get so little in return. After a $40,000 purchase we first receive a contract note and later a Holding Statement on a common sheet of A4 paper, both plastered with a few figures. They are not exactly a trophy talking point. We cannot consume them, display them, use them, or conveniently show them off as we could with a new car, a swimming pool or a house extension.

When we consider taking a loss – when the flimsy Holding Statement is suddenly worth $3,000 less than it was a day ago – it really does seem as if we are throwing money away. Lifelong attitudes to financial management subconsciously influence our decision, staying our hand when we should reach for the telephone and exit the position. Being able to take this loss takes emotional courage and most cannot do it without a whimper. Emotionally we freeze when rationally we should act.

By a variety of mechanisms, all of us consciously avoid situations where we lose money. We do not like losing money so many of us could not complete the mythical three-step traders' training course. Unless we do complete it – albeit metaphorically rather than literally – the chances of trading success are greatly reduced. Trading success demands we move beyond these attitudes.

Is the private trader doomed unless he develops a devil-may-care attitude to losing money? The answer lies in the difference between courage and fearlessness. The trader needs courage – an understanding of fear and the ability to overcome it. The trader without fear cheats financial death – for a limited time. This is not a path we want to follow.

We understand only too well the fear of losing money and often this fear keeps us in losing trades rather than executing our stop-loss. When we go too far, and too fast, fear overcomes our courage. The glimmer of an answer to the way we develop courage to efficiently execute stop-loss points is suggested by the ubiquitous slot machine found in casinos and clubs. They make a business of turning chicken wire nerves into steel.

Thresholds

Casino players hate losing even though this is an inevitable consequence of chasing jackpot rewards. The key to understanding how they run the gauntlet of loss is not the size of the inducement, but the size of the wager and the way loss is limited to the wager itself.

For those with a high resistance to losing money, the 5¢ slot machine is heaven-sent. Who will miss 5¢? We all have different thresholds of tolerance and the casino operators thoughtfully provide opportunities for everyone to operate as close to their threshold as they feel comfortable. We have the choice to step up from the 5¢ machine to a 20¢ machine, or to $1 or $10 machines. We can change games and play with $50 chips at the roulette or baccarat tables, or join the high rollers at $500 a throw. By these graduated steps the casino takes advantage of differing threshold tolerances for loss.

The trader can learn from this management practice. The casino entices because the losses seem small. Many gamblers accumulate large losses, little bit by little bit. The pain is reduced as every individual loss is affordable. In some important ways the process is the same as trading, except the trader actively monitors loss levels within an overall money management scheme designed to deal with uncertain rewards by containing risk. The casinos thrive because they match the tolerance for loss with the emotional maturity of their clients – and the number of slot machines accepting bets of a dollar or less says a lot about emotional maturity.

Many traders fail because they do not match the levels of loss, indicated by their stop-loss strategy, with their emotional ability to take them.

Each trader must first define how much he is prepared to lose should the trade turn against him. We have looked at some ways of mechanically calculating this, based on chart points and the 2% money management rule. However, the bottom line in practical terms depends on the individual trader. Some traders are comfortable with taking losses of several thousands of dollars while others feel extreme pain at several hundred.

Where is your pain level? All of us have a level of loss which we feel comfortable with. Once the loss grows beyond that threshold we increasingly find it difficult to pull the trigger on a trade. Our careful stop-loss planning is ignored. A loss of $100 is very easy to take. A loss of $1,000, or $10,000 less so. Every private trader should establish his tolerance for loss – his threshold – as early as possible. Every point is valid, be it constructed from chicken wire or steel. Knowing this figure in advance allows the trader to adjust his trading strategies so he does not expose himself to losses greater than he can bear.

This is an important additional consideration to include with the simple spreadsheet mechanics of the stop-loss calculations discussed in Chapters 13 and 14. In dollar terms the logical stop-loss points should be equal to or less than, our loss tolerance level. If the stop-loss point, in dollar terms, represents more loss than we are comfortable with then we are less likely to pull the trigger when the time comes.

The stop-loss may be perfectly logical, brilliantly analysed, superbly placed, but unless it touches the right emotional chord it is useless because we will not execute it. And then the little loss grows into a substantial loss, further reducing our ability to realise it by selling.

The mythical three-step trader's training program proposed moving from $100 to $1,000 and then to $10,000. The private trader adopts the same approach, teaching himself to tolerate larger losses. If larger losses are emotionally tolerable, then larger positions are taken consistent with wider money management objectives. As position size grows, so too does the dollar loss, even if the percentage loss remains the same.

For instance, a 2% loss on $4,000 of trading capital equals $80. Losing $80 is not the end of the world, and the trader can comfortably exit the trade and move into more profitable fields. If trading capital totals $100,000 then a 2% loss equals $2,000. This loss is of a different order emotionally, particularly when much of the $100,000 represents trading profits. Placing the sell order and taking this $2,000 loss is much more difficult to do, even though it still represents exactly the same percentage failure as the smaller account. Beginners find it difficult to fully convince themselves that it is the percentage figure that counts and not the dollar figure.

When they look at the trading calculation screen used in Chapter 13 they glimpse the dollar loss figure on a $100,000 account and flinch. Despite having $98,000 remaining, emotionally the loss of $2,000 is too difficult to contemplate. So the loss is permitted to grow, and with each dollar increase beyond $2,000 the chances of the closing the position and realising the loss are diminished. If they cannot act on a $2,000 loss, then it is much more difficult to act when it grows to $3,000 or $5,000. Trading success demands we turn from this grim reality and develop strategies to overcome this emotional paralysis.

A Trading Course

Changing deeply-held emotional attitudes is a difficult task. The film *What About Bob?* popularised the concept of baby steps — taking many small steps towards a distant objective. The trader emulates this by determining his tolerance for 'throw away' money. If we know we will execute an exit when facing a $1,000 loss, but cannot really pick up the phone when the loss is $1,500 then we need to make sure our trading tactics reflect this knowledge.

The trader needs to take positions where the dollar loss — in this case $1,000 — is at least equal to the logical stop-loss point. This is decided by manipulating the trade calculation screen to determine the position size to match the emotionally acceptable figure. The starting point is provided by the logical stop-loss point based on chart analysis.

Figure 18.1 shows two steps in adjusting the position size to reflect an ability to act on stop-loss points. We show three sample traders, Advanced, Beginner and an Emotional Loser. In all cases the logical stop-loss point, based on chart analysis, is at $4.10 and total trading capital available is $100,000 with the proposed entry at $4.30.

Trader Advanced has no problems with taking losses of $2,000 so the limiting factor is the 2% of equity figure. He matches the 2% loss level of $2,000 with position size. The calculations show an entry at $4.30 and position size limited to 7,000 shares or $30,702. With this combination the calculated dollar loss figure coincides with the $4.10 stop-loss level derived from the chart.

Trader Beginner is less experienced. From previous trades he knows once the loss grows beyond $1,000 he has great emotional difficulty in closing the position. Like Trader Advanced his available trading capital puts the maximum loss at $2,000 using the 2% rule, but he wants to limit any potential loss to $1,000. To do this he reduces his position size to 3,500 shares or $15,351. This combination still calls for an exit at $4.10 — the chart-derived logical stop-loss point. With only $1,000 at risk if the trade does turn against him, Trader Beginner is now more confident he will execute his stop-loss.

In setting the stop-loss point both sample traders matched their emotional tolerance for a loss in dollar terms with the logical stop-loss point based on chart analysis. Trader Emotional Loser only looks at the chart-derived stop-loss so the problem rapidly becomes serious.

Fig. 18.1

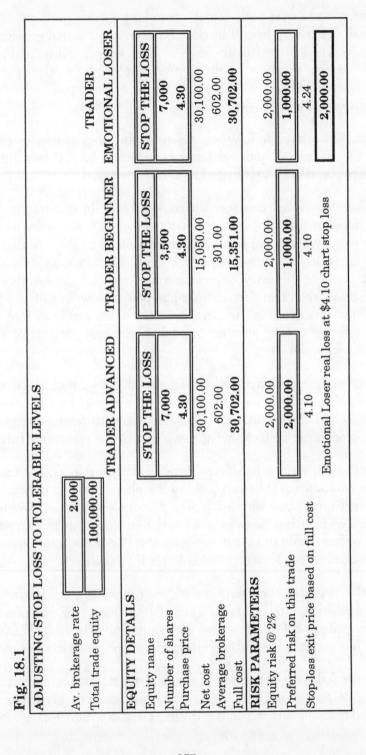

ADJUSTING STOP LOSS TO TOLERABLE LEVELS

Av. brokerage rate		2.000
Total trade equity		100,000.00

	TRADER ADVANCED	TRADER BEGINNER	TRADER EMOTIONAL LOSER

EQUITY DETAILS

Equity name	STOP THE LOSS	STOP THE LOSS	STOP THE LOSS
Number of shares	7,000	3,500	7,000
Purchase price	4.30	4.30	4.30
Net cost	30,100.00	15,050.00	30,100.00
Average brokerage	602.00	301.00	602.00
Full cost	30,702.00	15,351.00	30,702.00

RISK PARAMETERS

Equity risk @ 2%	2,000.00	2,000.00	2,000.00
Preferred risk on this trade	2,000.00	1,000.00	1,000.00
Stop-loss exit price based on full cost	4.10	4.10	4.24
		Emotional Loser real loss at $4.10 chart stop loss	2,000.00

Trader Emotional Loser fools himself by taking a large position size coupled with a small dollar stop-loss. If he does act on the exit signal generated by the dollar loss — when price falls to $4.24 — he is whipsawed in and out of the position time after time just by the normal range of daily price action. Before long he concludes this is a losing strategy so he selects the chart stop loss point as the exit trigger.

The consequences are fatal. When prices do fall, they pause, or consolidate around $4.10. Trader Emotional Loser now faces a $2,000 loss. Emotionally he is paralysed and ends up trapped in a losing position.

Most of us have visited this scenario at some time in our trading career. It generally happens this way. When prices fall to $4.24, just a few cents below our entry price, we lose our emotional maximum of $1,000. With 14¢ left to reach the chart-derived stop-loss point we hold on, convincing ourselves that prices will pause at this level. We make a fake promise to ourselves to exit if prices fall below the chart-derived stop-loss point. Now an exit at $4.10 costs $2,000. When prices do fall to here, we hold tight unable to face the extra loss. We quibble, making another fraudulent personal promise to exit when prices rally back to $4.24.

This scenario does not disappear by itself and unless we take action we return to it again and again until we no longer have the money for the entry fee. We avoid this scenario by manipulating position size with reference to the logical stop-loss point so the dollar value at risk is within our emotional threshold.

When Trading Beginner is able to consistently take a $1,000 loss calmly, quickly, unemotionally; if he can pick up the phone, sell the position without his voice quavering, and without feeling rotten about himself when he puts the phone down; if he can watch the order executed on the screen in real time with only a sniffle or morsel of regret, then he is ready to move on. Now he is emotionally ready to accept larger losses if required.

Just like the mythical three-step trader's training program, Trader Beginner increases the dollar amount he is prepared to lose. This is done in small increments, perhaps $500 in this case. The jump from $1,000 to $2,000 may be too much. It is very much a trial and error process fine-tuned to suit every trader.

The key is the dollar size of the loss. In searching for real trading success we match the theoretical money management and risk management objectives with our practical ability to initiate the loss. It is the latter that determines the position size.

Perhaps our trading capital gives $5,000 as an outer limit under the 2% risk rule. If the trader finds he cannot tolerate more than a $4,000 loss on any position, then he should limit his position size to a level where $4,000 is the dollar value of the potential stop-loss.

We do not change the stop-loss level, moving it up so it hangs in mid-air, unrelated to any logical stop-loss point. It is always based on chart analysis of logical stop-loss points. This includes making use of support areas, or using a countback technique to set a trailing stop-loss in an open position. Instead of changing its level, on entry, we manipulate our position size so the dollar loss is within the practical rather than theoretical limits. Emotions are powerful influences on behaviour, and trading exposes people to the full range of the most powerful of them all — greed and fear. Understanding these emotions and the role they play in sabotaging, or supporting, our trading gives us an important trading edge.

Trading With Maturity

Trading is not just business by another name. Despite technical mastery of trading mechanics, many novice traders still fail. Private trading requires emotional maturity. This is reflected in many ways. Some of the young institutional traders and brokers splash their windfall earnings in glitzy shows of wealth and earn the opprobrium of the general public. These people trade OPM, usually pronounced 'opium', an abbreviation for Other People's Money. OPM is just as addictive and mind-bending as its sound-alike namesake. Do not confuse this bull market behaviour with the attitudes and skills required for private trading.

Private traders tend to be more restrained, reflecting the same emotional maturity to the display of wealth as they apply to the attainment of it. Next time you attend a trading seminar try to estimate the trading net worth of individual participants. It is difficult because there are few physical clues in dress or decoration. The only clues come from the quality of the questions asked.

If we find it difficult to act decisively on stop-loss points — and most of us have this problem initially — then develop this ability in small steps. In the beginning this appears to limit profits, but as we develop as traders we understand that this emotional maturity acts as a brake on losses and so allows profits to flow and grow naturally.

19

COMMAND AND CONTROL

S ize is a bully in the market. When an institution chooses to sell its holdings, the shares it unloads on the market create a solid resistance level. Buyers find no reason to bid higher when thousands of shares are on offer at $4.00. Because institutional traders are often patient there are also few bargains below $4.00 as bids of $3.99 leave the institution unperturbed. Of course, in a general market collapse the institutions are just as eager to unload as everybody else.

The unwise private trader has ample opportunities to bully the market down at the speculative end. We touched on the mechanics of this in Chapter 15. On the one hand low liquidity hinders our entry and exit strategy. We must adjust our position size so it equals, on average, the volume over previous weeks. The relationship between volume and position size is critical in low liquidity stocks and easily observed on depth of market screens as well as on the daily chart. When our buy order is first in line at $0.77, and with no trades today, the horizontal line on the bar chart seems to stretch infinitely into the future.

We also know, should we raise our bid to $0.79, or meet the ask at $0.80, that our action alone will be solely responsible for a new line on the chart, perhaps setting the high or low for the day. At first this idea is intriguing, but left unchecked it grows into a dangerous misconception that we can bully the market into doing what we want. Like a surreal Salvador Dali painting, in a particular light and at a certain angle, this picture turns ugly as a hidden bully emerges from the background.

How often have you had the dubious distinction of being the only buyer at the absolute high? Have you succumbed to the dangerous idea that your buying can create a countback line breakout, and, that by implication, others will follow? The fallacy here of course is that a countback line breakout, or a new high, are valid when set by the general market and not when set in anticipation by eager but misinformed individual traders. Wishing will not make it so, not even when backed with your capital.

As private traders we would never dream of such action with a large blue chip stock like Coles Myer, Coca Cola Amatil or ANZ bank. Our tiny order is swamped in high liquidity and heavy volume, so our market impact is reduced. With smaller stocks our orders have significance. The step from observing the impact of our orders to deciding our orders have impact is small, and dangerous.

Bullies Love Control

Quite obviously we need to avoid and discard this idea that we can have an impact on market behaviour out of proportion to our size. We would discard this in favour of more relevant trading issues if not for the fact that many private traders, at one time or another, fall victim to this idea. Nobody openly admits to believing they can control the market, but often their action speaks louder than their denials. This happens in three ways.

The first is when we step from the audience onto the stage as an actor. As soon as we place an order we are on stage. The trading shows at the small end of town provide the opportunity to play out the fantasy of the market bully. It is not recommended, and if undertaken deliberately and systematically to 'ramp' a stock price, such action is illegal.

Ramping a stock involves creating the illusion of price activity, usually by controlled buying and selling between several related parties. Volume increases and prices churn within a tight band. Other traders are attracted to the action, bidding up price based on the volume activity. The original traders ride the price action, selling into the growing strength. There are many variations on this theme – all illegal – and all based on creating unusual trading volume in a sleepy stock.

Such activity is substantively different from our observation as private traders that our buy or sell order does have an observable impact on the market when trading small speculative stocks. This is not control and when we try to bully the market we usually end up worse off. When we try to buy too much we push the price up. When we try to sell too much, the prices falls because we choke the market with our sell order. When our position size is greater than the average size of trades we run the risk of not being able to execute our trade at the best price.

The second way our actions speak louder than our denial of the bully charge comes when we slide, trade by trade, into gambling mode. The pathological gambler believes in his omnipotence and the gambling trader works with the same delusions. These issues are more fully explored in the following chapter.

It is the third approach we want to consider in this chapter. Fertile ground for this belief about ability to control the market is provided when we build the false link between success in the market and successful prediction. This belief grows into a particularly nasty weed when combined with the observed impact of our orders on stocks with low liquidity.

Insidiously and erroneously the idea grows that we are somehow able to control or improve the outcome of our position by superior predictive analysis. The command and control fallacy entices when profits follow prediction.

If this sounds unreasonable then consider any of your open positions currently showing a loss. Ask yourself why you haven't exited the trade – and answer truthfully. Despite good chart analysis and stock selection, too often we kid ourselves with excuses: "The sell off was overdone," or "This company is fundamentally sound with good management," or even the most optimistic and emotionally fraudulent of all: "Fools. Don't they realise the global potential for this product?"

This last excuse is sometimes presented by fund managers as a virtue because "there is always a handful, only a scant handful of investments across Australia and around the globe that have been mispriced by the markets," and by implication their funds management team has the skill to uncover these investments. When this approach is applied to private trading the effect is insidiously disastrous.

Satisfied with any of these excuses, just like a bully, we fight the market, pitting our ego against it trying to prove .... what? .... that we know better than the market. Stripped of the self-justifying rhetoric our actions sound feeble, so why do so many traders persist with this? Exploring the roots of our confusion hands us a trading edge. Paradoxically they are often entangled with the roots of business success.

Most private traders turn to the market after a successful career in business, or the professions. Initially, trading income is a supplement to their day job and because they are still working it is easy to confuse the command and control skills that breed success in one sphere with the skills needed for success in the other. Some strategies which bring success in business bring disaster in the market.

Consider as an example a successful housing developer who, in the start-up days, and in the recession-we-had-to-have, held on grimly only to emerge victorious and profitable. Success came from tenacity and the ability to control the external factors in his segment of the market and to outlast his competitors.

Certainly, our developer analysed the housing market and predicted a shortage of duplex units. This command of analysis gave him the power to control events by building duplex units to meet the identified demand. To him it seems superior analysis meant early action which gave control and this equates with success. This is the core message of many modern management books. The message is not heard in the financial market, but the idea is hard to shake because it gives our developer the wealth required to trade.

Past business success develops the unspoken conviction that if he understands key information he can control his local market and make a profit. From here it is a short insidious step to the idea of stock market control. Even a small string of trading successes are equated with successful market predictions. Bit by bit, trade by trade, he comes to believe in his ability to master the market by throwing money at it. The baby bully is born.

Baby Bullies

Business success sometimes breeds arrogance. In contrast, trading success always breeds humility. We do not need to be a successful businessman to become a baby bully. Any of us can shove the market around when volumes are low enough. All novice traders pass through a developmental stage. They flirt with the idea that their understanding of the market means that when they take a position, the market will move in their favour. Although this growth phase is often most marked in traders with a business background, none of us is immune.

Inevitably one of our favourite positions — usually the one perfectly selected by our database scan, the one superbly analysed and entered at just the right price — turns against us and when it does, we are stunned. So we hold on, waiting for the market to reverse and match our previous market call. We rationalise our inaction in the jargon of our business success. "I was right in the '94 slowdown so this will come good", or " Perseverance paid off when the Shanghai negotiations collapsed, so I will stay put." The longer we have traded the more likely we are to use the jargon of trading, telling ourselves and others, "The sell-off was overdone."

Even more perversely, some novice traders feel if they can carry a large loss it says something positive about their wealth. The 1987 crash showed how flimsy high net worth is as protection against the power of the market.

Stripped of fancy bravado, all these excuses are really attempts to exert personal control over the market via an open position. This quest for omnipotence can balloon into the gambler's friend, as shown in the next chapter. Most of us do not go this far, but our belief in our ability to control events is a serious impediment to better trading. Professional traders are not immune, as hubris lurks on every trading screen. For an extreme example of this phenomenon take a look at *Going for Broke* or *Rogue Trader*, the story of Barings Bank trader, Nick Leeson. Similar stories exist about the Japanese copper trader, Yasuo Hamanaka, but they are not as well-documented. Both show how traders can go bad in a very big way, but every day there are traders quietly doing the same thing on a smaller scale — financially backing their predictions against the market reality.

Right is Sometimes Wrong

We overcome this tendency when we accept that trading the market is not about being right. It is about being profitable. In an objective sense we have shown how a trade can match all our criteria, but still show such an unprofitable low-percentage return. In these circumstances we are right, but also wrong. In an emotional sense, when we manage a trade dominated by the need to be right we can be very wrong. This need to be right is a powerful barrier to profitability.

The need for control – the need to be right – produces some creative excuses for trading failure. Check your repertoire for matches.

"I bought too early, but I can see the bottom forming", or "I am surprised the market doesn't realise the potential of this stock. I will buy more now it has gone lower", or for technical analysts, perhaps "My Elliott wave count is out by one."

We generate these excuses when we falsify the links between success, prediction and control. No matter how foolish these excuses seem in retrospect and in the cold light of substantial loss, the wannabe trader has many reasons, often counted in dollars, to convince himself they are valid. To do otherwise is a larger threat to his self-esteem as a trader, and perhaps as a successful businessman and professional. Essentially he struggles to control the market because control of the business environment has bought him success in the past.

Control the Controllable

We cannot control the market, despite the illusion of our order impact in low-volume equities. We must accept the inevitability of powerlessness to develop the humility required for success. The similarity to some Asian philosophical concepts is striking. Richard McCall in *The Way of the Warrior Trader*, and others, follow this path to its extremities. It is too easy to be sidetracked by this philosophy at depth, but traders do benefit from an understanding of the relationship between self and unreasoning infinity. Those uncomfortable with the way of the Samurai may find more comfort in the existentialism of Camus, or at *The Edge of Chaos* with Bernice Cohen, or perhaps with Ian Stewart debating *Does God Play Dice?*

We want to believe in an ordered universe and all this implies. This suggests order does exist in complex and chaotic situations. It implies a key can be found to unlock the secrets of a chaotic market and the key is forged from superior analysis backed by cash. Success builds on predictive analysis that is right and is coupled with control over external events. This self-reinforcing system does build business success. It is not as useful in trading success.

The novice trader steps back from the tangled relationship between success and control by redefining what he means by control in terms of trading. Business success often comes from controlling events. Trading success usually comes from reacting to those events. The control required is personal rather than external.

Traders understand the only events we have control over are the timing of our entry and our exit. This does not destroy the need for analysis but it does change its relationship with control. An understanding of demand and supply factors, of management strengths and weaknesses, of statistical measures of performance, or of technical indicators used with charts is a vital part of the trading process. Good analysis helps to make the entry and exits much better.

But trading discipline – the timing of entry and exit – turns these skills into profits.

So what is our key? The trader truly understands his analysis does not shape the market. The length, the complexity, the time spent on the search bears little direct relationship to the outcome of the trade. Within reason, more research is better than less, better analysis and analysis tools are more effective than cheap software and gut trading decisions, but more does not automatically improve the chances of success.

Successful traders recognise these activities help us to define the market and a trading opportunity, but not to influence it. The trading wheel turns a half revolution so we stand directly opposite the business relationship between analysis and control.

Returning to our simple housing example, as a result of his analysis the developer takes control of events or activity by building duplexes. In contrast, the trader increases exposure to the housing market segment in reaction to price activity. More subtly, the trader may look for leveraged exposure via related economic activity through construction material manufacturers, suppliers of household goods and furnishings, or mortgage securitisation derivatives. The trader profits by controlling the time and place of his entry and exit, not the underlying building activity.

We make our profit by controlling our reactions to the market. We decide the time, the place and the size of our exposure to a dynamical system that is beyond our control in every other sense. We use an analytical framework to improve our understanding of a dynamical event so we can trade the market as it is. There is no long-term reward for the intellectual or financial bully.

Sometimes the market looks like a rich man's playground where size is king. Bullies aim for size, believing it confers control. Such belief is fatal because unlike the schoolyard, the penalty for bullies is not detention. The market, indifferent to your existence and survival, quietly accepts financial ruin as a just punishment.

Bullies are unable to say, "I believe the market is wrong, but I will trade the chart signals rather than my opinions." The consistent profits come from controlling the time of our entry and exit. The most successful traders are those who understand that the rules which allowed them to accumulate business wealth are not always the rules which favour trading profits. The key behaviour that saves us from the fallacy of market control is the way we consistently profit from trading ability rather than prophecy. Only then have we swapped fictitious control of the market for better control of our trading.

20

GAMBLER OR TRADER?

CONTRIBUTING AUTHOR: Paul I. Munves, Ph.D*

For many readers, trading is the most interesting and exciting activity they know. The excitement does not come from a frisson of fear nor from the horror, vicarious or otherwise, of loss and potential loss. It comes from the daily challenge to trade the market effectively by managing risk. The task of aggressively managing risk places trading activities in the room next to the one labelled gambling, but the connecting door should be forever locked.

Sadly, for some traders the door is left ajar, and the trader's relationship with risk slips out of control, sliding into the next room. This chapter briefly explores how you can recognise when real trading stops and when gambling in the financial markets begins. Very little research has been done in this area. Nonetheless, we are suggesting that when trading behaviour resembles gambling behaviour, the trading activity may reasonably be understood in the same way gambling is understood.

Later we look at some simple self-help measures to regain more appropriate control, but first we search for guiding clues helpful in recognising pathological gambling because these may be useful indicators of when trading starts to slip into gambling mode.

Professional Gambling

How do we distinguish trading from gambling? There are i[ ]
differences between the phenomena of gambling and of trading. (
selects defined events with known rewards and the gambler has n[ ]
over relatively unknown risks. It is an activity with a defined beginning and
end, such as a horse race, a throw of dice, or a hand of cards. The gambling
event itself creates and circumscribes risk, as it does not exist before or after
the event. Gambling provides multiple defined and transitory events from
which the gambler makes a selection.

In contrast, trading is very different. Trading is the practical limitation of risk
in pursuit of unknown reward. Traders participate in an ongoing, continuous
event where the beginning and end are entirely defined by the participant.
The trader manages a user-defined segment of risk that is already in existence
prior to his participation and which will certainly continue after the trader
withdraws from his position. The market thus provides continuous risk. The
trader selects the management strategies to control risk partly by achieving
control over himself. This is demonstrated in his ability to make controlled,
astute decisions about the point of entering and the point of exiting a trade.
Unlike gambling which relies upon predictions and betting, trading depends
upon managing and controlling risk. There are, therefore, extremely
important motivational differences between the gambler and the trader which
we shall discuss at greater length in what follows.

You might not agree with these distinctions built around behavioural
phenomena, but if you are serious about trading then please develop your own
consistent set of understandings so you can avoid the trap of gambling in the
financial markets while pretending you are trading. The definitions above are at
the core of the way we understand and discuss gambling below. The impact of
this distinction on traders varies. For some the impact is fatal, for others an
uncomfortably close shave, and for the serious traders, it provides a useful way to
understand and avoid financial oblivion while still enjoying their chosen pursuit.

We trade the financial markets to make money and this is the ultimate
criterion in deciding if our activities are warranted and successful. Reading
this book may be pleasurable, but you invest the time and effort in the hope
that it will in some way help you make money and preserve wealth. Whether
you are investing in the markets with relatively longer-term time horizons or

more actively trading in the markets with shorter-term time horizons, the primary goal should be the same — to make money. This is self-evident for the full-time professional trader, but even a part-time trader is quite 'professional' when his activities are guided by this simple and overarching principle.

The danger for both short-term traders and long-term investors is when their attitude towards risk deteriorates due to an emotional unwillingness or even psychological incapacity to manage it. The professional trader accepts risk as an inescapable fact of life in the markets, but he devotes himself to the task of controlling risk by becoming adroit at calculating and managing it assiduously. Calculated risks are taken as part of the business of trading in much the same way that a retailer takes calculated risks in purchasing inventory for his store.

In this way trading is akin to professional gambling where the professional gambler makes his living using gambling as his primary source of income. As with trading, there are far more 'wannabe' professional gamblers than successful ones. Those who are successful are devoted to calculating risk and controlling it in ways specifically applicable to the way gambling risk is packaged. These are individuals capable of extraordinary self-control and very capable of waiting for the 'best bet'. Similarly, successful traders will invariably become adept at developing and utilising a set of tools for calculating and managing risk. While successful traders may vary widely in their reliance upon diversification, asset allocation by percentage of total assets, percentage of cash equivalents in their portfolio, fundamental analysis, technical analysis, stop-loss techniques, system development, and orthodox, automated system trading, they will nonetheless be unwavering in their devotion to managing and controlling risk.

Both professional gamblers and traders rely on profits alone to evaluate whether their methodology is indeed worthwhile. They do not include an element of excitement or thrills in the reward calculation. Trading, then, is best understood to be a disciplined activity aimed at taking calculated, managed risks for profit in the financial markets. As Confucius wrote, "In all things, success depends upon previous preparation, and without such preparation there is sure to be failure."

Professional risk management is a common feature of professional trading and of professional gambling. It would be foolish to deny this commonality. It is equally foolish to then decide that both activities amount to the same thing. The novice trader often fails in trading because he brings to his trading activity an inappropriate attitude toward risk which is more similar to that seen in the usual understanding of gambling as simply a pass-time activity. It is this failure to manage risk that we most commonly associate in a pejorative way with gambling. It is this slipshod approach that we want to isolate, explore, and banish from our trading activities.

The Five E's of Gambling

When we use the term gambling and gambler in a pejorative sense we are not referring to the professional gamblers discussed above. Instead we mean the common-or-garden-variety gamblers, those who choke the casinos, rooted in front of a slot machine, draped over the roulette table, and clinging to the last hand of poker. Understanding this kind of gambling is our primary concern.

Pathological gambling in the financial markets is a strong term applied to the end product of several developmental stages. The variety of behaviours is a continuum as shown in Table 20.1. As in alcoholism, denial is often an important characteristic reaction. With denial, selected perceptions are rejected in the service of avoiding psychological pain. Inherent in maintaining the denial is the use of fantasy, so the pathological gambler believes, in the face of evidence to the contrary, that he can gamble in a normal and controlled manner. Furthermore, he will ignore past losses, no matter how heavy or continuous, and believe he can win at gambling.

Pathological gamblers routinely deny their loss of control, but this is not the first, nor the only, development suggesting that a pathological process is underway. We want to explore these psychological developments and attendant behaviours for their heuristic value, so we can avoid unlocking the door from the trading floor to the adjoining room where gambling takes precedence. Gambling in the financial markets will most assuredly result in self-destruction. Efforts at self-help will most likely fail if not buttressed by participation in Gamblers Anonymous and preferably with simultaneous treatment with a mental health professional specifically familiar with this kind of problem.

People gamble for a variety of reasons, often classified as the five 'E's' of gambling:

1 Entertainment
2 Excitement
3 Escape
4 Easy Money
5 Ego

Table 20.1 Types of Traders and Gamblers

TYPE OF TRADER	TYPE OF GAMBLER	DESCRIPTION	DEGREE OF CONTROL	LENGTH OF STAY AT THIS LEVEL
Well-functioning Trader	Professional Gambler	Trading/gambling is his primary source of income; makes his living trading/gambling. Note: There are more 'wannabe' professional traders and gamblers than successful ones.	Very controlled; patiently waits for the best trade/bet.	Indefinite.
	Antisocial Personality	Has a criminal mindset. Was committing crimes before gambling problem developed.	Committing crimes driven by criminal thought process.	Indefinite; gambling continues even in prison.
	Casual Social Gambler	Gambling is one of many forms of entertainment; gambles infrequently.	If he could not participate in gambling, he would rarely miss it.	Rarely escalates to a higher level; if he does move, it's in response to a trauma or fuelled by a Big Win.
	Serious Social Gambler	Gambles as a major source of entertainment; plays regularly at one or more types of gambling and does so with great absorption and intensity; comparable to a tennis or golf 'nut'; gambling is still just a past-time activity.	Can stop gambling but would definitely miss it	May be able to keep serious gambling under control. Is especially vulnerable to external factors that could cause him to escalate his gambling and become a pathological gambler
Deteriorating Trader	Relief-and-Escape Gambler	Trades/gambles to escape troubles in personal or business life. Spends more time trading/gambling than he did prior to his need to escape from personal problems. Differs from pathological trader/gambler in that he has some degree of control over his trading/gambling. If another solution could be found to relieve tension over his problems, he would probably trade/gamble less.	Can probably stop trading/gambling, but with more difficulty than the well-functioning trader or the professional and social gamblers who exhibit more control.	Is very vulnerable to slipping into becoming a pathological trader/gambler. Debts incurred by diverting bill money to trading/gambling may result in entering the 'chasing' phase of the pathological trading/gambling cycle.
Compulsive Pathological Trader	Compulsive Pathological Gambler	Driven by an uncontrollable urge to trade/gamble; trading/gambling seriously compromises, disrupts or damages personal, family, or career pursuits. May incur excessive debts, loss of family, loss of job, and may even commit crimes to continue trading/gambling	Difficult to stop trading/gambling without professional intervention no matter how hard he tries. Loss of control evident and indicative of a disorder of impulse control. These individuals are very likely to satisfy 5 of the 10 criteria for pathological trading or gambling seen in Table 20.3	Goes through Winning, Losing and Desperation Phases which may last for 15 years or longer. Left untreated, the disorder can ultimately destroy everything important to the compulsive pathological trader/gambler.

Adapted from the Texas Council on Problem & Compulsive Gambling, Inc.

All of us enjoy the contribution these five 'E's' make to our trading day, but they are not the primary motivation for trading. Traders who are primarily motivated by any or all of the five 'E's' are actually gambling. Traders who are pathological gamblers have permitted these needs to gain ascendancy over earned profits and contaminate their risk management capacities. This difference in the weighting of our motivations is the key factor in deciding if we have slipped from trading into gambling. When profits alone are not enough, we have begun to gamble.

In the casino a $2 slot machine delivers the five 'E's' at the push of a button. In the market delivery is just as certain, but comes at a much higher price. There are six types of gamblers, as described in Table 20.1. These can be used as a proxy to recognise gambling behaviour in traders. Perhaps the most important variable between types is the degree of control the trader has over his trading activity. The more he is involved with risk-taking to fulfil emotional needs, the more likely it is that he is gambling rather than trading.

Trading slips into gambling mode when it is predominantly engaged in for any or all of the five 'E's' listed above, rather than as a systematically-organised activity endeavouring to calculate and manage risk in the pursuit of profit in the financial markets. It is the devotion to managing risk that distinguishes trading as a professional activity. The less control an individual is able to exercise over his trading activity, the more likely it is that gambling better describes the activity than does the term trading.

Likewise, the greater the inability to control the activity in terms of time devoted to it, amount of risk taken, emotional involvement, and impact on lifestyle stability, the more likely it is that gambling may become a bona fide disorder of impulse control formally designated as pathological gambling. Pathological gambling quite frequently exhibits three distinct phases. Table 20.2 provides a formal summary of each phase and has been included to illustrate how a problem with gambling can evolve over time in an individual's life. Readers who recognise themselves should make every attempt to withdraw from the market and seek professional help. For those who see this process as reflecting what is going on with their 'trading', this could be the most important item addressed in this book, for their very survival could well be at stake.

Table 20.2 Phases in a Gambler's Career

CHARACTERISTIC	WINNING PHASE	LOSING PHASE	DESPERATION PHASE
REASON FOR GAMBLING	Gambling for entertainment, ego, excitement and easy money.	Gambling to recoup losses; has some wins but has more losses; chases losses to try and win back what he has lost.	Gambling because he cannot keep from it.
GAMBLING ATTITUDE	Plans careful and cautious bets.	Wagers are impulsive and rash; bets on things with high odds to maximise payoffs.	Unreasonable; panicky; bets hunches, super-situations, long shots.
MOOD	Eager; unreasonable optimism.	Frequently angry and depressed over losses; even winning does not make him happy.	Feels powerless; blames others; feels remorse and panic; becomes a zombie.
DRIVING FORCE TO GAMBLE	Euphoria of winning; consuming desire to perpetuate the high; fantasises about winning.	Overwhelming need to quell depression over losing; desperately trying to recapture the glow of the Winning Phase	May cheat, steal, lie and manipulate to stay in action. Tries to juggle dwindling resources between bills and gambling money
TIME SPENT GAMBLING	Gambling is a part-time, leisure activity.	Most of life devoted to chasing his losses	Dominant thing in life
WORK ACTIVITY	Works in usual pattern, although begins to spend working time thinking about gambling.	Begins to miss work to go to the track, casino or watch sports; conversely, may have two jobs to get more money.	Probably has been fired from his job; reputation ruined.
FAMILY LIFE	Begins to split his time between gambling activities and family.	Preoccupied with gambling; wife and children stay out of the way; home life is unhappy.	Life is out of control; alienated from family and friends.
SOURCE OF GAMBLING MONEY	Winnings and money allotted to entertainment or leisure activities.	Becomes a con man; starts to convert assets into cash; heavy borrowing; has outstanding debts and several loans	Gets money wherever he can; often resorts to criminal activity.
PERSONAL HABITS	Life continues in normal pattern; family enjoys presents and extra income from the gambling proceeds.	Frequent absences from home; virtually ignores children and wife; lying becomes full-time activity; personality changes; is irritable, restless, withdrawn; unable to pay debts.	Everything he does seems out of character; irrational and desperate thinking; little consideration for family or health.
LENGTH OF PHASE	Varies; usually no longer than 3 years.	Varies; up to 15 years or longer.	Usually shorter period.
HOW PHASE ENDS	May experience a 'Big Win' or what some gamblers think of as beginner's luck. This Big Win results in thinking he can win money often. However, he hits what he thinks is an unlucky streak and starts to lose instead of win.	Gambler runs out of sources of ways to get bailed out of his financial problems; his sources of getting money with which to gamble become more limited.	Either seeks help from Gamblers Anonymous or counselling or things continue to get even worse (family leaves, he loses his job, commits crimes, goes to jail, tries to commit suicide).

Adapted from the Texas Council on Problem & Compulsive Gambling

While normal gambling is a risk-taking activity aimed at satisfying normal desires for entertainment, excitement, escape into fantasy, good fortune, and winning, some people get hooked on risk-taking as an end in itself. Fyodor Dostoyevsky, himself a pathological gambler, knew this. In 1866 he wrote in *The Gambler*:

> *I am sure vanity was half responsible for this; I wanted to astonish the spectators by taking senseless chances and - a strange sensation - I clearly remember that even without any promptings of vanity I really was suddenly overcome by a terrible craving for risk ...*

The fascination with risk-taking as an end in itself can be understood in various ways. Although the emotional 'logic' may strain your credulity, gambling offers the possibility that anything may in fact happen, that one risk is essentially no greater than any other, and that someone may, therefore, not be accountable for the choices they have made. For some, the allure of risk, of the improbable, of the chance occurrence is that it affords them the delusion that they will escape accountability and guilt. There is yet another way gambling offers a psychological escape. The taking of huge risks may also be sought for the intensity of the experience it affords, for the adrenalin rush, and for the distraction from unwanted feelings such as stress, helplessness, guilt, anxiety, or depression.

Some satisfy these cravings by jumping out of perfectly sound aircraft at high altitude, bungee jumping, or driving expensive fast cars at three times the speed limit. Some of us find it more convenient to ring our broker.

By examining the extremes we are able to identify and manage the tendency in ourselves. An authoritative list of criteria for pathological gambling can be found in the Diagnostic and Statistical Manual, DSM-IV, of the American Psychiatric Association. We have included an adaptation of these criteria in Table 20.3 once again to familiarise the reader with criteria used by psychiatrists in assessing pathological gambling.

Why we gamble is an issue beyond the scope of this chapter. Broadly we note there is now a trend towards taking a multidisciplinary approach to the understanding of pathological gambling. Quite probably, sociological, psychological, and biological processes are involved in an interactive and complex fashion. A person's developmental experiences, personality structure and dynamics, as well as constitutional vulnerabilities may all be involved in the manifestation of this disorder of impulse control. Compulsive pathological gambling has also been likened to other addictive disorders as a dysfunctional attempt to resolve underlying emotional disturbances.

Table 20.3   Diagnostic Criteria for Pathological Trading and/or Gambling

A	Persistent and recurrent maladaptive trading or gambling behaviour as indicated by five (or more) of the following:

1. is preoccupied with trading or gambling (e.g., preoccupied with reliving past trading or gambling experiences, handicapping or planning the next venture, or thinking of ways to get money with which to trade or gamble)

2. needs to trade or gamble with increasing amounts of money in order to achieve the desired excitement

3. has repeated unsuccessful efforts to control, cut back, or stop trading or gambling

4. is restless or irritable when attempting to cut down or stop trading or gambling

5. trades or gambles as a way of escaping from problems or of relieving a dysphoric mood (e.g., feelings of helplessness, guilt, anxiety, depression)

6. after losing money trading or gambling, often returns another day to get even ('chasing' one's losses)

7. lies to family members, therapist, or others to conceal the extent of involvement with trading or gambling

8. has committed illegal acts such as forgery, fraud, theft, or embezzlement to finance trading or gambling

9 has jeopardised or lost a significant relationship, job, or educational or career opportunity because of trading or gambling

10. relies on others to provide money to relieve a desperate financial situation caused by trading or gambling

B	The trading or gambling behaviour is not better accounted for by a Manic Episode

These criteria, with minor revisions simply to include reference to trading activity, are adopted directly from the Diagnostic and Statistical Manual, DSM-IV, Code 312.31 of the American Psychiatric Association

Our concern here is early recognition of similar characteristics in traders and to indicate possible preventative action. Pathological gamblers will typically exhibit some, but not necessarily all, of the following narcissistic characteristics. We have added an example of a typical statement a trader might make when exhibiting the particular characteristic:

Grandiosity — "I take very large positions because I'm a better trader than most."

Omnipotent strivings — "I have been right before so this will come around."

Magical thinking — "I know this trade will work because it has to."

276

Exploitative tendencies — "If you really care you can help me by giving me your money to trade so I can make back the loss."

Poor reaction to criticism — "Who are you to judge?"

Excessive sense of entitlement — "Of course I want the benefit of the doubt on that Order."

Recurrent fantasies of unlimited success — "I'm going to trade myself right into a new car and a new house."

Chronic feelings of envy — "My turn for a lucky streak is certainly due now."

Notable deficits in capacity for empathy — "How can you ask me about the margin debit when you know I'm working off that last loss?"

Profound craving for attention and admiration — "It's no problem for me to let the loss run because I've got the courage and enough capital to wait for the market to turn."

Feelings of uniqueness — "The market doesn't understand the true value of this stock but I do."

"Black Or White" thinking and "All Or Nothing" tendencies in the way they view themselves and others — "Why take a small position when I know this stock has already completed its bottom?"

The common link here is a false feeling of omnipotence. Instead of managing risk, the trader begins to think he can somehow control the market. He adopts an illusion of power and control often intended to defend himself against intolerable feelings of helplessness, depression, or guilt. The tendency is to experience oneself as omnipotent or all-powerful at precisely those moments when one is actually most helpless and out of control. This is profoundly self-deceptive and maladaptive.

Simply put, such a sense of omnipotence is more likely born out of desperation. Richard J. Rosenthal suggests that "pathological gambling is basically an addiction to a false state of mind." Those readers who wish to explore this further will find Rosenthal's "The Pathological Gambler's System for Self-Deception" in the *Journal of Gambling Behavior* and his, "The Psychodynamics of Pathological Gambling: A Review of the Literature" in *The Handbook of Pathological Gambling* edited by Galski a useful introduction to this engrossing field. Additional references are in the annex at the end of this chapter.

Irrespective of whether the markets are the result of a random walk, of a pattern, of cycles, or a product of chaos, the trader makes his profit by controlling the only element he can realistically control — himself. He applies an analytical framework to improve his understanding of the market so he can make consistent decisions about how he is going to trade the market as it is rather than the way he would like it to be.

Mirror, Mirror on the Wall

Under the extraordinary light of pathological gambling our everyday trading foibles lose intensity but if your trading becomes prominently motivated by more than one or two of the five 'E's', it is time to recognise that what you may wish to think of as trading is, in fact, gambling behaviour. While you may still possess control over this form of gambling that is masquerading as trading, continued self-deception will blow you out of the markets. The similarity of these behaviours suggests ways to explore why the discipline of trading has given way to seeking entertainment, thrills, distraction, wishful thinking, and a variety of narcissistic needs. The list of twenty questions in Table 20.4 are a guide which can be used by traders to assess whether their trading has gotten out of control.

This list is adapted from the Gamblers Anonymous Twenty Questions which are usually accepted as the best layman's tool for purposes of self-assessment. A 'yes' answer to seven or more of these questions suggests that your trading is slipping towards gambling behaviour. Every trader can benefit from answering this list of questions as honestly as possible. We all have occasional lapses in self-discipline. Answering these questions will help traders to identify trading inclinations that interfere with maintaining optimal trading self-control.

The gambler's memory distorts the world in a way that written records cannot. Just as sound identification of trading opportunities points us in the direction where the balance of probabilities is weighted in our favour, so too does the careful identification of the tendencies that are interfering with the discipline of sound trading practices.

Table 20.4   The Traders Twenty Questions

1	Has trading routinely caused you to neglect necessities such as time with family, record keeping, leisure time activities, household maintenance, and so forth?	
2	Has trading ever made your home life unhappy?	
3	Has trading ever adversely affected your reputation?	
4	Have you ever felt remorse after trading?	
5	Have you ever traded to get quick and easy money with which to pay debts or otherwise solve financial difficulties?	
6	Do you resist efforts to carefully develop or follow a trading plan?	
7	After a losing trade do you feel you must trade again as soon as possible and win back your losses?	
8	After a winning trade do you have a strong urge to win even more regardless of your original trading plan?	
9	Do you ever trade with positions that are large enough to seriously damage your entire account?	
10	Do you ever borrow outside of your trading account to finance your trading or have you had difficulties due to margin calls?	
11	Have you traded just to prove you were right or to impress someone?	
12	Have you ever traded with money that you had previously allocated for payment of still obligatory non-trading expenditures?	
13	Has trading ever made you careless with regard to your own welfare or that of your family?	
14	Have you ever traded mainly for excitement rather than according to a trading plan?	
15	Have you ever traded to escape worry or trouble or even boredom?	
16	Have you ever committed, or considered committing, an illegal act to finance trading?	
17	Did trading ever cause you to have difficulty in sleeping?	
18	Do arguments, disappointments, or frustrations create within you an urge to trade?	
19	Did you ever have an urge to celebrate any good fortune in your life by trading?	
20	Have you ever considered self-destruction as a result of your trading?	

These questions are an adaptation of the Gamblers Anonymous Twenty Questions.
Seven or more affirmative answers to these questions would be considered to be an indication that trading activity is deteriorating and/or becoming pathological as described in Table 20.1 and Table 20.3

Pin the following list beside your trading mirror. The first two listed activities are valuable for any trader, and we would recommend they be retained as a matter of course. These notes can be written in the margin of a chart, then printed and pinned to the wall when each new trade is opened.

The activities further down the list are designed for those who fear they have a more serious problem where the slide from trading to gambling has begun in earnest. This is a slippery slope, but recovery is possible.

1 Keep a diary of feelings before, during, and after putting on a trade. Reflect upon why you think you had those feelings and whether they are a sound basis to make judgments about either market action or oneself.

2 Write down all of the reasons a disciplined, controlled, and systematic approach to trading is distasteful. Note all of the aversive thoughts and feelings that occur to you about the labour of calculating and managing risk.

This includes the inclination to have another cup of coffee, to walk the dog or hope the telephone rings. These diversionary tactics are designed to defer the more unpleasant tasks. Reflect carefully on how you think you came to have these feelings and whether in your considered judgment these feelings are an asset or a liability to your ability to trade. Although quite expensive, Tusche Chandes $ecure software is the first attempt to build a usable database of personal trading responses. A demo copy can be downloaded from the link on the Guppy Traders Site, www.ozemail.com.au/~guppy

3 Write down everything that you consider as a current source of stress and anxiety. Ask yourself if you can acknowledge feelings of helplessness as a normal part of the human condition. Seek appropriate understanding of and solutions to your frustrations rather than seeking escape, distraction, and pseudo power through a 'Big Win'.

Sometimes our sense of helplessness is engendered by the market itself. The market is infinite, uncontrollable, uncaring and unforgiving. At times traders try to impose their will on the market as discussed in Chapter 19. Successful traders accept this inherent uncontrollability and trade on the edge of the implied chaos. Those likely to be unsuccessful traders swap this existentialist existence for the fleeting power conferred by the trade of a lifetime. Be honest with yourself. If you feel uncomfortable with uncertainty, then trading is not a fruitful activity.

4 Write down all of the significant affronts to your self-esteem that have occurred in the past or currently. Write down how vulnerable you feel to these unwanted occurrences and what strategies you typically employ to cope with them. Write down how you maintain your feelings of self-worth and your emotional equilibrium. Reflect carefully on whether these tactics seem optimally appropriate and effective. Trading activity should not be employed as a strategy to cope with diminished self-esteem.

5 Repeat steps 1-4, noting how you think those who know you the best would have responded about each of the issues related to your functioning. Consider carefully how many of their imagined responses reflect your own best judgment about your own functioning.

6 Discuss steps 1-5 with at least one of your most trusted and reliable confidants. If fear or shame would deter you from discussing these items with anyone you know, consider seeking a consultation with a mental health professional.

Life is a Gamble, but Trading is Not

We have attempted to provide some guidance above to help you recognise when you stop trading and start to use the financial markets for gambling. For those well down the path we included some guides to recognising pathological gambling so you can decide if professional help is warranted.

Both trading and professional gambling rely on the effective management of risk. Emotions play a useful role in each activity, but they do not provide the dominant motivation or reward. In essence, trading becomes pathological gambling when there is a shift in the predominant motivational orientation accompanied by needs to alleviate psychological pain in an inappropriate, unrealistic, and compulsive manner. We all have our momentary lapses, our bouts with temptation, our narcissistic indulgences, and as we are all subject to the *"slings and arrows of outrageous fortune"*, we may not always be at our best. But these transitory occurrences are evidence that we are all more simply human than otherwise. If we can acknowledge our failings, if we can reflect honestly about how we all sometimes mishandle our feelings and deepest desires, we can learn from our indiscretions and imprudence, becoming even more adept at our task as traders which is the effective management of risk.

Superficially, in many ways the trading floor is next to the gambling floor. At times the smooth glow of numbers on the trading screen is almost indistinguishable from the soft rattle of electronic slot machines. Good trading demands we look beyond the superficial. The two floors are in rooms decorated with different patterns of risk and the connecting door should always remain locked.

---

*ABOUT THE AUTHOR

Paul I. Munves, Ph.D. earned the Certificate in Psychoanalysis at the William Alanson White Institute in New York and returned to his hometown of Dallas, Texas in 1982. He established the Dallas Society for Psychoanalytic Psychology and served as its President for two terms. The Dallas Society for Psychoanalytic Psychology awarded him the Distinguished Psychologist Award in 1984. He continues to serve as Associate Professor in the Division of Psychology at the University of Texas Southwestern Medical Center and maintains a private practice devoted to working with adults. He very actively follows the markets and his observations are based upon his experience with market participants.

Annex to Chapter 20

References

Lesieur, Henry R. and Rosenthal, Robert J. (1991), "Pathological Gambling: A Review of the Literature" (Prepared for the American Psychiatric Association Task Force on DSM-IV Committee on Disorders of Impulse Control Not Elsewhere Classified). *Journal Of Gambling Studies*, 7 (1), 5-42.

Rosenthal, Robert J. (1986), "The Pathological Gambler's System For Self-Deception". *Journal Of Gambling Behavior*, 2, 108-120.

Rosenthal, Robert J. (1987), "The Psychodynamics Of Pathological Gambling: A Review Of The Literature". In T. Galski (Ed.), *The Handbook Of Pathological Gambling* (pp. 41-70), Charles C. Thomas; Springfield, Illinois.

For Further Reading

Journal Of Gambling Studies. Henry R. Lesieur Ph.D. (Ed.), Human Sciences Press, Inc.; Subscription Department, 223 Spring Street, New York, NY 10013-1578.

The Psychology Of Gambling. Edmund Bergler, International Universities Press; New York, 1958.

Behind The Eight Ball. Linda Berman and Mary Ellen Siegel, Simon & Schuster; New York, 1992.

When Luck Runs Out. Robert L. Custer And Harry Milt, Facts On File Publications; New York, 1985.

The Chase: Career Of The Compulsive Gambler. Henry R. Lesieur, Ph.D., Schenkman Books; Cambridge, Mass., 1984.

Compulsive Gambling: Theory, Research, And Practice. Edited By Howard J. Shaffer, Sharon A. Stein, Blase Gambino and Thomas N. Cummings, Lexington Books; Lexington, Mass., 1989.

Where to Turn for Help

Gamblers Anonymous/Gam-Anon, Level 2, The Wesley Centre, 210 Pitt Street, Sydney NSW 2000, Australia.

Gamblers Anonymous/Gam-Anon, St. Luke's Anglican Church, Dorcus Street, South Melbourne Victoria 3205, Australia.

Australian National Council On Compulsive Gambling, P.O. A270, Sydney South NSW 2000, Australia.

Australian National Council On Compulsive Gambling, P.O. Box 114, St. Paul's NSW 2031, Australia.

Australian National Association For Gambling Studies, c/o Dr Mark Dickerson, Psychology Department, University Of Western Sydney, Campbelltown NSW 2560, Australia.

In The United States

The National Council On Problem Gambling, Inc., 445 West 59th Street, New York NY 10019, USA: (212) 765-3833, (800) 522-4700.

Institute For The Study Of Gambling And Commercial Gaming, University Of Nevada, Reno Nevada 89557-0016, USA: (702) 784-1477.

Gamblers Anonymous, P.O. Box 17173, Los Angeles California 90017, USA: (213) 386-8789.

Gam-Anon, P.O. Box 157, Whitestone NY 11357, USA: (718) 352-1671.

Institute Of Certified Financial Planners, Two Denver Highlands, 10065 East Harvard Avenue, Suite 320, Denver Colorado 80231, USA.

International Association Of Financial Planners, Two Concourse Parkway, Suite 800, Atlanta Georgia 30328, USA.

Internationally

Canadian Foundation On Compulsive Gambling (Ontario), 505 Consumers Rd, Suite 605, Willowdale Ontario M2J 4V8, Canada: (416) 499-9800 (Business Hours), (416) 222-7477 (After Hours).

Gamblers Anonymous/Gam-Anon, 17-23 Blantyre Street, London SW 10 ODT, England.

The Society For The Study Of Gambling, c/o Dr David Miers, Cardiff Law School, P.O. 427, Cardiff CFI 1XD, Wales, United Kingdom: 0222-87400.

Jellinek Consultancy, Ostende 9, 1017 WT Amsterdam, The Netherlands: 020-6220261.

21

INSIGHT AND IRONY

This prospecting expedition was about finding nuggets of trading opportunity. We expected to find nothing else — or so it seemed. Chaucer's company of pilgrims in the *Canterbury Tales* expected to wend their way to Canterbury ostensibly *"The holy blisful martir for to seke"* and nothing else. With sustained insight and irony Chaucer exposes a multitude of expectations, some of which are only loosely associated with such pious ambitions.

The market allows both insight and irony and our prospecting expedition is no exception. Working in our home office we may think we are prospecting alone, but we are part of a new gold rush. Linked by the power of information, equipped with electronic tools, and connected to a market beyond the power of any individual, organisation, or government to control, we travel with a company of prospectors working the same ground.

Chaucer talks of *"a compaignye of sondry folk, by aventure yfalle in felaweship, and pilgrimes were theyalle."* Pause for a moment, forget the institutional traders, and survey the company of fellowship at our level, clustered not in a tavern at Southwerk, but dispersed in market cyberspace.

Some wannabe traders are really prospecting for thrills. Their jungle adventure is not about survival. They look for a near-death experience as an antidote to an otherwise dreary working life. When charting software empowers these people they reach stupid decisions much faster.

A few are excited by the sheer risk of it all. These gamblers pose no serious competition. The stakes are too high for them to survive more than a few trades. Their prospecting technique involves scattering money at random with the demented excitement of the truly financially insane. Their behaviour is mildly infectious so we are well advised to observe them from a distance.

Other prospectors are tradesmen. We tell them by their expensive software tools and the suite of technical indicators spread across half a dozen charting and analysis packages. Some of them are so enchanted by screen patterns that they fail to see the nuggets in plain view. Their technical virtuosity must match the reality of the market, but does not always do so. These prospectors improve their chances of success by their mastery of tools rather than processes.

The huddle of screen jockeys jammed next to a monitor confuse action with profitability. For many getting closer to the action — a real-time feed — is a substitute for an inability to trade well. Some are temperamentally suited to day trading. Others, like moths to a flame, are drawn towards it because they cannot trade successfully on longer time scales.

Skulking in a corner, looking for victims, are the command and control kings. They would wrench a nugget of opportunity from the market's reluctant grasp — if only they could make it so. We tell them initially by the wad of cash and sheer brute force they bring to the delicate task of discovery and exploitation. Like the others above, they are led by ambition.

At the back of every prospector's mind is always an ambition to 'strike it rich' or 'hit the jackpot'. This ambition has carried us beyond the daily grind of work for wages and at the start of this expedition it now demands a revision of established relationships. Harnessed properly, this ambition drives us forward. Unharnessed it leads to unpredicted destinations.

We all want the opportunity to prove that money can make us happy. If we were honest with ourselves, and we rarely are in public, then we acknowledge this as the primary motivation in this market-driven treasure hunt. These ambitions are no different from those that fuelled the Australian gold rushes of the 1850s; that enticed Spanish peasants to destroy a civilisation in their search for the man of gold — El Dorado; that encouraged men to push wheelbarrows across the Nullabor desert to the goldfields of West Australia or to hack through the jungles of Borneo looking for another Bre-X. How we use this ambition, not our prospecting tools, decides our success or failure.

Scattered amongst the soon-to-be disheartened and defeated prospectors are a few successful traders, not necessarily distinguished by wealth. Ambition harnessed as a driving force, they combine technical mastery of their tools with an artistry that at first glance appears intuitive. Closer inspection reveals they carry, in addition to the basic pick and shovel charts and metal detecting technical indicators, spreadsheets for risk calculation and financial analysis.

They are risk managers comfortable with the enormity of the market and their personal insignificance in it. It is this acceptance more than any other factor which facilitates the identification, and successful exploitation of, trading opportunities when equipped with even the most basic of tools. They have asked the question "I am a trader because ...." and found the answer does not begin with $$$. This is the group we wish to emulate.

These are our fellow travellers on this prospecting expedition. It is not just a pilgrimage on a trail of wealth any more than Chaucer's company sought only spiritual enlightenment. As private traders we participate in the most fascinating modern expedition of all, but watch out for the irony.

Search hard and trade well.

Appendix

FOREIGN JUNGLES

Understanding of the way orders to US brokers are structured improves systematic trading on these exchanges and in markets derived from the US. A comparison of the order execution structure is given in Figures A1, A2 and A3. In the same way that depth of market information discussed in Chapter 15 gives the Australian trader important information, US order terms are also helpful. A brief outline follows and additional detail is covered in *The Compleat Day Trader* by Jake Bernstein.

Fast Markets – a License to Maim

A fast market is formally declared as a warning to screen traders when the trading floor is having trouble coping with the flow of orders. The people recording the transactions cannot keep up with the pace of price changes. What you see on the screen is not what you get. Victor Sperandeo writing in *Trader Vic – Methods of a Wall Street Master* advises that "in a fast market, the (screen) information is totally unreliable."

Rules are relaxed in anticipation of a higher error rate. Brokers return trading orders as 'unables' and the slippage between the order and the fill grows. In the scramble for prices, expect to be maimed.

Market Orders and Market On Close

Many traders see them as a license to steal because it costs the trader at least a tick, and sometimes two or three or even more when trading S&P futures. They are best used when riding a large profit where the trader can afford to give a little back in return for a quick exit.

Market on Close orders, or 'murder on close' can be filled at almost any price in the last minute of trade. In a thin market such an order is certain trouble.

Fill Or Kill (FOK) Orders

The pit broker will attempt to fill your order three successive times at the requested price. If there is no fill the ordered is immediately killed. Not all exchanges nor all brokers accept FOK orders and under certain market conditions FOK orders may be refused.

If you use the acronym watch your pronunciation carefully as US brokers don't always appreciate the humour.

Market If Touched Orders

These orders are placed as a buy just below the market, or just above the market if selling. The Market If Touched order becomes a market order when it is hit and will usually be filled at or near your order price.

This order is used when you have a specific price target, often based on support or resistance levels. Trading these targets on the ASX is done using Good Till Cancelled orders.

Good Till Cancelled Orders

This orders remains in the market until cancelled or filled. Usually the broker cancels them at the end of the month and you must re-instate them. An ASX Good Till Cancelled order remains in place indefinitely until cancelled by the trader, or until it exceeds the allowable percentage range away from the current traded price. Some Australian brokerages have started automatically removing GTC orders after nine weeks irrespective of the original client instruction. Check for this. It could cost you significant profit.

Stop Orders

These are the infamous stop-loss orders so often written about. When trading from the long side they are placed below the market price to protect profits. But here is the catch. In a fast market they will not necessarily be filled because sharp and sudden turns result in considerable slippage of buy and sell stop orders.

Stop Limit Orders

These are the thinking traders' stop-loss orders. A stop limit order at 6000 with a limit of 6015 means you will accept a fill within these ranges. Bernstein argues "the good part of such an order is that it permits the floor broker more leeway in filling you and .... improves the odds that you will be filled."

Any exchange that relies on market makers is a long way from the trading efficiencies of the SEATS system used by the ASX. Constructing an order to please the broker is not, and should not be, a consideration in an efficient securities market. A brief overview of the differences in the major exchanges is given in Figures A1, A2 and A3.

One Cancels the Other

Here the cancellation of one order is dependant upon the execution of another. This is dangerous trading in any market unless you can afford to carry both open positions should the order be misapplied. Not all exchanges accept this order format.

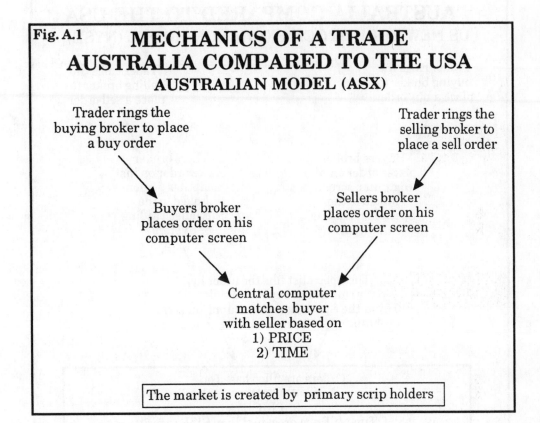

Fig. A.1

MECHANICS OF A TRADE
AUSTRALIA COMPARED TO THE USA
AUSTRALIAN MODEL (ASX)

Trader rings the
buying broker to place
a buy order

Trader rings the
selling broker to
place a sell order

Buyers broker
places order on his
computer screen

Sellers broker
places order on his
computer screen

Central computer
matches buyer
with seller based on
1) PRICE
2) TIME

The market is created by primary scrip holders

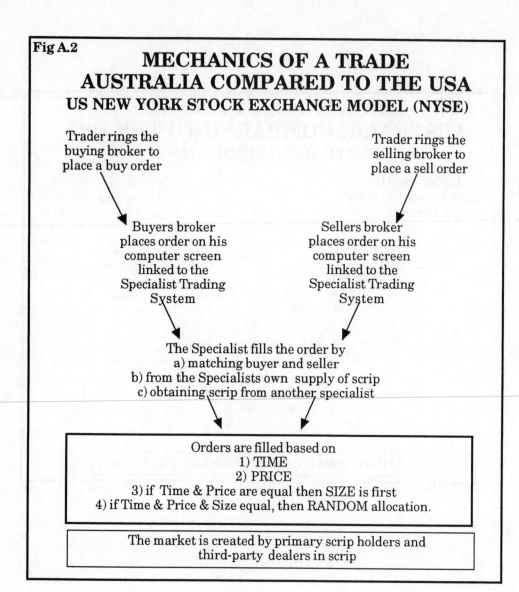

Fig A.2

MECHANICS OF A TRADE
AUSTRALIA COMPARED TO THE USA
US NEW YORK STOCK EXCHANGE MODEL (NYSE)

Trader rings the
buying broker to
place a buy order

Trader rings the
selling broker to
place a sell order

Buyers broker
places order on his
computer screen
linked to the
Specialist Trading
System

Sellers broker
places order on his
computer screen
linked to the
Specialist Trading
System

The Specialist fills the order by
a) matching buyer and seller
b) from the Specialists own supply of scrip
c) obtaining scrip from another specialist

Orders are filled based on
1) TIME
2) PRICE
3) if Time & Price are equal then SIZE is first
4) if Time & Price & Size equal, then RANDOM allocation.

The market is created by primary scrip holders and
third-party dealers in scrip

Fig. A.3

MECHANICS OF A TRADE
AUSTRALIA COMPARED TO THE USA
US NATIONAL ASSOCIATION OF SECURITY
DEALERS AUTOMATED QUOTATION SYSTEM
(NASDAQ)

Trader rings the
buying broker to
place a buy order

Trader rings the
selling broker to
place a sell order

Buyers broker
places order on his
computer screen
linked to the
Market Maker for
that market

Sellers broker
places order on his
computer screen
linked to the
Market Maker for
that market

The Market Maker fills the order by
a) drawing from the Market Maker's own supply of
scrip. (This leads to wide spreads because this is how
the market makers are profitable.)
b) buy or selling from the market

Orders are filled based on
1) NEGOTIATION
Time & Price are variables, but are not a determined sequence
for matching buyer and seller.
Type of order, Limit, Fill All or None, or At Market, plays a
more important role in executing a trade.

The market is created by third-party dealers in scrip

INDEX

DISCOUNT COUPON – TRADING WORKSHOPS

10% off the regular seminar fee — single and group rates
(These workshops are held in all Australian capitals and also in Asia.)

Trading looks easy, but it takes skill. How best to approach your market and survive is a skill that can be learned, and improved. Trading success means knowing how to GET IN by identifying a trade. It means knowing how to manage the trade so you GET OUT with an overall profit.

You can become a better trader by attending a half-day workshop because Daryl Guppy will teach you how to understand the market from a private trader's perspective, how to use those advantages, and how to manage a trade to lock in capital profits.

All traders — those considering entering the market and those who want to improve their trading — will benefit from this workshop.

Nobody can give you the ultimate trading secret, but Daryl Guppy will show you, using local examples selected by the audience on the day, how a private trader identifies and manages a trade. You will enter the market better informed than your competitors.

Daryl Guppy holds regular Trading Workshops. Dates and details are posted on www.ozemail.com.au/~guppy eight weeks before each workshop.

How to claim your workshop discount

When you book your seminar mention that you own *Trading Tactics* and get 10% off the advertised fee. Bring this book with you to confirm your discount. It can be autographed for you if you wish.

Some comments from workshop participants

"The workshop, like your book, was practical and informative. I enjoyed it, and more importantly, I learned from it. For me it brought a lot of the theory into perspective. Let me know when the next one is scheduled so I can mark it in my diary."
—Private equity trader

"If you get one good idea from a seminar, it is worthwhile. Your workshop gave me two very profitable ideas."
—Futures 'local' floor trader